WITHDRAWN

D1737217

# ALBUQUERQUE
# REMEMBERED

The Albuquerque home of Governor Manuel Armijo in the 1840s is shown as it appeared in about 1900. Located a short distance southeast of the Old Town Plaza, it was demolished in 1910. Courtesy the Albuquerque Museum Photoarchive, PA1980.152.3. Miller collection. Donated by Mr. and Mrs. Mickey L. Miller.

# ALBUQUERQUE
## *Remembered*

## HOWARD BRYAN

University of New Mexico Press
Albuquerque

PRINTED IN THE UNITED STATES OF AMERICA

YEAR                                    PRINTING
12  11  10  09  08  07  06       1  2  3  4  5  6  7


Library of Congress Cataloging-in-Publication Data

Bryan, Howard.
   Albuquerque remembered / Howard Bryan.— 1st ed.
      p. cm.
   Includes bibliographical references and index.
   ISBN-13: 978-0-8263-3782-5 (pbk. : alk. paper)
   ISBN-10: 0-8263-3782-1 (pbk. : alk. paper)
   1. Albuquerque (N.M.)—History.  I. Title.
   F804.A3B79 2006
   978.9'61—dc22

                          2005028927

Book design and composition by Damien Shay
Body type is Utopia 9.5/13
Display is Aquitaine Initials and Amazone

# Contents

# *Introduction*

It is the intent of this book to both inform and entertain the general reader regarding some of the important (and a few unimportant) events that helped shape the growth and character of Albuquerque during the three centuries of its history. Attention also is given to dramatic events that occurred in the vicinity before Albuquerque's founding in 1706.

Under the flags of Spain, Mexico, the United States, and, for a brief period, the Confederate States, Albuquerque grew from a small farm and ranch village in the northern reaches of New Spain to the thirty-fifth-largest city in the United States. Each period of its history is filled with dramatic and unusual events.

Special attention is given to some of the colorful characters that abound in the city's history, sometimes at the expense of less colorful business and civic leaders who shunned publicity about themselves and their important accomplishments. Humorous episodes and anecdotes, as related in early newspapers, are scattered throughout the text to balance some of the dramatic and often violent events that occurred in Albuquerque over the years.

Compiling three centuries of Albuquerque history has required reliance on a great many varied sources, ranging from the published accounts of eighteenth-century visitors to my twentieth-century interviews and conversations with city pioneers and my personal experiences as a newspaper reporter. Most of this research occurred during my forty-two years (1948–1990) as a reporter and historical columnist for the *Albuquerque Tribune*.

During my early years with the newspaper I became acquainted with many Albuquerque pioneers who entertained me with their recollections of Albuquerque's earlier days. They included William A. Keleher, D. K. B. Sellers, Erna Fergusson, J. R. Galusha, Gilberto Espinosa, John Milne, Joseph Barnett, Julia B. Gallegos, Harry O. Strong, Chester French, Fred Kirkpatrick, and Allesandro and Pompilio Matteucci.

Much of the text is based on articles and advertisements appearing in a wide variety of Albuquerque newspapers dating back to the 1860s. Most of these historic newspaper files may be viewed on microfilm at the Albuquerque Publishing Company in Albuquerque.

Books that have been helpful in preparing this history include:

Adams, Eleanor B., ed. *Bishop Tamaron's Visitation of New Mexico, 1760.* Albuquerque: Historical Society of New Mexico, 1954.

Alberts, Don E. *Balloons to Bombers: Aviation in Albuquerque, 1882–1945.* Albuquerque, NM: Albuquerque Museum, 1987.

Bolton, Herbert E. *Coronado, Knight of Pueblos and Plains.* Albuquerque: University of New Mexico Press, 1949.

Ciotola, Nicholas B. *Italians in Albuquerque.* Chicago: Arcadia, 2002.

Dewitt, Susan. *Historic Albuquerque Today: An Overview of Historic Buildings and Districts.* Albuquerque, NM: Historic Landmarks Survey of Albuquerque, 1978.

Domínguez, Fray Francisco Atanasio. *The Missions of New Mexico 1776: A Description.* Translated and annotated by Eleanor B. Adams and Fray Angélico Chávez. Albuquerque: University of New Mexico Press, 1956.

Hackett, Charles W., ed. *Revolt of the Pueblo Indians of New Mexico and Otermín's Attempted Reconquest, 1680–1682.* 2 vols. Albuquerque: University of New Mexico Press, 1942.

Johnson, Byron A., and Sharon P. Johnson. *Gilded Palaces of Shame: Albuquerque's Redlight Districts, 1880–1914.* Albuquerque, NM: Gilded Age Press, 1983.

Keleher, William A. *Turmoil in New Mexico, 1846–1868.* Santa Fe, NM: Rydal Press, 1951.

Kendall, George W. *Narrative of the Texan Santa Fe Expedition.* 2 vols. Austin, TX: Steck, 1935.

Oppenheimer, Alan J. *The Historical Background of Albuquerque, New Mexico.* Albuquerque, NM: Planning Department, City of Albuquerque, 1962.

Simmons, Marc. *Albuquerque: A Narrative History.* Albuquerque: University of New Mexico Press, 1982.

Winship, George P. *The Coronado Expedition, 1540–1542.* Chicago: Rio Grande Press, 1964.

*Chapter One*

# BEFORE ALBUQUERQUE

## The Rise and Fall of the Pueblo Indian Province of Tiguex

### The Prehistory: 10,000 BC–AD 1540

Modern Albuquerque, covering an area of more than 130 square miles in the Rio Grande Valley of central New Mexico, occupies land that has known periodic human habitation for at least twelve thousand years. Archaeologists say the city covers several thousand prehistoric sites representing various stages of human development in the region.

Near the close of the last ice age, by about 10,000 BC, small bands of Paleo-Indians ("ancient" Indians) of the so-called Clovis culture camped here and hunted such prehistoric and now extinct beasts as the elephant-like giant woolly mammoths and mastodons. They were followed by primitive hunters of the Folsom culture, who from about 8500 to 7500 BC hunted giant bison and big game other than the already extinct mammoths and mastodons. Long wooden spears, tipped with sharp projectile points of chipped stone, were the favorite hunting weapons of these Paleo-Indians. The spears were often launched with a handheld wooden device known as an atlatl, by means of which the spear is thrust back and then thrown forward.

Of these earliest inhabitants we know practically nothing, the only evidence of their existence being the projectile points and other stone implements they left behind at a few scattered locations. The cultural names we have given these ancient hunters, Clovis and Folsom, stem from the names of New Mexico communities near where their artifacts were first found and identified. The finely chipped Folsom points are distinguishable by grooves on each side for ease in attaching them to wooden shafts.

Gradually, over the centuries, the once cool and wet climate became warmer and drier, most big game animals became extinct, and the early hunters were replaced by Indians of the Desert culture, known as hunters and gatherers, who hunted small game with bows and arrows and gathered seeds and other edible plant products. Eventually, they began planting small crops of corn, beans, and squash, enabling them to settle down in small clusters of dome-shaped huts, and later in pit houses, shallow dugouts roofed with poles, sticks, and mud mortar. Weavers of fine, waterproof baskets, they are known to us as Basket Makers. By about AD 400, they were making pottery of molded and baked clay.

Between AD 700 and 900, these prehistoric Indians began building and occupying small, above ground communal buildings of sun-baked mud and stone, compact structures containing living quarters and storage rooms for a number of families. Beginning in about AD 900, Indian towns began to proliferate throughout the entire region, particularly in the high desert country northwest of the Rio Grande Valley, where major apartment dwellings of stone masonry, some terraced to heights of four and five levels, and containing more than one thousand rooms, began to take shape on canyon floors, high mesa tops, and in cavities of steep cliffs. These early stone masons have been designated in recent years as the Anasazi, a controversial Navajo word first thought to mean "ancient ones," but a more likely translation is "enemy ancestors," or "enemies of our ancestors," a designation considered meaningless by the descendants of the early builders.

A long and severe drought in the thirteenth century forced the Anasazi to abandon their major centers in the arid region, and many, including those who had built the magnificent stone structures in and about Chaco Canyon, migrated eastward to establish adobe towns along the Rio Grande and its tributaries.

By the beginning of the sixteenth century, the present Albuquerque locale was the scene of at least a dozen riverside Indian towns, consisting of compact communal dwellings of various sizes, which eventually became known as pueblos, and the inhabitants as Pueblo Indians, *pueblo* being the Spanish word for "town." This designation distinguished these Indians from Native Americans who led nomadic lives.

Soon, the lifestyles of these town-dwelling Indians, over a wide area of New Mexico, were to be altered forever with the arrival of European strangers from the south.

### The Coronado Expedition, 1540–1542

Albuquerque was yet 165 years in the future when the first Europeans visited and described the locale during the early 1540s. They were members of the Coronado Expedition, a large Spanish force that was exploring the northern and uncharted regions of New Spain, as Mexico was known at the time, in search of gold and the great wealth that was believed to exist there.

The principal object of the expedition was to investigate rumors that the legendary Seven Cities of Cíbola, said to be rich in gold and other valuables, were located in the unexplored regions a thousand miles north of Mexico City, capital of the viceroyalty of New Spain. That such a place might exist did not seem unreasonable to the Spanish conquistadors, who previously had discovered great wealth while conquering the New World civilizations of the Aztecs and the Incas.

Selected to lead the expedition as captain-general was Francisco Vásquez de Coronado, a thirty-year-old native of Salamanca, Spain, who was serving as governor of the province of Nueva Galicia, northwest of Mexico City. He had arrived in New Spain in 1535 at the age of twenty-five, and two years later he married doña Beatriz de Estrada, a wealthy young heiress whose late father had been treasurer of New Spain.

The treasure-hunting expedition assembled at the town of Compostela, in the western coastal region of present-day Mexico, and began a slow, northward trek, in scattered segments, on February 23, 1540. It consisted of more than three hundred mounted soldiers and infantrymen, hundreds of Mexican Indian servants, four or five Franciscan friars, several women, and more than five hundred horses and mules.

The soldiers wore a variety of medieval helmets and body armor, and were armed with swords, lances, crossbows, harquebuses (early muskets), and a few small bronze cannons. Although most of the soldiers were Spanish, several other nationalities were represented as well, including a Scotsman, a German, two Italians, and several Portuguese.

Accompanying the expedition as a guide was Fray Marcos de Niza, an adventurous Franciscan missionary, who claimed that he had seen Cíbola from a distance the year before, while leading a small expedition

3

into the northern wilderness, and had viewed a city that appeared to be large and wealthy. He had retreated south after learning that his guide Esteban, a colorful black Moorish slave, had entered Cíbola and was put to death by the inhabitants.

Coronado and the vanguard of his expedition, after slow progress northeast through present-day Arizona, reached Cíbola during the first week of 1540, but instead of finding cities rich in treasure, they found six or seven Zuni villages of mud and stone, just inside the western border of present-day New Mexico, and containing nothing of value to the hungry explorers other than stores of food. Fray Marcos was sent home in disgrace.

Arriving at Hawikuh, westernmost of the Zuni pueblos, Coronado attempted to enter into peaceful negotiations with the Indians, but they were no more hospitable to these visitors than they had been to Esteban, whom they referred to as the "black Mexican." They challenged the Spaniards to cross a line of cornmeal they drew on the ground, some skirmishing developed, and the Zunis fortified themselves in Hawikuh, a multistoried pueblo surrounded by a wall.

Coronado ordered an assault on the pueblo, and the Indians, from positions on the rooftops, rained rocks and arrows down on the soldiers, aiming many of the missiles at Coronado, highly visible in his gilded armor and shiny, plumed helmet. He was knocked unconscious and carried from the field.

After a brief battle, the Zunis asked for peace, abandoned the pueblo, and Coronado and his men moved in and began feasting on the food stores. Coronado established his temporary headquarters at Hawikuh, which he called Granada. From Cíbola, as the Zuni villages were called at the time, Coronado began dispatching small groups of explorers into the surrounding region. One, led by Pedro de Tovar, reached the Hopi villages in northern Arizona, and another, led by García López de Cárdenas, continued on west to reach the rim of the Grand Canyon, this being the first group of Europeans to view this natural wonder.

Hernando de Alvarado, captain of artillery, left Zuni on August 29 to explore the unknown country to the east, accompanied by about twenty soldiers and Fray Juan Padilla, a Franciscan missionary. They visited Acoma Pueblo, situated atop a high mesa, and continuing east they reached the west bank of the Rio Grande, in the vicinity of present-day Albuquerque, on September 7, 1540. Since it was the eve of the Feast Day of Our Lady, Alvarado promptly named the river the Río de Nuestra Senora, the "River of Our Lady." The name didn't stick.

In describing what was to become the Albuquerque locale, Alvarado wrote:

> This river of Our Lady flows through a very wide open plain sowed with corn plants; there are several groves, and there are twelve villages. The houses are of earth, two stories high; the people have a good appearance, more like laborers than a warlike race; they have a large food supply of corn, beans, melons, and fowl in great plenty; they clothe themselves with cotton and the skins of cows [buffalos] and dresses of feathers of the fowls [turkeys]; they wear their hair short.
>
> Those who have the most authority among them are the old men; we regarded them as witches, because they say that they go up into the sky and other things of the same sort.

The twelve riverside villages that Alvarado referred to, as well as several others at some distance from the river, were inhabited by Pueblo Indians who spoke the Tiwa (spelled "Tigua" in Spanish) language, and the towns were known collectively as the Province of Tiguex (pronounced "tee-wesh," although commonly pronounced "tee-guay" today). Alvarado wrote that there were seven other villages in the province that had been destroyed and depopulated by "Indians who paint their eyes" and who lived in straw houses in the same region as the "cows," apparently a reference to the Indians from the broad buffalo plains to the east.

Albuquerque today occupies the center of what was once the Province of Tiguex, all evidence indicating that these Indian pueblos extended along the east and west banks of the Rio Grande within a thirty-five-mile stretch between the present-day towns of Los Lunas on the south and Bernalillo on the north. Alvarado wrote that the people of these villages greeted him and his party with friendship, that they exchanged gifts, and that Fray Juan Padilla erected some Christian crosses.

Continuing their explorations with Indian guides to the north and northeast, Alvarado and his men learned that there were seventy or eighty Indian pueblos in the region, and that they did not share a common language but spoke in a variety of tongues. Among the larger Indian towns they visited was one called Braba, present-day Taos Pueblo, and one called Cicuye, later known as Pecos Pueblo, the extensive ruins of which are preserved today in Pecos National Historical Park southeast of Santa Fe.

Meanwhile, Alvarado had sent a messenger to Coronado at Cíbola (Zuni) with word that the Province of Tiguex was an ideal place for him to establish winter headquarters for the expedition. Sent from Zuni to Tiguex to prepare the winter quarters was a group of Spanish soldiers and Indian allies led by García López de Cárdenas, captain of cavalry, who had returned from his journey to the Grand Canyon.

Upon reaching the Rio Grande, apparently near the southern edge of the Indian province, Cárdenas and his men began preparing lodgings for the expedition near one of the pueblos. As winter approached, and it began to snow, the Spanish explorers began suffering from the cold, and they asked the Indians to vacate one of their pueblos and move in with friends at other pueblos.

Without resistance, but with much resentment, the Indians vacated the pueblo the Spanish called Alcanfor, or Coofor, said to be the southernmost Tiguex pueblo on the west bank of the Rio Grande. Although the exact location of this now vanished pueblo is unknown today, it probably was located in the vicinity of present-day Isleta Pueblo, a short distance south of Albuquerque. Cárdenas and his men took over the abandoned pueblo and began preparing it for the arrival of Coronado and the still scattered remnants of the expedition.

Coronado, accompanied by thirty of his soldiers, left Zuni late in November and headed east for the Rio Grande, arriving at Tiguex in December after first visiting an Indian province of eight pueblos called Tutahaco to the south. Coronado established his headquarters at Alcanfor, where he waited for the arrival of the remainder of his expedition, led from Zuni by Captain Tristán de Luna y Arellano.

Among the Spanish soldiers arriving at Tiguex at this time was Pedro de Castañeda, who twenty years later wrote a detailed account of the Coronado Expedition. Describing the Province of Tiguex, he wrote:

> Tiguex is a province with twelve villages on the banks of a large, mighty river; some villages on one side and some on the other. It is a spacious valley two leagues [about five miles] wide, and a very high, rough, snow-covered mountain chain lies east of it. There are seven villages in the ridges at the foot of this, four on the plain and three situated on the skirts of the mountain.

The mountain chain Castañeda referred to consisted of what are known today as the Sandia and Manzano mountains, and the seven villages may have been those known later as the Salinas pueblos, near the southeastern foot of the Manzanos, which were abandoned in the 1600s.

North of Tiguex, Castañeda wrote, was another province of seven villages, known as Quirix, a reference to the Keres or Keresan pueblos north of present-day Bernalillo that include such existing pueblos as Santa Ana, San Felipe, Santo Domingo, and Cochiti. To the northwest, he continued, was yet another province of seven villages, called Hemes. These seven villages were later consolidated into the present Jemez Pueblo.

Castañeda's narrative provides some interesting details about the Province of Tiguex and its people during the sixteenth century when the first Europeans arrived on the scene. Along the banks of the river were fields of corn, beans, and melons, the cornfields attracting large numbers of cranes, wild geese, crows, and starlings. There also were some small cotton fields, the cotton used by men to make articles of clothing.

Men and women worked together to build their villages, the women preparing the earthen mixture and erecting the walls, the men hauling in wood and setting it in place. The houses belonged to the women, and the young men lived in large underground *estufas*, or "kivas." Young women went about entirely naked, even in cold weather, until they were married, while the men wore long robes over shirts made of deerskin. "The men spin and weave," Castañeda continued, "while the women bring up children and prepare the food."

The pueblos had separate rooms where the women prepared food and ground cornmeal with stones, he wrote, adding:

> A man sits at the door playing a flute while they grind, moving the stones to the music and singing together. They grind a large quantity at one time, because they make all their bread of meal soaked in warm water, like wafers. . . . In all these provinces they have earthenware glazed with antinomy and jars of extraordinary labor and workmanship, which are worth seeing.

These people were not cruel, Castañeda wrote, and they did not eat human flesh, nor make sacrifices of it. But, as events were soon to prove, they did not have unlimited patience.

Coronado's arrival at Tiguex in December 1540 coincided with what proved to be a very severe winter, with much snow and frigid temperatures, causing the Rio Grande to freeze from bank to bank. The Spanish soldiers, unaccustomed to bitter cold, found that the shelter at Alcanfor did not satisfy all their needs. They wanted warmer clothing and blankets.

Communication between the Spaniards and the Tiwas was difficult, however, there being no language interpreters, and was carried out by gestures and a makeshift sign language. Better communication might have averted the crises that soon were to follow.

Summoned to Alcanfor by Coronado was a prominent Tiguex leader whom the Spaniards called Juan Alemán, because he resembled a man by that name in Mexico City. Coronado told Alemán that he must arrange for the Indian province to furnish him with more than three hundred articles of clothing for his men. Alemán answered that he was unable to do this, that the Spaniards would have to visit and deal separately with each of the pueblos in the province.

Coronado dispatched delegations of his men to each of the pueblos to collect clothing and other provisions. At some pueblos the collectors angered the Indians by making immediate demands for clothing and other articles, on some occasions stripping cloaks off their backs. Since the expedition was under orders not to take anything from Indians without reimbursement, these Indians may have received some petty merchandise in exchange.

Only a short time before, tension between the Indians and the Spaniards had increased when an Indian from a pueblo the Spaniards called Arenal, about five miles north of Alcanfor, approached Cárdenas with a delegation of his friends and complained in sign language that a Spanish soldier had entered his home and had violated, or had attempted to violate, his wife. He received no satisfaction, however, as he was unable to identify the soldier.

Without warning, early one morning late in December, the Indians of Tiguex launched a revolt against their now unwelcome visitors. The first indication came when a Mexican Indian who had been guarding the expedition's herd of horses near Alcanfor ran to the pueblo and reported that the Indians had killed his companion and were driving horses north toward their pueblos. Seven or eight mounted soldiers, led by Captain Cárdenas, followed the trail of stolen horses north up the river valley, finding along the way more than twenty-five dead horses and seven dead mules, all killed by Indian arrows. They drove the live horses they found back to the horse camp at Alcanfor.

On a more ominous note, Cárdenas found that a small pueblo the Spaniards called Alameda, about a mile north of Alcanfor, had been abandoned, and that many Indians had gathered and fortified themselves at Arenal, and at a pueblo called Moho, about ten miles farther north, both pueblos now surrounded by palisades. At Arenal, Cárdenas could hear the defiant Indians running stolen horses and shooting them with arrows inside the stockade.

Cárdenas attempted to bring a peaceful solution to the revolt, informing the Indians at Arenal that they could be forgiven for stealing and killing the horses, as the Spaniards had many of them. The Indians remained defiant, however, jeering and shouting war cries from the rooftops of the pueblo, and waving as banners the tails of the horses they had killed.

When other attempts to negotiate a peaceful settlement failed, Coronado ordered Cárdenas to attack Arenal and bring the defiant Indians to submission. Cárdenas proceeded north to Arenal with about sixty horsemen, some infantry, and some Mexican Indian allies. The horsemen surrounded the pueblo, Cárdenas once again asked the Indians to submit peacefully, and then he ordered an assault on the fortified town.

In a fierce afternoon battle that lasted several hours, the Spanish soldiers fought their way through the barricades and gained the roofs of the first and second floors of the terraced pueblo, their muskets and crossbows proving more than a match for the Indian arrows and other missiles. By nightfall, when the fighting ceased temporarily, thirteen or fourteen of the Spanish soldiers had been badly wounded, and a number of their Indian allies had been killed.

When the battle resumed the next morning, the Indians fought from the protection of interior rooms in the upper level of the pueblo, aiming their arrows through small openings. When attempts to dislodge them by force failed, Cárdenas devised a plan to smoke them out. Using battering rams, the soldiers knocked holes in the doorless and windowless ground floor of earthen pueblo and ignited smudge fires below the upper levels. Dense smoke, rising into the small rooms above, began suffocating the occupants, and they ran out into the open air where some were killed by the soldiers. The others threw down their arms and asked for peace, which was granted. They were led outside the pueblo to a tent occupied by Cárdenas.

Cárdenas, who had been ordered by Coronado not to take any prisoners alive, and claiming later that he did not know that the Indians had put down their arms and asked for peace, ordered that two hundred stakes be prepared to burn them alive. When Indians in the tent saw that the Spaniards were binding and beginning to burn some of their companions, they began to struggle and defend themselves. Foot soldiers attacked the tent, and the Indians fled in panic, only to be chased and cut down by the Spanish cavalry. At battle's end, few if any of the more than two hundred defenders of Arenal remained alive. Cárdenas led his soldiers back to Alcanfor, where he was greeted warmly by Coronado.

It was snowing the next day when Captain Arellano and the main body of the expedition arrived from Zuni, bringing along the expedition's supply of sheep and cattle. Their arrival brought the population of the former Indian pueblo of Alcanfor to more than three hundred Spanish soldiers, which was comforting to Coronado as the Tiguex revolt was not yet over.

Early in January (1541) Coronado sent scouting parties up the river valley to assess the situation. Forty cavalrymen and some foot soldiers, let by Cárdenas, crossed to the east bank of the river and trudged north through snow past a succession of abandoned pueblos, some of them abandoned hastily when the occupants saw the soldiers approaching. The Spaniards found seven or eight dead Spanish horses at the northernmost pueblo they visited, a small and abandoned one on the east bank. They burned a portion of the pueblo in retaliation, and returned to Alcanfor.

Coronado learned that many of the Indians who had abandoned their homes had gathered at the pueblo called Moho, said to be the largest and best fortified pueblo in the Province of Tiguex. Moho, also referred to as Tiguex by the Spaniards, was located on an elevation near a spring, on the west bank of the river about fifteen miles north of Alcanfor. The exact location is unknown today, but the site most likely is within the present city limits of Albuquerque.

The leader of the Indians fortified at Moho was the man the Spaniards called Juan Alemán, who initially had been on friendly terms with them. Since the Spaniards had negotiated successfully with Alemán in preceding months, Coronado sent Cárdenas and thirty horsemen to Moho in an attempt to negotiate a peaceful settlement with the insurgents.

Cárdenas and his escort drew up outside the pueblo, Alemán appeared among his warriors on the rooftops, and Cárdenas informed him by signs and a few words that they both understood that the Spaniards desired peace with the Indians and would treat them kindly. Alemán responded that he was willing to emerge from the pueblo and greet the captain in friendship, but only on the conditions that Cárdenas dismount, leave his soldiers behind, and approach unarmed. Cárdenas agreed to the conditions, and walked forward to meet Alemán, who left the pueblo accompanied by two men.

"Juan Aleman approached and embraced him [Cárdenas] vigorously," Castañeda wrote in his narrative, "while the other two who had come with him drew two mallets which they had hidden behind their backs and gave him two such blows over his helmet that they almost knocked him senseless." The Indians attempted to drag the struggling Cárdenas through a narrow opening into the pueblo, but his cavalrymen, rushing forward and braving a shower of arrows and rocks, rescued their captain and carried him off to safety. After Indians at another fortified pueblo nearby rejected his peace proposals, Cárdenas returned to Alcanfor to report to his commander.

Coronado, believing that he could not resume his explorations until the Tiguex revolt was put down, marched north to Moho with his entire force, camped at the spring that furnished the pueblo's water supply, and ordered his men to surround the fortified village. When his repeated demands for submission were met with jeers, he ordered a full-scale assault on the pueblo.

Moho proved to be a far tougher nut to crack than Arenal. After breaking through the palisades, the soldiers attempted to breach the outer walls of the earthen pueblo, only to find that the walls were reinforced with heavy tree trunks that they could not penetrate. They began to scale the walls with makeshift ladders to engage the Indians who were assembled on the rooftops, but as Castañeda wrote, "they threw down such quantities of rocks upon our men that many of them were laid out, and they wounded nearly a hundred with arrows, several of whom afterwards died on account of bad treatment by an unskilled surgeon who was with the army." Many of the arrows were poisoned with rattlesnake venom.

Unable to dislodge the defenders of Moho, Coronado began a siege of the fortified town, hopeful that the Indians would surrender when their water ran out. The pueblo was well supplied with corn and other foodstuff. Although cut off from their water supply, the besieged Indians managed to hold out for weeks by melting snow from a series of snow-storms that passed over the region. When water from melted snow became scarce, they began digging a deep well inside the pueblo, only to have the walls cave in, trapping and killing about thirty of the workers.

Coronado launched another assault on the pueblo late in February, but it, too, was unsuccessful. Among the Spaniards killed in the assault was Captain Francisco de Ovando, one of the expedition's most popular officers.

In the effort to conserve their dwindling water supply, the Indians asked the Spaniards during the middle of March for permission to release the women and children to their custody. Permission was granted, and about one hundred women and children filed out of the besieged pueblo and were received kindly by the Spaniards, one of the soldiers, Lope de Urrea, gathering the children in his arms.

About two weeks later, their water supply now exhausted, the besieged Indians made a break for freedom. Stealing out of the pueblo in the early morning darkness, they killed several Spanish soldiers before their presence was noted. The alarm was given, and cavalrymen began chasing down and killing the fleeing Indians. Some of the Indians plunged into the cold and swiftly flowing waters of the Rio Grande, which the Spaniards were calling the Río Tiguex, and some made it across to the east bank, where they fell exhausted and were soon captured. A portion of the vacated pueblo was burned.

An estimated two hundred Indians were killed during the siege of Moho, which was said to have lasted about eighty days, and those who were captured were made servants of their conquerors. With the fall of another nearby pueblo where Indians had fortified themselves, the Tiguex War, perhaps fought entirely within the present limits of Albuquerque, was over.

With the Province of Tiguex now in shambles, and no longer a threat, Coronado was ready to resume his explorations of the Tierra Nueva, the "new land." An Indian captive whom the Spaniards called El Turco, or "the Turk," persuaded Coronado to explore the plains country far to the northeast of Tiguex where he claimed there was great wealth. Alvarado had brought the Turk to Tiguex from the pueblo of Pecos, called Cicuye at the time, where he had been the slave of some Indians who had captured him.

In his homeland on the northeastern plains, the Turk told the Spaniards, were wondrous countries rich in gold and silver, including one called Quivira, where the people ate off gold and silver plates, where the emperor was lulled to sleep by the twinkling of golden bells suspended from tree limbs, and where there was a large river containing fish as big as the Spaniards' horses.

Determined to investigate this fabulous land called Quivira, Coronado gathered his entire force, and with the Turk as a guide, left Tiguex on April 23, 1541. A march of about sixty miles to the northeast brought them to Cicuye (Pecos), which Castañeda described as "a pueblo containing five hundred warriors and is feared throughout the land." From here, in terms of modern geography, the large expedition plodded slowly east across New Mexico into the Texas Panhandle, pausing along the way to bridge a narrow and swift-moving river before heading north into central Kansas, the supposed location of Quivira.

Quivira proved to be even a greater disappointment than Cíbola. No trace of gold, silver, or other riches, but seemingly endless plains, filled with buffalo herds, and inhabited by "primitive" Indians who lived in round huts made of thatched grass. The Turk, confronted by the Spaniards, admitted that he had lied about the wealth of Quivira, and confessed that the Indians of Cicuye had persuaded him to lead them far into the trackless plains with the hope that they would become lost and never return. Soldiers strangled and buried the Turk on the spot, and the disheartened explorers made their way back to Tiguex, arriving in the middle of September. Coronado established winter headquarters once again at Alcanfor, and began debating his future course of action.

On December 27, 1541, Coronado and one of his officers, Rodrigo de Maldonado, were racing their horses side by side near Alcanfor when Coronado's saddle girth broke, causing him to plunge to the ground beneath the hoofs of Maldonado's horse. Suffering severe head wounds, Coronado was carried to his quarters, where he lingered near death for days. "It was while he was in this condition," Castañeda wrote, "that he recollected what a scientific friend of his in Salamanca had told him, that he would become a powerful lord in distant lands, and that he would have a fall from which he would never be able to recover. This expectation of death made him desire to return and die where had a wife and children."

Coronado never fully recovered from his head injuries. Discouraged and disillusioned, he spent the remainder of the winter at Alcanfor and began making plans to lead his expedition back to Mexico. It was early in April of 1542 that the weary explorers gathered their belongings and began the trek home, retracing the route by which they had come. The captured Tiguex Indians they had held as slaves or servants were released.

Left behind, at their own requests, were several Franciscan friars and their servants, including Fray Juan Padilla, who returned to Quivira where he reportedly was killed by Indians upon his arrival, and Fray Luis de Escalona, who returned to Cicuye (Pecos Pueblo) and was never heard from again. Also remaining behind were some of the expedition's Mexican Indian allies.

Coronado, who resumed his position as governor of Nueva Galicia, later was cleared of charges that he mismanaged the expedition. García López de Cárdenas returned to his home in Spain where he was imprisoned and fined on charges that he had inflicted cruelties and other offenses on the Indians, particularly the burning of Indian prisoners following the attack on the pueblo of Arenal.

Coronado, in a letter to the King of Spain, wrote that it would be impossible to establish a Spanish settlement at Tiguex, where Albuquerque is located today, because the winters were too cold, and it was too distant from any seaports. Coronado, however, spent no summer months at Tiguex. He died in 1554 and was buried in Mexico City.

### Later Spanish Expeditions, 1581–1591

Following Coronado's departure from Tiguex in the spring of 1542, the region remained without any organized Spanish presence for nearly forty years. Then, in the summer of 1581, a small Spanish expedition consisting of three Franciscan friars, nine mounted Spanish soldiers, and nineteen Mexican Indian servants moved north up the Rio Grande in what was intended to be a mission to convert Pueblo Indians to the Christian faith.

Known as the Chamuscado-Rodríguez Expedition, the missionary enterprise was organized by Fray Agustín Rodríguez, who was authorized by Spanish authorities in Mexico City to penetrate the little known northern regions with an escort of solders under the command of Captain Francisco Sánchez Chamuscado. Accompanying Fray Agustín were two other friars, Fray Francisco López and Fray Juan de Santa María.

Pausing at one of the Piro-speaking Indian pueblos on the Rio Grande near the present-day town of Socorro on August 21, 1581, the party took possession of the land in the name of the King of Spain, designating it as the Province of San Felipe, and naming the river

Guadalquivir, after a river by that name in Spain. Continuing up the river valley, across the land now occupied by Albuquerque, the Spaniards identified and assigned names to more than sixty Indian pueblos. The names they gave the province, the river, and the pueblos, however, did not outlast their visit.

Fray Juan de Santa María left the expedition in September, determined to return to Mexico alone, and was killed by Tiwa Indians within two to three days of his homeward journey. The two remaining friars, after visiting pueblos over a wide area of the region, decided to begin their missionary work at Puaray, on the Rio Grande near present-day Bernalillo. One of the northernmost Indian pueblos of Tiguex, Puaray was described as containing 123 houses (apartments) and terraced to three stories in height.

Chamuscado and the soldier escort left Puaray for the return trip to Mexico on January 31, 1582. Soon after their departure, the Indians fell upon and killed Fray Agustín Rodríguez and Fray Francisco López. The fate of the martyred friars was unknown until early in 1583 when a small relief expedition from Mexico, on a mission to determine the welfare of the padres, moved north up the Rio Grande to the Province of Tiguex. The expedition was led by Antonio de Espejo, a prominent merchant and rancher, and included Fray Bernardino Beltrán, fourteen Spanish soldiers, and some Indian servants.

Espejo learned before reaching Puaray that the Franciscan friars had been killed. The Indians of Tiguex, fearing retribution, left their pueblos as the Spaniards approached and fled east to the safety of the mountains. Determined to explore the region for mineral wealth, Espejo led the expedition west into Arizona before returning to the Rio Grande.

Arriving at Puaray in June, the Spaniards found that most of the inhabitants had fled east to the mountains, except for about thirty who shouted insults from the rooftops when asked for food. The soldiers attacked the pueblo, set fire to a kiva in which some of the Indians had sought protection, then led sixteen captives out of the pueblo and executed them. The Espejo Expedition returned to Mexico by journeying into New Mexico's eastern plains and following the Pecos River south.

Early in 1591, a detachment of fifty Spanish soldiers commanded by Captain Juan de Morlete marched north through the Tiguex province, their mission not to deal with the Indians, but to find and arrest one of their countrymen. The object of their search was Gaspar Castaño de Sosa, lieutenant governor of the Mexican province of Nuevo León, who without proper authorization was attempting to settle a group of Spanish colonists in New Mexico.

Without waiting for official permission from the Spanish government, Sosa had headed north into New Mexico the previous summer with about 170 men, women, and children, carrying their belongings in two-wheeled carts drawn by oxen. They followed the Pecos River north to Pecos Pueblo, where they fought a brief skirmish with the inhabitants, then headed west, searching for a suitable site for the proposed colony.

Morlete and his men, moving upstream from the Tiwa pueblos, found the illegal colonists camped at the Keresan pueblo later called Santo Domingo, on the east bank of the Rio Grande. Sosa was placed in chains, and the soldiers marched him and his followers back to Mexico. Convicted in Mexico City of rebelling against the lawful authority of New Spain, Sosa was exiled to China. Later, the Council of the Indies in Spain exonerated him, but his vindication came too late, for by this time he had been killed in a mutiny on a Chinese junk.

## Spanish Colonization

In the summer of 1598 the Pueblo Indians of the Province of Tiguex were startled to see a long procession of hundreds of Spanish men, women, and children moving slowly north along the east bank of the Rio Grande across the site of present-day Albuquerque. Many of the Indians, frightened by the large invasion force, fled their pueblos and went into hiding. The procession, which stretched out for several miles, included family groups, single men, soldiers, and Franciscan friars, their possessions transported in about eighty wagons and carts. Herders drove along about seven thousand head of livestock, including horses, mules, beef cattle, sheep, and goats.

Leading the procession was don Juan de Oñate, a native of Zacatecas, Mexico, who with the title of governor and captain general had been given official permission by King Philip II of Spain to take possession of and colonize the kingdoms and provinces of New Mexico and to convert the region's Pueblo Indians to Christianity. The Spanish colonists were nearing the end of a long and difficult journey that for months had taken them hundreds of miles across deserts and rugged terrain from the interior of Mexico.

The Province of Tiguex, according to an expedition report, consisted of many pueblos, farms, and planted fields on both sides of the Río del Norte (River of the North) as the Rio Grande in New Mexico was known at that time and for centuries to come. Tiguex, however, was not the goal of these Spanish colonists, and they continued north out of the province, to the probable relief of the Tiwa people.

Oñate, who was moving in advance of the main caravan with a small group of soldiers and Franciscan friars, arrived at the Tiwa pueblo of Puaray, near the northern edge of the province, on June 27, 1598. Among those in the advance party was Captain Gaspar Pérez de Villagrá, who later was to publish an account of the expedition in his epic book, *A History of New Mexico*. In telling of the surprise that awaited them at Puaray, he wrote:

> We halted at the pueblo of Puaray, where we were well received. The Indians took the priests to the quarters that had been prepared for them. The walls of their rooms had been recently whitewashed, and the rooms were cleanly swept.
>
> The next day, however, when the whitewash had dried, we were clearly able to see, through the whitewash, paintings of scenes which made our blood run cold. God always finds a way to make known the story of those who suffer for his Holy Faith.
>
> There, pictured on the wall, we saw the details of the martyrdom of those saintly men, Fray Agustin [Rodríguez], Fray Juan [de Santa María] and Fray Francisco [López]. The paintings showed us exactly how they had met their deaths, stoned and beaten by the savage Indians.

Oñate told the group not to look at the wall paintings, or let the Indians know that they had seen them, Villagrá continued. Fearing trouble, the Spaniards filed silently out of the pueblo during the middle of the night, while the Indians were sleeping.

Continuing upstream, Oñate and his followers visited the Keresan pueblos of San Felipe, Santo Domingo, and Cochiti, north of present-day Bernalillo, pueblos that had escaped the warfare and clashes with Spaniards that had ravaged their southern neighbors at Tiguex since the arrival of Coronado nearly sixty years before. Found living at Santo Domingo were two Spanish-speaking young men, Tomás and Cristóbal, who had accompanied the Castaño de Sosa expedition to the region in 1591 as Mexican Indian servants. Since they had learned the Keres language, they proved invaluable to Oñate as interpreters.

At a July 7 council meeting at Santo Domingo, Oñate told a delegation of Pueblo Indian leaders that he was bringing the Christian religion to them for the salvation of their souls. The Indians pledged allegiance to the Spanish Crown.

The Oñate colonists ended their long journey at the Tiwa-speaking pueblo of Ohke, on the east bank of the Rio Grande near present-day Española. Oñate gave the Indian pueblo a new name, San Juan de los Caballeros, today's San Juan Pueblo. Establishing his headquarters here, Oñate began assigning Franciscan missionaries to the various Pueblo Indian provinces, Fray Juan Claros being the first missionary assigned to the Tiguex province.

A short while later, Oñate moved his colonists to the west bank of the river, opposite San Juan, and established the Spanish community of San Gabriel as New Mexico's first capital. After touring the many Indian pueblos in the region, Oñate estimated that there were about seventy thousand Pueblo Indians living in New Mexico. It soon became evident that many of these Indians resented the Spanish presence in their lands.

Early in 1599, Oñate's forces stormed and sacked the lofty pueblo of Acoma, about sixty miles west of Tiguex, in retaliation for the killings there a few weeks before of nearly a dozen Spanish soldiers, including Oñate's nephew, Juan de Zaldívar. Early in 1601, the Spanish soldiers fought a fierce battle and defeated rebellious Indians of the Salinas pueblos, near some salt lakes along the southeast fringes of the Manzano Mountains. Meanwhile, the Spanish colonists at San Gabriel were showing signs of discontent and mutiny in the new land. Deserters were tracked down and executed. Oñate, in his far-ranging travels throughout the region, was disappointed in not finding any valuable minerals.

Suspended from office in 1607, Oñate later stood trial on a number of charges, including the severe treatment of Indian captives following the destruction of Acoma. Although exonerated of most charges, he was banished from New Mexico for life. He died in Spain in 1626.

Succeeding Oñate as governor of New Mexico was don Pedro de Peralta, who arrived with additional colonists, soldiers, and missionaries to reinforce the dwindling population of San Gabriel. He abandoned San Gabriel in 1609 or 1610 and moved the colonists about twenty-five miles south to establish a new capital, Santa Fe, on the banks of a small stream in an uninhabited locale in the shadow of the Sangre de Cristo Mountains.

Spain had decided to maintain New Mexico primarily as a missionary colony for the conversion of Pueblo Indians to Christianity, and the Franciscan missionaries went about their work with great zeal. Upon their arrival at various Pueblo Indian provinces, they began depopulating the smaller pueblos and consolidated the Indians in one or two of the larger pueblos, where they were put to work building substantial mission churches and convents.

Fray Alonso de Benavides, custodian of the New Mexico missions from 1623 to 1629, reported in a memorial to the Spanish Crown in 1634 that the Province of Tiguex, which he called the Tioas (Tiwas) Nation, contained about fifteen or sixteen pueblos consisting of about seven thousand souls, all baptized. There were spacious and attractive churches and convents at Isleta and Sandia pueblos, he continued, where the Tiwa Indians were taught to read, write, and sing.

"Fray Esteban de Perea and Fray Juan de Salas have worked a great deal in this province and nation, both in congregating these Indians in pueblos and converting them to our holy Catholic faith, as they were great sorcerers, superstitious, and very belligerent," he wrote. "Today they are very docile and well instructed, not only in their living and all kinds of crafts but also in things spiritual." "The Rio del Norte [Rio Grande] flows through the center of the province for about thirty miles," Benavides continued, "which causes the friars much hardship in crossing the river each time their ministering demands it, since the river is very swift and subject to bad floods."

During the 1600s, many Spanish colonists began establishing small farms and ranches in the Rio Grande Valley north and south of Santa Fe. The settled region north of Santa Fe was called the Río Arriba, or upstream country, while the region to the south, including the site of present-day Albuquerque, was called the Río Abajo, or downstream country.

By the 1670s, there were more Spanish colonists living on scattered farms and ranches in the Río Abajo than were living in Santa Fe. Spanish colonists who farmed and ranched in the Tiguex district maintained a peaceful coexistence with the Tiwa Indians, often attending religious services at mission churches at the Tiwa pueblos of Sandia, Alameda, and Puaray at the northern edge of the Indian province, and at Isleta on the southern edge.

A prolonged drought, followed by famine and pestilence, ravaged New Mexico in the late 1660s and early 1670s, causing much hardship to

Spanish colonists and Indians alike. Nomadic Apaches began raiding and looting Indian pueblos, particularly those in the Salinas District along the southeastern fringes of the Manzano Mountains. Abandoning their pueblos and mission churches forever, and migrating east to the Rio Grande Valley, were the inhabitants of Quarai, Abó, Las Humanas (Gran Quivira), and other nearby pueblos.

These catastrophes, coupled with the harsh efforts of Spanish government officials and Franciscan friars to stamp out all vestiges of native religions the Indians had practiced for centuries, brought increasing anger and discontent among the estimated eighteen thousand Pueblo Indian converts living in New Mexico.

A crisis about religions differences began to escalate in 1675 when don Juan Francisco de Treviño, the twenty-fourth Spanish governor of New Mexico, captured forty-seven Pueblo Indian medicine men who were accused of sorcery and witchcraft, hanged three of them, and released the others after they had suffered severe floggings. Among those released was Popé (pronounced "po-pay"), a San Juan Pueblo medicine man, who sought revenge by establishing a base of operations at Taos Pueblo where he began formulating plans for a full-scale revolt against the Spanish presence in New Mexico.

In 1680 Popé and his coconspirators dispatched messengers to the various Indian pueblos, each messenger carrying a cord tied in a series of knots. Leaders at each pueblo were told to untie a knot each day, and when they had untied the last knot, they were to rise in rebellion against the Spaniards and their religion.

Don Antonio de Otermín, who had succeeded Treviño as Spanish governor in 1677, described what happened next as "a lamentable tragedy such has never before happened in the world."

### Revolt of the Pueblos, 1680

On the morning of August 10, 1680, Pueblo Indians of New Mexico unleashed a violent revolt against Spanish rule and the Christian religion that brought death and destruction over a wide area of the province. The Pueblos, assisted by some Apache allies, devastated the region from Taos Pueblo south to Isleta Pueblo, a distance of about 130 miles, while the rebellion was felt as far west as the Hopi villages in northern Arizona.

The first targets of the rebelling Indians at each pueblo were the resident Franciscan missionaries and their mission churches. Many of the missionaries were killed at the outset of the revolt, the churches ransacked and set on fire, and religious objects associated with Catholic worship destroyed or desecrated.

Pueblo warriors, armed with bows, arrows, lances, and shields, streamed out of their villages to attack outlying Spanish farms and ranches, slaughtering men, women, and children, ransacking their homes, and driving off their livestock. Indians from the northern pueblos swarmed into Santa Fe, where the citizens took refuge and fortified themselves in the thick-walled Palace of the Governors. The revolt spread quickly to the Keresan and Tiguex pueblos in the Río Abajo district south of Santa Fe, where an estimated 120 Spanish men, women, and children were killed and their homes ransacked.

Sandia Pueblo, with a population of about three thousand Indians, was the center of the revolt in the Tiguex province. From this pueblo, and the smaller and neighboring pueblos of Puaray and Alameda, the rebelling Indians vented their wrath on Spanish colonists living on scattered farms and ranches on both sides of the Rio Grande on land now occupied by Albuquerque.

Alonso García, lieutenant governor of New Mexico and commander of the Río Abajo district, led a small rescue force along the river valley that gathered up about fifteen hundred survivors. They proceeded south to Isleta Pueblo, which was occupied by about two thousand Tiwa Indians who had not taken an active part in the revolt. Believing that all the Spanish colonists in and around Santa Fe had been killed, the Río Abajo refugees, led by García, left Isleta and began retreating south towards El Paso, a distance of nearly three hundred miles.

In Santa Fe, Otermín and about one thousand Spanish citizens and soldiers remained under siege in the government buildings. Soldiers ventured out into the streets on several occasions to inflict heavy casualties on the Indians who occupied the capital. Cut off from the outside world, however, with no hope of any assistance, the Spaniards collected what possessions they could carry and on August 21 filed unmolested through battle-littered streets to begin a retreat south to El Paso. What had been the Spanish capital of New Mexico for seventy years had now become an Indian pueblo.

During the retreat south, the Spaniards found that Sandia Pueblo was abandoned and that an attempt had been made to burn the church. Otermín ordered his men to torch the entire pueblo. The Santa Fe refugees found a scene of desolation as they continued down the east bank of the Rio Grande across land now occupied by Albuquerque.

Indians, standing off at a distance, jeered and taunted the retreating Spaniards as they passed by abandoned and ransacked Spanish haciendas. The bodies of slain men, women, and children, some of them stripped of their clothing, were found at intervals along the trail.

The Santa Fe refugees joined forces with the retreating Río Abajo refugees south of Isleta Pueblo, and all of the approximately twenty-five hundred Spaniards continued south out of New Mexico. Upon reaching the vicinity of present-day, river-separated cities of El Paso, Texas, and Juárez, Mexico, they established temporary settlements on both banks of the Rio Grande.

The Pueblo Revolt had succeeded in driving all the Spanish colonists and missionaries out of New Mexico. The Spanish death toll in the revolt was listed at more than 380 citizens and twenty-one Franciscan missionaries.

### Spanish Invasions and Reconquest, 1681–1696

Antonio de Otermín, the Spanish governor who lost New Mexico, had early ambitions of being the governor to reconquer the lost Spanish province. He had to wait for reinforcements, however, as many of the Spanish refugees who had accompanied him out of New Mexico had deserted the El Paso settlements and migrated south into Mexico.

On November 6, 1681, little more than a year after his retreat out of New Mexico, Otermín headed north out of El Paso with a force of less than three hundred men, consisting of 146 soldiers, more than one hundred Indian allies, some servants, and a few Franciscan friars. A march of nearly two hundred miles brought the Spanish expedition to the Piro pueblos, on the banks of the Rio Grande, and all were found to be abandoned and partially destroyed, apparently the victims of Apache attacks. Otermín ordered his soldiers to burn the pueblos of Socorro, Senecu, Alamillo, and Sevilleta.

Early on the morning of December 6, 1681, Otermín and seventy handpicked men reached and surrounded Isleta Pueblo, southernmost of the Tiwa pueblos, and the first occupied pueblo encountered on the march. The Spanish soldiers, encountering only token resistance, stormed into the pueblo without firing a shot to find the village occupied by more than five hundred Indians. The Indians said they had offered brief resistance because they thought they were being attacked by Apaches.

Franciscan missionaries with the expedition absolved and baptized 511 men, women, and children, including some Piros who had taken refuge there. The Indians said the rebels from the northern pueblos had forced them to renounce the Christian religion and return to their old ways.

Juan Domínguez de Mendoza, lieutenant general of cavalry, was ordered by Otermín to reconnoiter the country north of Isleta with sixty mounted Spanish soldiers and some Indian allies on foot. Leaving Isleta on December 8, they camped that night at Mendoza's former and abandoned home in the Atrisco jurisdiction, now a part of present-day Albuquerque.

The Mendoza force reached the northern Tiwa pueblos of Alameda, Sandia, and Puaray the next day to find that all had been recently abandoned except for a few elderly Indians who told them that the remainder had fled east into the Sandia Mountains. The church at Alameda had been burned to the ground. At these and other abandoned pueblos the Spaniards gathered up ceremonial objects the Indians used in the observance of their religion and burned them.

Continuing north into the Keresan province, the Spaniards learned that many of the Indians had left their pueblos on the Rio Grande to occupy defensive positions on top of high and steep-sided mesas. At San Felipe Pueblo, they found that the church was unroofed and the monastery torn down, while at Santo Domingo Pueblo, both the church and the monastery had been demolished.

The Spanish force continued upstream to Cochiti Pueblo, northernmost of the Keres-speaking pueblos, about twenty-five miles south of Santa Fe. The pueblo was deserted, but hundreds of Pueblo Indian rebels who were gathered near the pueblo shouted at the Spaniards and engaged in warlike demonstrations. They represented nearly all of the New Mexico pueblos that had taken part in the revolt.

Mendoza established his camp in the pueblo, and the Spaniards began a series of negotiations with the Indians, including two of the revolt leaders, don Luis Tupatú of Picuris Pueblo, near Taos, and Alonso Catiti, Indian governor of the Keresan pueblos. Peace pacts were arranged whereby the Indians said they would return to their pueblos and engage in peaceful pursuits. But the Indian rebels, the Spaniards soon learned, had no intention of adhering to these pacts. The rebels, it was learned, planned to send attractive young Indian women to Cochiti to mingle with and seduce the Spanish soldiers, while Keres and Jemez warriors would attack the pueblo and kill the soldiers while they were engaged with their female companions. Mendoza gathered his force and retreated south.

South of San Felipe Pueblo, they met and joined forces with Otermín and the remaining Spanish force that had been moving north from Isleta. The Otermín force had just finished burning the Tiwa pueblos of Alameda, Sandia, and Puaray. The Mendoza force had not destroyed any of the Keresan pueblos. The combined force retreated south to Isleta, where it was found that the Indian population had dwindled to 385 men, women, and children, the remainder apparently having joined the rebels.

Believing that any further attempt to reconquer New Mexico from the Indians would be futile, the Spaniards burned Isleta on January 1, 1682, and began the long trek back to El Paso, accompanied by the Isleta Indians. Following their arrival at El Paso, the Indians established a new pueblo, Isleta del Sur (Isleta of the South) on the north bank of the river.

The net result of the Otermín expedition was the burning of eight Indian pueblos and the sacking of three others, all in the Tiwa and Piro provinces. Mendoza later was criticized for holding parleys with revolt leaders at Cochiti instead of capturing them. With the destruction of the remaining Tiwa pueblos in what is now the Albuquerque area, the once thriving and populous Province of Tiguex ceased to exist, as did the Piro province to the south.

Two Keresan pueblos on the Jemez River, a western tributary of the Rio Grande, became targets of Spanish military expeditions that penetrated New Mexico in the late 1680s, led by governors who had succeeded Antonio de Otermín. In 1686 don Pedro Reneros de Posada led a force that attacked and burned Santa Ana Pueblo when the inhabitants refused to surrender. In 1689, eighty Spanish soldiers under don Domingo Jironza Pétriz de Cruzate attacked Zia Pueblo, farther upstream, and killed many of the inhabitants.

Spaniards on these expeditions learned that the rare unity displayed by the Pueblo Indians at the outbreak of the revolt had by now dissipated. Popé had been deposed as their leader, and the Indians were wracked by inter-Pueblo warfare, civil strife, and attacks by Apache raiding parties. The Tiwas of Sandia Pueblo, and some of their neighbors, had migrated west to live among the Hopi Indians in northern Arizona. To the Spaniards, it appeared to be an ideal time to undertake a major reconquest of New Mexico.

Assuming duties at El Paso in 1691 as governor and captain general of New Mexico was Diego de Vargas, or to give his full and formal name, don Diego José de Vargas Zapata y Luján Ponce de León y Contreras. A native of Madrid, Spain, with a solid military and political background, he immediately began making plans to reconquer New Mexico for the Spanish Crown and the Catholic Church.

Vargas left El Paso in August 1692 and headed north into New Mexico with a force consisting of fifty soldiers, ten armed citizens, three Franciscan friars, and about one hundred Pueblo Indian allies who were living in the El Paso vicinity. Reaching Santa Fe, which was occupied by about one thousand Indians, Vargas and his followers entered the occupied New Mexico capital without encountering serious resistance and took formal possession on September 14. Finding the Indians who held Santa Fe in a conciliatory mood, and receiving peaceful submission from Indians at other pueblos in the region, Vargas led his force back to El Paso after what appeared to be a bloodless conquest.

In order to begin the Spanish resettlement of New Mexico, Vargas left El Paso again on October 4, 1693, and headed north with one hundred Spanish soldiers, seventy families of colonists, and eighteen Franciscan missionaries, numbering about eight hundred persons in all. Some of the families consisted of blacks or mestizos, the latter of mixed Spanish and Indian blood.

The expedition of soldiers and colonists reached Santa Fe on December 16, and the Indian occupants, probably alarmed by the arrival of Spanish colonists, refused Vargas's demands that they vacate the town. Spanish soldiers stormed into the town and in a two-day battle drove the Indians from the New Mexico capital they had held for thirteen years.

Spanish citizens once again occupied Santa Fe, but Vargas was forced to embark on a series of military campaigns in the region before bringing all the rebellious Pueblo Indians to submission. Peace was short-lived, however, for the Pueblo revolt flared again on June 4, 1696, when the Indians killed five Franciscan friars and twenty-one Spanish settlers. Vargas embarked on more military campaigns before bringing an end to the revived revolt.

With the end of Pueblo-Spanish hostilities, and the arrival of more Spanish colonists, Spaniards again began resettling the uninhabited Rio Grande Valley in the vicinity of present-day Albuquerque. Atrisco, on the west bank of the Rio Grande in what is now Albuquerque, was settled in about 1703 on a Spanish land grant that Fernando Durán y Chaves, a soldier under Vargas, had petitioned for and received in 1692. His father had lived there before the 1680 revolt.

Bernalillo, on the east bank of the river to the north, was a Spanish settlement as early as 1696. It was here that Vargas died in 1704 after being stricken ill while campaigning against Apaches south of Santa Fe. He was buried in Santa Fe, where he lies today in an unmarked grave.

The Spanish families who settled on the Atrisco grant were soon to have Spanish neighbors on the uninhabited opposite bank of the river.

## *Chapter Two*

# ALBUQUERQUE UNDER SPANISH RULE, 1706–1821

### Uncertain Beginnings, Neighboring Settlements, and Indian Raids

**The Founding of Albuquerque, 1706**

Details concerning the founding of Albuquerque are rather vague due to a lack of documentary evidence. Spanish officials at the time were required to make detailed reports concerning such activities, but researchers have searched Spanish archives in vain for the required instrument of founding, sometimes referred to as Albuquerque's charter, or birth certificate.

Credit for Albuquerque's founding, however, belongs to Francisco Cuervo y Valdés, a Spanish nobleman who served as acting governor of New Mexico from 1704 to 1707. A native of Santa María de Grado, in the province of Asturias in northern Spain, Cuervo arrived in New Spain in 1678 and served as lieutenant governor of Sonora and military governor of the provinces of Nuevo León and Coahuila.

Cuervo was appointed governor of New Mexico in 1704 by the viceroy of New Spain, Francisco Fernández de la Cueva Enríquez, the eighth Duke of Alburquerque, and a native of Spain with headquarters in Mexico City. Cuervo arrived in Santa Fe early in 1705 to succeed Diego de Vargas, who had died in office in Bernalillo the previous year.

In a formal document dated April 23, 1706, Governor Cuervo notified the Spanish Crown and the Duke of Alburquerque that he had founded a town south of Santa Fe and had named it in honor of the viceroy, his immediate superior. In keeping with the spelling of the duke's title, the official name given to the new town was Alburquerque, but the extra *r* eventually was lost. Although the origin of the word is uncertain, it is believed to stem from an Iberian corruption of the Latin words *albus* and *quercus*, meaning "white oak."

"I certify to the king, our lord, and to the most excellent senor viceroy, that I have founded a villa on the banks and in the valley of the Rio del Norte in a good place in regards land, water, pasture and fire-wood," Cuervo wrote. "I have given it as patron saint the glorious apostle of the Indies, San Francisco Xavier, and called it and named it the Villa of Alburquerque."

The governor wrote that thirty-five families, comprising 252 adults and children, had already taken up residence in the town. According to Spanish law, at least thirty family heads were necessary to establish a villa, a legal Spanish municipality. Cuervo went on to say that a spacious church had been completed, a house for the priest was well underway, the settlers had completed their houses, and a start had been made on government buildings that would serve as an administrative center for the region. Irrigation ditches were open and running, he added, crops had been sown, and the town was in good order and well arranged.

Accompanying the first settlers to the new town was a detachment of ten soldiers commanded by Captain Martín Hurtado, who was designated the first alcalde of the villa. Some of the soldiers were accompanied by their dependents. It was their duty to guard the small settlement against attacks by small groups of Indian raiders.

The Albuquerque site had been selected by General Juan de Ulibarrí during a scouting trip along the Rio Grande, still called the Río del Norte. Near the site were some haciendas that had been abandoned since the outbreak of the Pueblo Revolt in 1680. Close to the site was the abandoned hacienda of a widow, doña Luisa Trujillo, and a grove of cottonwood trees called the Bosque Grande de doña Luisa.

The site stood astride El Camino Real, "the Royal Road," a long and primitive trail that linked Santa Fe with Spain's colonial capital of Mexico City, about fifteen hundred miles to the south. Pioneered by the don Juan de Oñate colonists in 1598, the trail served as New Mexico's primary life and supply line to Mexico and the outside world for more than two centuries. About twelve miles east of the site was the Cañon de Carnuel, later called Tijeras Canyon, a pass through the Sandia-Manzano mountain chain to the eastern plains.

Cuervo's report on his founding of Albuquerque was met with mixed reactions in Mexico City. Spanish colonial officials noted that the acting governor had not been authorized to found any villas, or to grant lands to settlers, but since the deed had already been done, they acknowledged the new villa but changed the name of the patron saint from San Francisco Xavier to San Felipe, patron saint of the Spanish king. This change of patron saints was unknown to Albuquerque residents for decades to come.

Cuervo was ordered not to found any more new towns, but he had no opportunity to do so, anyway, for he was informed that the King of Spain had sold the New Mexico governorship to a wealthy Spanish admiral, don José Chacón Medina Salazar y Villaseñor. Governor Cuervo, the founder of Albuquerque, returned to Mexico City in 1707 and faded into obscurity.

Meanwhile, some questions arose concerning Cuervo's claims about his founding of Albuquerque, and in 1712 the viceroy ordered Juan Ignacio Flores Mogollón, governor of New Mexico at the time, to conduct an official inquiry regarding the circumstances surrounding the founding. Conducting the investigation, and taking testimony from witnesses, was General Juan Páez Hurtado, who soon learned that Albuquerque was not all that it was claimed to be.

Witnesses testified that there were only nineteen original families, comprising 103 men, women, and children, fewer than were necessary to found a villa, plus ten soldiers and their dependents. It was also learned that the original families had not built their own homes, but had moved into haciendas that had been abandoned since the Pueblo Revolt, which stretched more than two miles along the river. No mention was made of a spacious church, although a small one apparently existed at the time, and no town plaza or streets had been designated. Instead of being a compact town, as Cuervo had claimed, Albuquerque consisted of a collection of riverbank farms.

Also investigated was Cuervo's claim that he had founded yet another villa north of Santa Fe that he named Santa María de Grado, after his hometown in Spain. No such town was ever found.

The viceroy, after reviewing the findings, agreed to maintain Albuquerque's designation as a villa. No charges were brought against

Cuervo, who was not the first or the last politician to exaggerate or embellish his accomplishments.

Still another version of the founding of Albuquerque was written in 1776 by Juan Candelaria, an eighty-four-year-old Albuquerque resident and a son of one of the founding families. His recollections about the founding of Albuquerque and other New Mexico communities were unknown until the 1920s when found by researchers in Mexico City. In telling of the founding of Albuquerque, Candelaria wrote:

> On the seventh day of February, in the Year of Our Lord 1706, this Villa of Alburquerque was incorporated under the name of San Francisco Xavier. Don Francisco Cuervo y Valdes was governor. Friar Juan Minguez was the first minister of this Villa. He had come as a missionary.
>
> Twelve families and the soldiers from the garrison residing in the town of Bernalillo came to colonize it. The heads of these twelve families were Cristobal Jaramillo, Juan Barela, Francisco Candelaria, Feliciano Candelaria, Nicolas Lucero, Baltazar Romero, Joaquin Sedillo, Antonio Gutierrez, Cristobal Barela, Pedro Lopez del Castillo, Dona [*sic*] Bernardina Salas y Trujillo, a widow, and Juana Lopez del Castillo.
>
> The soldiers were Captain Don Martin Hurtado, who commanded, chief alcalde of the place; his secretary, Juan Pineda, Francisco Garcia, Pedro de Chavez Duran, Andres Montoya, Sebastian de Canseco, Antonio de Silva, Jose de Salas, Tomas Garcia and Xavier de Benavidez.
>
> The Duke of Alburquerque was the Viceroy at the time of its founding and derived its name from him.

Many Albuquerque residents today trace their ancestry to some of these founding families.

## Neighboring Settlements and Indian Raids

Although Albuquerque was founded in the heart of what had been the populous Province of Tiguex, all but one of the dozen or so Tiwa-speaking Indian pueblos were in ruins and uninhabited at the time. The lone exception was the pueblo of Alameda, about ten miles upstream to the north.

A group of about fifty Tiwa Indians had started rebuilding and reset-tling the pueblo in 1702, but abandoned the project in 1708 or 1709 and moved south to join other scattered groups of Tiwas in rebuilding and resettling the larger pueblo of Isleta, about fifteen miles south of Albuquerque and near the site of an earlier pueblo that had been called Alameda by members of the Coronado Expedition in the early 1540s.

The tract abandoned by the Tiwas of Alameda Pueblo north of Albuquerque was granted in 1710 to a Spaniard, Francisco Montes Vigil. He sold it to Juan Gonzáles Bas, who erected a home and chapel on the grant. Other Spanish settlers established the small community of Alameda on the grant, *alameda* being the Spanish word for "cotton-wood grove."

Just south of the Alameda Grant, a strip of land extending from the Rio Grande east into the Sandia Mountains was granted in 1712 to Captain Diego Montoya and conveyed a short while later to widow Elena Gallegos. After her death in 1731, the fertile river valley portion of the huge Elena Gallegos Grant was divided into narrow strips of farmlands by her descendants and heirs.

Spanish settlers who inherited or bought these farm strips irrigated their crops by diverting water from the Rio Grande through a system of irrigation ditches, called acequias, as was common throughout the river valley. They established several small communities near the river, includ-ing Los Poblanos, Los Ranchos, and Los Gallegos, known collectively as Los Ranchos de Albuquerque. Beyond the river valley, that portion of the Elena Gallegos Grant that extended eastward into the Sandia Mountains was designated common grazing lands for the grant settlers.

Meanwhile, small Spanish settlements began taking shape in the river valley south of Albuquerque, beginning with Los Padillas in 1710 and Pajarito in 1711, on the west bank of the Rio Grande north of Isleta Pueblo.

South of Isleta Pueblo, the village of Tome was established in 1739 on the east bank of the Rio Grande near the site of a hacienda that had been abandoned by Tomé Domínguez de Mendoza at the outbreak of the Pueblo Revolt in 1680. Valencia, a short distance north of Tome, was set-tled in 1751.

Belen, on the west bank of the Rio Grande about thirty miles south of Albuquerque, was settled in 1741 by Diego de Torres and Antonio de Salazar, the settlers including both Spaniards and *genízaros*, who were Hispanicized Indians who had been captured or purchased as children from nomadic tribes.

Sandia Pueblo, a former Tiwa village on the east bank of the Rio Grande about fifteen miles north of Albuquerque, had been abandoned and in ruins for more than sixty years when it was reestablished in 1748 through the efforts of a Franciscan missionary, Fray Juan Miguel Menchero.

During the turmoil of the Pueblo Revolt, many Indians of this pueblo had migrated more than two hundred miles to the west to establish a Tiwa pueblo, called Payupki, among the Hopi Indian villages in what is now northern Arizona. Efforts to return these Indians to the Rio Grande Valley in 1742 had proved unsuccessful, some of them taking up temporary residences at Jemez and other scattered New Mexico pueblos.

The task of rebuilding and resettling Sandia Pueblo in 1748 was accomplished by about 350 Indians, mostly Tiwas, but including some Hopi families who had accompanied them to the Rio Grande. They were given a grant of land extending from the Rio Grande eastward into the Sandia Mountains, bounded on the north by the opposite end of what was commonly called Cañada del Agua (Water Canyon), and on the south opposite the mouth of the Cañada Juan Taboso, the latter name, since shortened to Juan Tabo, of uncertain origin.

*Sandía* is the Spanish word for "watermelon" and the word first applied to the pueblo, apparently because of the melon patches there, and later to the mountains directly to the east. Spanish authorities had urged the reestablishment of Sandia Pueblo, believing that it would help protect Albuquerque from Apache and Comanche raiders and war parties that often entered the locality from that direction.

Albuquerque, as well as other small Spanish settlements in the Rio Grande Valley, for years had been the target of periodic raids by bands of nomadic Indians from surrounding regions who stole livestock and occasionally abducted women and children. Particularly troublesome during the early 1700s were Apaches of the Faraón band, who inhabited the Sandia Mountains east of Albuquerque, and Navajos who lived in the semiarid country to the west.

The detachment of ten soldiers that had accompanied Albuquerque's original settlers in 1706 were withdrawn to Santa Fe the following year by the Marqués de Peñuela, who had succeeded Cuervo as governor of New Mexico. In 1708 two prominent Albuquerque residents, Fernando Durán y Chaves and Baltazar Romero, petitioned the governor for the return of the soldiers, saying that since their departure the Indians had been running off livestock from corrals on a daily basis.

In the following years, various New Mexican governors led small military expeditions against the marauders with varying degrees of success. Albuquerque was sometimes used as a staging point for these expeditions, which were comprised of Spanish soldiers and Pueblo allies.

The early Apache and Navajo raids on the Rio Grande settlements paled in comparison to a growing menace from the plains country to the northeast. Far-ranging Comanche war parties, sometimes several hundred strong, began descending upon New Mexico settlements, bringing death and destruction to Spanish settlements and Indian pueblos alike from Taos south to Tome, a distance of about 150 miles.

A large force of Comanches swept through the Taos Valley on August 4, 1760, killing seventeen settlers and destroying their farms. About two hundred Comanches attacked Albuquerque on June 18, 1774, killing five men, capturing four sheepherders, and running off the settlement's horse herd. Indians of the fortified Sandia Pueblo managed to repel an attack by a large force of Comanches in June 1775 but thirty-three men of the pueblo who followed the retreating attackers were all ambushed and slain.

Fray Andrés García, the parish priest for both Albuquerque and Tome, reported that on May 26, 1777, he buried at Tome twenty-one settlers who had been killed by Comanches, and thirty more on June 3, 1778. According to legend, the Comanches ravaged Tome when a Spanish father there reneged on his promise to give his daughter in marriage to a Comanche chief when she came of age. The Franciscan friar also reported that ten men and one woman in Albuquerque were killed by Comanches on August 27, 1777.

While the thick-walled mission churches in Albuquerque and other settlements provided a safe haven for settlers living nearby during Indian raids, those farmers and ranchers living at some distance from the churches most often fell victim to the raiders. The small village of San Miguel de Carnué, which some Albuquerque settlers had established in 1763, was abandoned in 1770 due to Indian raids and not reestablished until 1818. Also abandoned were some small farm and ranch settlements on the Rio Puerco about twenty miles west of Albuquerque.

Comanche depredations in the Rio Grande Valley ceased after a governor of New Mexico, Juan Baustista de Anza, led a military force of six hundred men into what is now southeastern Colorado late in 1779, defeated the Comanches on their home ground, and later signed a lasting peace with them.

**Visiting Prelates, 1760 and 1766**

Pedro Tamarón y Romeral, the sixteenth bishop of Durango, paused in Albuquerque in 1760 while visiting Franciscan missions throughout his vast diocese. The diocese, headquartered in Durango, Mexico, extended more than one thousand miles north to include the Province of New Mexico. A native of Spain, Bishop Tamarón was sixty-three years old when he embarked on his long and arduous journey that took nearly two years. His entourage consisted of sixty-four men, including forty-one regular, citizen, and Indian soldiers, and his personal servants.

The villa of Albuquerque, he reported, was composed of Spanish citizens and Europeanized mixtures. The parish priest, he noted, was a Franciscan friar who also served the village of Tome downstream. There were 270 families with 1,814 persons, he wrote, indicating that these figures also included the priest's parishioners in Tome.

Bishop Tamarón gave no physical description of Albuquerque, and did not mention the church, but appeared concerned about the welfare of the parish priest, writing:

> Because some of his parishioners are on the other side of the river, this parish priest of Albuquerque, called Fray Manuel Rojo, is obliged to cross it when summoned. This kept him under apprehension, and above all he emphasized to me that when the river froze, it was necessary to cross on the ice. He elaborated this point by saying that when the ice thundered, he thought he was on the way to the bottom, because when one crosses it, it creaks as if it were about to break.

La Isleta, the bishop continued, was a pueblo of the Tigua (Tiwa) Indians and settlers with San Agustín as its patron saint. The population consisted of 107 families of Indians, with 304 persons, and 210 families of settlers, including those of Belen, downstream, with 620 persons. "It is called Isleta because it is very close to the Rio Grande del Norte, and when the river is in flood, one branch surrounds it," he wrote. "It is not inundated because it stands on a little mound."

Sandia Pueblo, the bishop wrote, was a new pueblo of Tigua (Tiwa) and converted Moqui (Hopi) Indians who lived apart in their tenements. The Tiwa tenement housed fifty-one families with 196 persons, and the Hopi tenement housed sixteen families with 95 persons. The Franciscan missionary also administered thirty-six families of settlers with 222 persons, he said.

A much more detailed account of Albuquerque and its nearby settlements and pueblos was provided sixteen years later by Fray Atanasio Domínguez, commissary visitor to the Franciscan missions of New Mexico, who visited Albuquerque in 1776. A native of Mexico City, Domínguez was about thirty-six years old when he journeyed north to visit and inspect the New Mexico missions in a region reeling from Comanche and Apache attacks.

The villa of Albuquerque, he reported, stood on a plain and so near to the Río del Norte that the church and the convent were about two musket shots from it. "The villa itself consists of twenty-four houses near the mission," he said. "The rest of what is called Albuquerque extends upstream to the north, and all of it is a settlement of ranchos on the meadows of the said river for a distance of a league [about two and one-half miles] from the church to the last one upstream." These lands were watered by the river through wide and deep irrigation ditches, crossed by little beam bridges, he continued, and the crops included apricots, apples, peaches, pears, melons, and watermelons.

Albuquerque, he said, consisted of 157 families with 763 persons, of all classes and walks of life and speaking the local Spanish.

Domínguez said the single-naved church was of adobe construction with very thick walls, with the main door facing east. A small arch above the door contained two broken, middle-sized bells. The convent extended south from the church, he said, and a walled cemetery extended around the church and convent. The parish priest was fifty-eight-year-old Fray Andrés García, who had served thirty years as a Franciscan missionary at a number of New Mexico missions.

Domínguez also said that the altar screen in the church contained three paintings, the one in the center representing St. Francis Xavier, who was firmly believed to be the titular patron. "I have established, and know for certain, that it is San Felipe de Neri," he wrote. "I therefore ordered that an image of this saint be put in place, and it is a large oil painting on canvas in a wooden frame, which the King gave, and it is now in poor condition from age."

Domínguez wrote that Alameda, upstream to the north of Albuquerque, was a settlement of farms and ranches containing sixty-six families with 388 persons. Located here was a small chapel, facing south with a little belfry containing two small bells, which had been built years before by Juan Gonzáles Bas, and was owned by his heirs.

Lower Corrales, on the west bank of the river north of Albuquerque, was a settlement of ranches containing twenty-six families with sixty persons, he said. It was bordered on the north by Upper Corrales, across the river from Sandia Pueblo, and consisted of ten families with forty-two persons.

Domínguez found what he called deplorable conditions at Sandia Pueblo, which had been resurrected twenty-eight years before. Efforts to restore the mission church, partially destroyed during the Pueblo Revolt, had failed, he said, and all that remained was a roofless structure with only the walls remaining to indicate the original appearance. Religious services were held in a room that had originally been the church baptistery, the one entrance to which was from inside the church ruins. Church adornments were old and in bad shape. The church itself faced east, and had two small towers containing broken bells. The convent, also in ruinous condition, extended south from the church.

Domínguez said that the pueblo contained ninety-two families with 275 persons, most of them Tiwas, and the remainder Hopis. They lived apart and spoke their own languages. The Tiwas lived in three building blocks east of the church, he said, while the few Hopis lived in some small, badly arranged houses above the church to the north.

Domínguez referred to Atrisco, on the west bank of the river opposite Albuquerque, as Atlixco, probably the original name of the settlement, being a Mexican Indian word meaning "upon the water." The settlement, located on a sandy plain, consisted of fifty-two families with 288 persons.

As Bishop Tamarón had noted before, Domínguez said that Isleta Pueblo received its name because it became situated on a little island when the Rio Grande overflowed and left its bed north of the pueblo. "The pueblo consists of three beautiful blocks of dwellings, separated from one another at the corners, which are located in front of the church and convent, and form a very large plaza there to the south of them," Domínguez reported. At various distances outside the plaza, he said, there were about twenty houses, which if joined together would be as large as one block, or tenement. "Everything is of adobe, very prettily designed and much in the Spanish manner," he continued.

The church, San Agustín de la Isleta, was of adobe construction with very thick walls and a bare earth floor, Domínguez reported. It faced south, and on each of the front corners was a small turret, one of which contained a middle-sized bell.

Isleta Pueblo contained 114 families of Tiwa Indians with 454 persons, he said. A large number of settlers were administered by the mission, including those at Pajarito to the north, with thirty-seven Spanish families, and Belen, downstream, with ninety-six Spanish families and forty-nine families of genízaros.

In addition to his task of inspecting New Mexico's Franciscan missions, Domínguez was instructed to study the possibility of opening a wagon road between Santa Fe and Monterey, on the California coast, about nine hundred miles to the west. Joining him in this venture was Fray Francisco Silvestre Vélez de Escalante, a young Franciscan missionary and native of Spain who had served at a number of New Mexico missions.

The Domínguez-Escalante Expedition, consisting of the two Franciscans and eight other men, left Santa Fe on July 29, 1776, and headed northwest up the Chama River valley into southwestern Colorado, then west into central Utah. With winter approaching, supplies were running low and because of unreliable guides, the explorers headed south into Arizona, fording the Colorado River at a point since known as the Crossing of the Fathers.

The expedition then headed back east into New Mexico, reaching the Rio Grande at Isleta Pueblo on December 23, 1776, and arriving back in Santa Fe on January 2, 1778. During a period of five months, the expedition had traveled through nearly two thousand miles of virgin wilderness.

The adobe church at Albuquerque that Domínguez visited and described had fallen into such a state of disrepair by the early 1790s that it was deemed necessary to replace it. A new and larger church was erected, this one facing south, as it does today. Since the earlier church faced east, there has been some question as to whether that church was demolished and a new one built at a different location, or whether it was incorporated as a part of a larger church that was oriented to face south.

### Visit of Zebulon Pike, 1807

A small group of U.S. soldiers, with a Spanish military escort, paused in Albuquerque on March 7, 1807, while en route south to Chihuahua City where they were to be questioned about their intentions. They considered themselves prisoners of war, but their courteous captors insisted that they were merely guests of the Spanish government, noting that they were permitted to keep their sidearms and were free to roam about the villages they passed through.

The leader of the group was Lieutenant Zebulon Montgomery Pike, a twenty-eight-year-old New Jersey native, whose journal of his experiences, published in 1810, gave citizens of the United States their first glimpses of New Mexico.

Pike and twenty-two men had headed west from St. Louis in July 1806 with instructions to explore the southwest regions of the newly acquired Louisiana Purchase, which doubled the territory of the United States. Although the boundaries were indefinite, the lands purchased from France bordered lands claimed by Spain.

In what is now central Colorado, Pike reached but failed an attempt to scale a high mountain peak in November that was later named Pikes Peak in his honor. Reaching southern Colorado in early February 1807 Pike and his men paused to build a stockade on the Rio Conejos, a western tributary of the Rio Grande.

It was here, on February 26, that Pike and his men were apprehended and taken into custody by a force of one hundred Spanish soldiers, commanded by Lieutenant Ignacio Saltelo, who informed them that they were trespassing on Spanish lands. Pike said that he did not realize that he had entered Spanish territory, which may or may not have been the truth.

Pike was told that the governor of New Mexico would like to have a few words with him, and he and his men were escorted south to Santa Fe. Governor Joaquín del Real Alencaster questioned Pike at length about his mission, entertained him at dinner, and told him that the Spanish authorities in Chihuahua would like to have a few words with him, too.

Pike and his men, with a Spanish escort, left Santa Fe on March 4 and headed south along the east bank of the Rio Grande, pausing at Santo Domingo and San Felipe pueblos, reaching the latter pueblo by crossing the river on an eight-arch bridge with a pine log floor. They spent the night of March 6 at Sandia Pueblo, which Pike wrote as "St. Dies" in his journal.

Continuing south through what Pike called "a country better cultivated and inhabited than any I had yet seen," the U.S. citizens arrived in Albuquerque on March 7 and were entertained at the new San Felipe de Neri Church. "We were received by Father Ambrosio Guerra in a very flattering manner, and led into his hall," Pike wrote. "From thence, after taking some refreshments, we went into his inner apartment where he ordered his adopted children of the female sex to appear.

> They came in by turns—Indians of various nations, Spanish,
> French, and finally two young girls, from whom their com-
> plexion I conceived to be English. On perceiving I noticed
> them, he ordered the rest to retire, many of whom were beau-
> tiful, and directed those to sit down on the sofa beside me.
>
> Thus situated, he told me that they had been taken to
> the east by the Tetaus [Comanches] and passed from one
> nation to another, until he purchased them, at that time
> infants; they could recollect neither their names nor lan-
> guage, but concluding that they were my country women, he
> ordered them to embrace me as a mark of their friendship,
> to which they appeared nothing loath.
>
> We then sat down to dinner, which consisted of various
> dishes, excellent wines, and, to crown all, we were waited on
> by half a dozen of those beautiful girls who, like Hebe at the
> feast of the gods, converted our wine to nectar, and with
> their ambrosial breath shed incense on our cups.

Pike and his men, with their Spanish military escort, left
Albuquerque the same day, which Pike wrote was the beginning of the
spring irrigation season:

> Both above and below Albuquerque, the citizens were begin-
> ning to open canals, to let in the water of the river to fertilize
> the plains and fields which border its banks on both sides;
> where we saw men, women and children, of all ages and
> sexes, at the joyful labor which was to crown with rich abun-
> dance their future harvest and insure them plenty for the
> ensuing year.

Spanish authorities in Chihuahua, after questioning Pike about his
mission, confiscated his personal papers, maps, and journals, and
ordered that he and his men be escorted back to U.S. territory. Later,
Pike became a major general and was killed in the War of 1812 while leading an American attack against the British in Canada.

Meanwhile, the viceroyalty of New Spain was soon to become a thing
of the past with the end of Spanish rule.

# Chapter Three

# ALBUQUERQUE UNDER MEXICAN RULE, 1821-1846

## The Controversial Career of Manuel Armijo

### The New Republic

A successful revolt against Spanish rule in the lower provinces of the viceroyalty of New Spain led to independence in 1821 and the establishment of the republic of Mexico, officially the United Mexican States. The new republic, with Mexico City as its capital, stretched from Guatemala north into what is now the southwestern regions of the United States, including Texas, New Mexico, Arizona, and California.

It is not known if the citizens of the small agricultural community of Albuquerque observed independence from Spain with any formal celebrations. In Santa Fe, however, about sixty miles to the north, independence was celebrated in fine style.

Don Facundo Melgares, the last New Mexico governor under Spanish rule, received orders from Mexico City to stage an independence celebration in New Mexico's capital and to make a full report of it. His report was published in a Mexico City newspaper several months later.

Melgares reported that the Santa Fe celebration occurred on January 6, 1822, and opened with the ringing of church bells, salvos of artillery, and music. After a mass in the parish church, men, women, and children participated in a triumphal procession through the streets, carrying palms and flowers, and wearing tricolor sashes reading "Long Live the Independence of the Mexican Empire."

Musicians played patriotic tunes, the governor continued, and Indians from Tesuque Pueblo performed dances on the plaza. During the evening, speeches and poetry recitations were delivered from a stage that had been set up under the portal of the Palace of the Governors. The celebration wound up with a dance and entertainment in the palace that began at 8 P.M. and continued until 4:30 A.M. Moderation prevailed throughout all the events, the governor said.

Moderation, however, was not the way a young American visitor, Thomas James, described the Santa Fe celebration in his book, *Three Years among the Mexicans and the Indians*, published twenty years after the event. He wrote that the celebration consisted of five days and nights of "universal carousing and revelry," continuing until everybody fell from exhaustion.

Independence had only a small initial effect on the citizens of Albuquerque, most of whom lived at scattered farms and ranches throughout the river valley. An elective town council was organized, and the central plaza in front of the church was officially designated as the Plaza de la Constitución.

An 1822 census, authorized by the council, gave the population of the Albuquerque jurisdiction as 2,302 men, women, and children, including 297 farmers, 121 day laborers, 15 merchants, 13 craftsmen, 3 teachers, and 1 priest. The jurisdiction extended north and south along the Rio Grande for about eight miles, and east and west for about thirty-three miles, the east–west section being mostly uninhabited and used for grazing and the gathering of firewood. The Albuquerque jurisdiction included a number of small plazas and chapels in the river valley, both north and south of the central plaza. Named for prominent families in the vicinity, these neighborhood plazas included Los Barelas, Los Duranes, Los Candelarias, and Los Griegos.

An Albuquerque volunteer militia, consisting of about 360 men, had been organized to protect the settlers and their livestock from Navajos to the west whose raids on outlying farms and ranches were increasing in intensity. The militia, consisting of both cavalry and infantry companies, sometimes joined other New Mexico militias in wide sweeps through Navajo country.

Warfare between the settlers and the Navajos included numerous killings, livestock thefts, and the taking of captives. Captured Navajo women and children were often sold to prominent New Mexico families for use as servants, and young New Mexicans captured by the Navajos were often adopted into families and used as herders for the large flocks of sheep they had accumulated over the years.

Independence from Spain in 1821 coincided with the opening of the Santa Fe Trail, a nine-hundred-mile wagon route that extended from Missouri's western frontier to Santa Fe and that opened New Mexico to foreign trade that had been forbidden under Spanish rule. Soon, wagon caravans loaded with merchandise from the United States were arriving in Santa Fe where the traders enjoyed large profits selling manufactured goods and accumulating Mexican silver coins.

When Santa Fe became saturated with American goods, the Missouri traders continued south along the historic Camino Real through Albuquerque to richer Mexican markets in Chihuahua and Durango. Albuquerque, astride the Chihuahua Trail, as the northern section of the historic highway was known, played host to streams of foreign visitors as the mule- and ox-drawn wagons passed up and down the Rio Grande Valley through the farming community.

Prominent New Mexican families in Albuquerque and its vicinity were quick to take advantage of the profitable foreign trade, assembling wagon trains of their own and hauling merchandise from Missouri with the advantage of avoiding Mexican tariffs that the Missouri traders were obliged to pay upon their arrival in Santa Fe. This trade resulted in a proliferation of mercantile stores in small New Mexico communities. Albuquerque area families engaging in the overland trade included the Armijos, Pereas, Chávezes, Oteros, and Bacas. Some made small fortunes driving thousands of sheep to markets in Chihuahua.

It was an Albuquerque resident, Manuel Armijo, who was destined to become the dominant figure in New Mexico affairs during the quarter century of Mexican rule. Born during the early 1790s at the Plaza de San Antonio, on the northern outskirts of Albuquerque, he was among the youngest of many children of Vicente Armijo and Bárbara Durán y Chaves, wealthy landowners and merchants.

One of the most controversial figures in New Mexico history, Armijo won the admiration of his fellow New Mexicans, but his volatile political and military career caused him to become vilified by outsiders who had unpleasant dealings with him. Most assessments of his character, which remain in print today, were written by his enemies rather than by his friends.

Armijo's active role in Albuquerque's civil and military affairs, and his boundless determination, helped lead him to three separate terms as governor of New Mexico. His first term, beginning in 1827, was rather uneventful, and he resigned in 1829 in an apparent effort to avoid an investigation into alleged irregularities concerning the conduct of his office.

A bloody insurrection against an unpopular New Mexico governor in 1837 propelled Armijo back into the governor's chair for a second term. It is believed he had a prime role in instigating the insurrection, which he managed to crush in a counter-revolution.

The unpopular governor was Albino Pérez, a lieutenant colonel in the Mexican army, who assumed the governorship in 1835 when New Mexico was becoming a department rather than a province of the republic of Mexico. Many New Mexicans resented the fact that an aristocratic military officer, a man they considered an outsider, was sent north from Mexico City to assume the governorship in Santa Fe.

An early account of Pérez and his problems was given in 1863 by Judge Kirby Benedict of Santa Fe in a talk delivered to the Historical Society of New Mexico. In describing Pérez, he said:

> He was a person tall and graceful. His address was courteous and polished. He was a man of education, and of middle age. He was fond of social life, and prodigal of expenses in procuring its gratifications. This was one source of his disasters.

The prime source of his disasters, however, came as a result of his orders from the Mexican government to begin a system of direct taxation on New Mexico citizens. His enemies began spreading false rumors about the scope of this taxation, claiming, among other things, that married men would pay a luxury tax for the privilege of sleeping with their wives, and that farmers would be taxed for each egg their chickens laid.

Open revolt flared in Mexican villages and Indian pueblos north of Santa Fe in August 1837 and Pérez moved north from Santa Fe with a small militia force in an effort to quell it. Defeated by the rebels in some skirmishing, the governor and a few of his followers retreated to Santa Fe, followed by several thousand of the insurgents.

Judge Benedict, in his 1863 address to the historical society, told what happened next:

> From here, Perez and some of his friends fled toward the
> south, but were overtaken, one after another, at various dis-
> tances below here [Santa Fe], and cruelly butchered.
>
> After Perez was killed, his head was cut from his body.
> The insurgents had camped outside of town, near the
> church Rosario now standing. The head was borne to them
> in triumph, and one whole night the conquerors held an
> inhuman orgy, and amused their bloody vengeance in offer-
> ing indignities to the head of the governor, and kicking it in
> derision over the grounds.
>
> While these things were transpiring at night, a friend of
> Perez stole to where the body was laying, at the hour of mid-
> night, and brought it to this city, from where it was taken to
> the Campo Santo, nearby upon the hills, and there buried,
> and all that remain of the ashes of the unfortunate governor
> sleep there to this day.

The insurgents proclaimed José Gonzáles, an illiterate Taos farmer and buffalo hunter, as governor of New Mexico.

It did not take Manuel Armijo long to seize a golden opportunity to regain power. Leading a large force of counter-revolutionaries north from Albuquerque and vicinity, he soon defeated the insurgents and ordered the immediate executions of Gonzáles and other rebel leaders. Armijo brought his success to the attention of the Mexican government, which praised him as a patriot and appointed him governor of New Mexico for a second term with the military rank of general.

It reportedly was Armijo who, while serving as New Mexico's chief exec-utive, remarked, "Poor New Mexico. So far from heaven, so close to Texas." His second term as governor was highlighted by what he consid-ered a serious threat to New Mexico sovereignty by neighboring Texas.

The new Republic of Texas, which bordered New Mexico on the east and southeast, had won its independence from Mexico in 1836 in a revolt led by American citizens who had settled there. In determining the boundaries of the new republic, it was believed that the Rio Grande, which formed its southern boundary, should also form its western boundary, where it flowed south through New Mexico. This plan would have put such New Mexico communities as Albuquerque, Santa Fe, and Taos in Texas.

More than three hundred citizens of the Republic of Texas, consisting of men, boys, and uniformed dragoons, left a rendezvous point near Austin in June 1841 for a journey to Santa Fe that would take them across little known plains country inhabited by hostile Comanche and Kiowa Indians. They took along wagons filled with trade goods, a herd of beef cattle, and some artillery pieces.

The Texans claimed that this was essentially a trading expedition for the purpose of opening up a trade route between the new republic and Santa Fe. It was agreed, however, that they would raise the Texas flag over Santa Fe, providing that reports should prove true that Santa Fe citizens desired such a change of allegiance.

Armijo, however, considered the Texas expedition to be an armed invasion of his domain by a hostile force, and began taking steps to deal with the situation. Wearing a resplendent uniform, and mounted on a large mule, the governor-general let a group of New Mexico regulars and militia east out of Santa Fe to deal with the enemy.

Rounding up the Texans on New Mexico's eastern plains was not a difficult task, for they were exhausted from their long trek, straggling along in groups, demoralized, and half-starved. They surrendered their weapons without resistance, and Armijo wanted to execute them all on the spot. Cooler heads prevailed, however, and they were taken to the Pecos River village of San Miguel, southeast of Santa Fe, where several were executed. From here, Armijo ordered that the prisoners be marched on foot to Mexico City, a distance of about two thousand miles. A soldier escort under the command of Captain Damasio Salazar was selected to lead them south down the Rio Grande Valley as far as El Paso del Norte, present-day Juárez, Mexico.

Among the prisoners was George Wilkins Kendall, a newspaperman and co-owner of the *New Orleans Picayune*, who had joined the expedition as an observer. His account of the expedition, and the suffering and ill treatment of the captives, was first published in 1844 in a two-volume set of books entitled *Narrative of the Texan Santa Fe Expedition*.

Kendall wrote that the Texas prisoners—187 in all—were escorted by the guards out of San Miguel on October 17, 1841, and that a difficult three-day march brought them to Santo Domingo Pueblo, on the east bank of the Rio Grande north of Albuquerque. Here the Indians treated them kindly, furnishing them with tortillas, pumpkins, and corn. The same hospitality was shown them at San Felipe and Sandia pueblos as they continued downstream toward Albuquerque.

Captain Salazar, meanwhile, was taking a sadistic delight in torment-ing and mistreating his helpless prisoners. At Algodones, near Sandia Pueblo, they were jammed together for the night in two small and unven-tilated rooms, causing them to nearly suffocate; and at Alameda, on the northern outskirts of Albuquerque, they were herded together in an open corral with no protection from the cold.

The prisoners reached Albuquerque on October 22, 1841, but their stay was to be a short one. "About noon we entered Albuquerque, some-what famed for the beauty of its women, besides being the largest place in the province of New Mexico, and the residence of Armijo part of the year," Kendall wrote.

> As we were marched directly through the principal streets
> the inhabitants were gathered on either side to gaze at the
> *estrangeros*, as we were called. The women, with all kindness
> of heart, gave our men corn, pumpkins, bread, and every-
> thing they could spare from their scanty store as we passed,
> and had Salazar allowed us to remain but an hour, all our
> immediate wants would have been supplied, but the hard-
> hearted wretch appeared to delight in acts of cruelty, and
> drove us through with scarcely a halt of ten minutes.

Kendall devoted two pages of his narrative to describing the beauty of a teenaged Albuquerque girl he saw standing on a mud wall, supporting a large pumpkin on her head with her right hand, while her left hand was gracefully resting upon her hip. "Among the crowds of beauty her image will stand out in bold relief, and not one of those who saw her on the day we passed through Albuquerque will ever forget her," he concluded.

The Texas prisoners who survived the long march to Mexico City were released by the Mexican government and allowed to return to their homes.

+══ ══+

Governor Armijo left office in 1844, for obscure reasons, but returned to the governorship in 1845 for a third term. He soon faced a far greater threat to his domain than a few hundred straggling Texans.

The United States declared war on Mexico on May 13, 1846, and by August an American army of about sixteen hundred men was moving down the Santa Fe Trail for the conquest of New Mexico. The Army of the West, as it was called, reached the New Mexico town of Las Vegas on

August 15, 1846, and the commander, General Stephen Watts Kearny, mounted a rooftop and took possession of New Mexico on behalf of the United States. Still following the trail, the army left Las Vegas and headed west for Santa Fe, about sixty-five miles away.

In Santa Fe, Armijo announced that he would defend his domain, and led a force of regulars and militia east about fifteen miles to the mouth of Apache Canyon, where they began digging in to repulse the invaders. Then, in an apparent change of heart, Armijo decided against defending the capital, and began a lone flight south out of New Mexico to Chihuahua. The Army of the West entered and took possession of Santa Fe on August 18 without encountering any resistance.

Armijo had been visited in Santa Fe on August 12 by two Americans, James Magoffin, a veteran Santa Fe trader, and Captain Philip St. George Cooke, and there is evidence that he accepted a large sum of money in exchange for his agreement not to resist the American advance. The Americans hoisted the Stars and Stripes over the Santa Fe plaza and began making plans for a provisional government for New Mexico.

Albuquerque felt the full impact of the American occupation on September 5, 1846, when Kearny and about seven hundred soldiers arrived in the town on a jaunt down the Rio Grande Valley. Albuquerque residents, having long felt neglected by Mexico's central government in Mexico City, greeted the newcomers with rousing cheers. The American dragoons assembled in parade formation on the central plaza facing the church, and members of the Albuquerque militia fired a twenty-gun salute with muskets from the roof of the church. Addressing the crowd of Albuquerque citizens, Kearny administered to them the oath of allegiance to the U.S. government. The American flag was hoisted over the plaza.

Kearny and his men continued downstream as far as Tome before returning to Santa Fe. During this excursion the Americans found that the Rio Grande Valley was thickly populated from Algodones south to Tome, a distance of nearly sixty miles, and that Albuquerque itself stretched for seven or eight miles up and down the river.

Kearny and the main body of his force headed west out of New Mexico on September 25 to assist in the conquest of that part of Mexico known as California. Other American troops began arriving in New Mexico to establish garrisons in various communities to help protect the inhabitants from Indian raids. The U.S. government established a small military post in Albuquerque on November 17, 1846, quartering officers and men in existing adobe buildings west of the plaza that were rented from Albuquerque citizens. The initial rent paid for all the buildings was $165 a month.

Albuquerque did not take an active part in a brief but bloody revolt against American rule that swept through northern New Mexico early in 1847. American troops from Santa Fe crushed the revolt in a battle at Taos Pueblo. Among those killed in the revolt was Charles Bent, who had been appointed the first civil governor of New Mexico under U.S. rule.

Texas, meanwhile, which late in 1845 was admitted to the union as the twenty-eighth state, still wanted to claim the Rio Grande in New Mexico as its western boundary. With New Mexico in transition from Mexican to American rule, Texas thought it was an opportune time to stake its claim.

Spruce M. Baird, a native of Kentucky, was practicing law in Nacogdoches, Texas, in 1848 when Texas governor George T. Wood appointed him "District Judge of Santa Fe County, Texas," embracing the entire eastern half of New Mexico. Baird arrived in Santa Fe on November 10, 1848, but failed to convince any Santa Fe residents that they were Texans.

When Texas relinquished its New Mexico claim for $10 million, Baird decided to stay in New Mexico and practice law. He established a ranch home on the east bank of the Rio Grande about six miles south of Albuquerque, which became known locally as El Rancho del Chino Tejano, or "the Ranch of the Curly Texan. He served in various political capacities in New Mexico until the Civil War when he returned to Texas.

Manuel Armijo was acquitted at a court-martial in Mexico on charges of cowardice and desertion in connection with the loss of New Mexico. Returning to New Mexico, he settled in Lemitar, about seventy miles south of Albuquerque, where he died on December 9, 1853. He was buried in the San Miguel Catholic Church at nearby Socorro.

The New Mexico Legislative Assembly in Santa Fe on December 13 offered its "most sincere condolences to the family and friends of General Armijo and to the Territory for the loss of one of its greatest benefactors."

# Chapter Four

# ALBUQUERQUE UNDER AMERICAN RULE, 1846–1862

## A Lively Military Town

### The Albuquerque Military Post, 1846–1862

Following the signing in 1848 of the Treaty of Guadalupe Hidalgo, which ended the war between the United States and Mexico, New Mexico remained under American military control until 1851 when it became a territory of the United States. The military post in Albuquerque, which had been established in 1846, ceased operations in 1851 but was regarrisoned in 1852 as a military department headquarters and quartermaster depot.

In the early 1850s, the post was garrisoned by eighty officers and men of the First and Second Dragoons who were in quarters rented from civilians. Rent for all buildings used by the post amounted to more than $2,000 a year.

Thirteen Albuquerque civilians were employed by the quartermaster. These included five laborers, four teamsters, one herder, and one ferryman. The ferryman operated a small ferryboat across the Rio Grande. The boat was a crude, bargelike craft that was propelled across the stream by poles and ropes.

Some recollections of Albuquerque and the military post, as they existed in the 1850s, were furnished to the *Albuquerque Weekly News* in 1898 by an unidentified pioneer who referred to himself only as "Billy." He first visited Albuquerque in 1851 while serving with troops under the command of Colonel Edwin Vose Sumner.

The pioneer recalled that some of the adobe homes in Albuquerque had solid cottonwood doors, while others had no doors at all, with the only entrances through the roofs. Most Albuquerque men wore brown shirts and drawers, he said, adding that the women dressed simply, too. Wild geese and ducks were thick in the area, he said, and coyotes strolled across the plaza as if they belonged there. Tons of grama grass could be cut on any of the surrounding mesas, he said, but fresh water was scarce.

A ferryboat that hauled people and vehicles across the Rio Grande was located about a half mile north of where the Barelas Bridge later was erected, the pioneer continued. There was quite a community at the river crossing known as Placers, but it later was washed away by floodwaters. The ferryboat was owned by the government, he said, and was operated under contract by a man named Chávez and his son, who were paid by the month. He said the boat was built by a soldier named Church, a former ship's carpenter, who was being held in the local guardhouse for desertion. The soldier did such a good job building the small boat that he was pardoned with honors. Church also built the first permanent flagstaff that was erected on the Albuquerque plaza in the 1850s.

The pioneer said the Rio Grande changed its course many times between 1851 and 1898, and estimated that the riverbed rose four feet during that period. He said the river flowed much closer to the Albuquerque church and plaza in 1851 than it did in 1898, having shifted some distance to the west.

The pioneer also said that Captain Richard S. Ewell, an army officer stationed at Los Lunas, about twenty miles south of Albuquerque, was one of the most famous Indian fighters in New Mexico in the 1850s. "Captain Ewell's command at Los Lunas consisted of some of the roughest looking men you ever saw in the army," he said. "They didn't shave, and wore all sorts of old hats. Often they left Los Lunas with 10 days rations and didn't return for a month, living off the country when their rations gave out."

A sergeant and four enlisted men of the command were attacked one day by Apaches at the mouth of Hell's Canyon east of Los Lunas, the pioneer continued. A relief party found the five men filled with arrows, "and the least number of arrows found in any one man was thirteen." The wounded soldiers were taken to the military hospital in Albuquerque, he said, where all but one of them died.

Captain Ewell left New Mexico to become a prominent Confederate general during the Civil War, as did Major James Longstreet, who served as paymaster at the Albuquerque military post before the war. Ewell and Longstreet were two of General Robert E. Lee's three corps commanders at the 1863 Battle of Gettysburg.

The arrival of a railroad survey party in Albuquerque on October 5, 1853, signaled the beginning of five weeks of rest, relaxation, and partying for the weary travelers. Members of the government-sponsored expedition established a tent and wagon camp west of the plaza and began mingling with the townspeople.

The expedition, led by Lieutenant Amiel W. Whipple of the U.S. Topographical Engineers, was surveying a possible railroad route from Fort Smith, Arkansas, west to Los Angeles, California, roughly along the thirty-fifth parallel. The seventy members included men who were knowledgeable in such scientific fields as geology, botany, astronomy, meteorology, and engineering.

It had been nearly four months since the expedition left Fort Smith and it was running short of supplies, but the acting commissary at the Albuquerque military post was unwilling to take the responsibility of releasing needed supplies in the absence of General John Garland, the post commander, who was on a tour of observation in southern New Mexico. It was not until October 21 that the general returned and released provisions so that the expedition could resume its survey.

Whipple, in his detailed account of the expedition, wrote:

> Albuquerque contains less population than Santa Fe. Its situation, however, is more central with regard to the inhabited portions of New Mexico, and it has been select-ed by General Garland for the headquarters of this military department.
>
> Nearly the whole valley of Rio del Norte is capable of yielding good crops; but between Bernalillo and this place are the finest ranchos and vineyards to be found in the Territory.
>
> The number of inhabitants in Albuquerque and its environs, including the ranchos, is estimated at 2,500. This is exclusive of Atrisco, which lies opposite upon the right bank of the river.

An 1850s sketch of Old Albuquerque, looking east across the town plaza, attributed to Lieutenant Colonel Joseph Eaton of the Albuquerque military post. Author's collection.

> The houses are of one story, built of adobes, and the appearance of the town is similar to that of others in New Mexico. The presence of the troops, however, creates an unusual air of animation about it.

Whipple, in his account, referred to the river as both the Río del Norte and the Rio Grande, indicating that the names were interchangeable at the time. He also used the spelling "Zandia" for the Sandia Mountains. "Several reconnaissances have been made during our stay here, in the vicinity of the Rio Grande," Whipple continued. "The botanist and geologist passed through the canyon of Carnuel to San Antonio, and ascended to the top of Zandia mountain; which, from measurement by triangulation from Albuquerque, is found to be seven thousand feet above the valley of the river, and twelve thousand feet above the sea." (They overestimated the height above sea level by about fifteen hundred feet.)

Providing more details about the Albuquerque visit was Heinrich B. Mollhausen, a German artist and naturalist who accompanied the expedition, and whose account later was published in Germany. "Albuquerque," he wrote, "lies about five hundred yards from the Rio

Grande, and has a rather ruinous aspect; the only building at all conspic-
uous is the church, which, with its two towers, might lead to the expectation of a more important settlement. Church, houses, barracks, and
the stables of the garrison are all built of the same material, namely,
adobe, or bricks dried in the air in the usual Mexican fashion."

Mollhausen wrote that the stores of the traders exhibited a curious
variety of all imaginable articles in ordinary use, including clothing, medicines, dried fruits, linens, pastries, brandy, and iron goods. The traders
accepted only hard cash, and paper money was not taken. Expedition
members learned the names of the few streets, where the best wine was
to be had, and where pleasures of the fandango were to be enjoyed, he
continued. They also learned the names of persons of distinction, "and
above all, of every handsome senorita."

Shortly before the expedition left Albuquerque, Mollhausen wrote,
the members gave a "grand féte" for Albuquerque citizens "and lovely
citizenesses" in appreciation for the hospitality that had been shown
them and the frequent balls that had been given for the entertainment
of the visitors. Invited, he wrote, were "all the good folks of
Albuquerque whom we could regard as at all educated and presenta-
ble." Expedition members scoured the country, even as far as Santa Fe,
for meats and drinks, and even came up with such delicacies as canned
oysters. The "night of revelry," as Mollhausen called it, proved to be a
tremendous success.

Whipple hired Antoine Leroux, a French-Canadian resident of Taos,
to help guide the expedition westward across little known regions of
Arizona, which at the time was the western half of the territory of New
Mexico. Augmented by twenty-five troops from Fort Defiance, the expedition headed west out of Albuquerque on November 10, 1853, with 114
members, sixteen heavy wagons, and a herd of sheep.

### Albuquerque's First Newspaper, 1853

The visit of the railroad survey party to Albuquerque in the autumn of
1853 coincided with the brief publication of Albuquerque's first newspaper. The full name of the weekly paper was *El Amigo del Pais y la Voz del
Pueblo*, the English translation being "The Friend of the Country and the
Voice of the Town," or "People."

Little is known today about the appearance or content of this weekly paper, as there are no known issues in existence today. The newspaper's principal claim to fame, however, is that it published an article or

articles that resulted in the tragic death a year later of one of New Mexico's most prominent and colorful figures.

The debut of the Albuquerque newspaper was noted by the *Santa Fe Weekly Gazette* on August 20, 1853. Under the headline reading "A New Paper," the newspaper published this item:

> We are requested to state that a new paper is to be published in Albuquerque, the first number of which will be issued next week, entitled El Amigo del Pais y la Voz del Pueblo.
>
> We are not advised as to who are the proprietors of Amigo del Pais; Don Facundo Pino is the agent in this city and is now soliciting subscribers. We will notice this stranger more at large when it makes its appearance among us.

The *Santa Fe Weekly Gazette* ignored the Albuquerque newspaper in following weeks, however, an indication that James L. Collins, the editor, learned that it was being published by his political enemy, Colonel Richard H. Weightman of Santa Fe.

Weightman, a native of Maryland who had been expelled from the U.S. Military Academy for slashing another cadet with a knife, had arrived in New Mexico in 1846 as a captain with the Missouri Light Artillery. Discharged in 1849 with the rank of colonel, he set up a law practice in Santa Fe and served as New Mexico's delegate to Congress in 1851–1852.

The *Gazette* attacked Weightman continually, contending that he was sympathetic to Texas's claims to all of New Mexico east of the Rio Grande, and that he was in "cahoots" with Judge Spruce M. Baird, whom Texas had sent to New Mexico in 1848 to press her land claims. Baird had established a residence near Albuquerque, and there was evidence that he assisted Weightman in the publication of the Albuquerque newspaper.

The folding of the Albuquerque newspaper was noted by the Santa Fe newspaper on December 10, 1853. Under a headline reading "The Amigo del Pais," the newspaper said:

> We understand that the life of this interesting paper is considered beyond the hope of recovery. Soon after its arrival in Albuquerque, it gave evident signs of declining health, and although it was closely watched and kindly cared for by a

few, very few, devoted friends, they were unable to prevent a paralysis that has for a time suspended animation.

The climate of Albuquerque, it is thought, was not congenial to a constitution so delicate, and it has been thought best to remove the favorite to this city, where we understand it is to be placed under the direction of a skillful quack, but unless it can receive the nourishment of a little government pap, its restoration is considered impossible.

On the final demise of the patient we will prepare an obituary in which we will try to do justice to the memory of the departed favorite, and to offer such consolation to its friends that a bereavement so heart rending must require.

The fate of *Amigo del Pais* was recalled a decade later in the initial issue of Albuquerque's second newspaper, the *Rio Abajo Weekly Press*, which was established on January 20, 1863.

Weightman, according to the article, sold the newspaper to Judge Baird, who had been appointed public printer for New Mexico, and the newspaper was moved to Santa Fe. The article went on to say:

Judge Baird was no printer, although the Legislative Assembly voted that he was one, and in becoming the proprietor of a printing office, he found himself in the condition of a man who won the elephant in the raffle—unable to sustain it. The Amigo del Pais did not long survive the change of locality and attendant circumstances.

During its brief existence in Albuquerque, the *Amigo del Pais* published an interview with Francis X. Aubry that offended the colorful French-Canadian adventurer, wagon freighter, and trail blazer. Aubry claimed that statements attributed to him in the interview were false. He was not about to forget it.

Born in Quebec in 1824 as Francois Xavier Aubry, he left home at the age of nineteen and made his way to St. Louis, Missouri, where he found employment as a clerk at a store that dealt in dry goods and groceries. In 1846 he bought some trade goods and accompanied a wagon train to Santa Fe, where he sold the goods and remained one month.

In following years, the energetic young French Canadian operated his own merchandise-loaded wagon trains from Independence, Missouri, to Santa Fe, making two and three round trips each year when other traders were making only one. When not engaged in the Santa Fe trade, Aubry occupied himself exploring new routes west to California and east into Texas, and driving thousands of head of sheep to California where they were sold at a handsome profit.

In 1848, as the result of some wagering that he couldn't do it, Aubry set a Santa Fe Trail speed record by riding horseback from Santa Fe to Independence, a distance of about eight hundred miles, in five days and sixteen hours. On this record trip, according to newspaper accounts, he encountered twenty-four consecutive hours of rain, muddy trails, and swollen rivers, broke six horses, walked twenty miles, slept only two and one-half hours while strapped to his saddle, and ate only six meals.

Aubry was fluent in three languages, French, English, and Spanish. He was described as being of medium height with small hands and feet and a jet black mustache. An unidentified Santa Fe pioneer who knew him recalled that he was "handsome, a boon companion and a dashing cavalier, popular among men and more popular among women, equally at home on a dance floor or in a boxing ring, and a dead shot with a pistol or rifle."

It was on the afternoon of August 18, 1854, that Aubry, upon his arrival in Santa Fe from a trip to California, tied his horse in front of the Mercure brothers' saloon and walked inside. The saloon, which was midway along the block on the south side of the plaza, was operated by Joseph and Henry Mercure, who, like Aubry, were French Canadians.

Weightman, who was seated on the southeast corner of the plaza, saw Aubry's arrival, and walked to the saloon to greet him. Entering the saloon, where Aubry was being greeted by friends, the two greeted each other cordially and conversed pleasantly for several minutes.

Aubry asked Weightman, who was sitting on the bar facing him, what had happened to the newspaper he had published in Albuquerque the year before.

"It died for a lack of subscribers," Weightman replied.

"Any such lying papers ought to die," Aubry retorted.

Weightman asked Aubry what he meant by such a remark.

"Last fall you asked me for information about my trip to California, which I gave you, and you afterwards abused me," Aubry replied.

Weightman said this was not so, and Aubry, slamming his fist down on the counter, exclaimed, "I say it is so!"

Weightman got off the counter, picked up a tumbler that was about one-third full of whisky and water, and threw the contents in Aubry's face. He then stepped back from the counter and placed his hand on his belt.

The two men began to struggle, Aubry drew a five-shot Colt pistol from his belt, and the gun discharged prematurely, sending a bullet into the ceiling. Weightman drew from his belt a Bowie knife, the same with which he had slashed a cadet at West Point, and plunged it into Aubry's abdomen. Aubry sank to the floor and died within ten minutes.

Tried for murder, Weightman was acquitted on grounds of self-defense. He returned to Missouri, where he was killed in 1861 while leading a Confederate charge at the Battle of Wilson's Creek.

Aubry was buried at the parochial church, on the site of Santa Fe's present-day St. Francis Cathedral, where his exact resting place is unknown and unmarked today.

## The Wayward Padre

Padre José Manuel Gallegos, pastor of the San Felipe de Neri Catholic Church in Albuquerque from 1845 to 1852, was quite popular with most of his parishioners in spite of his unorthodox lifestyle. It was his extracurricular activities that brought about a major crisis at the church and a new career for the padre.

A native New Mexican, Gallegos was born in 1815 at the village of Abiquiu, on the Rio Chama north of Santa Fe. As a young man he attended a parochial school operated by Padre Antonio José Martínez at Taos, and he later studied for the priesthood at the College of Durango in Mexico, where he was ordained in 1840.

During his seven years as pastor of the Albuquerque church, Padre Gallegos exhibited a love of drinking and gambling, and was the convivial crony of leading traders and politicians. At times he could be seen riding around Albuquerque in a handsome carriage, smoking cigars and accompanied by attractive senoritas.

For his housemate, and probably mistress, he took in a woman with three children who had been the mistress of two Mexican officers in turn. Together, they opened a general mercantile store, which, to the dismay of some, remained open all day on the Sabbath. In connection with the store, the padre also owned a wagon train, with which he made frequent trading trips to Mexico. The 1850 census listed him as a thirty-five-year-old priest with assets worth $8,000.

Life for Padre Gallegos began to change in 1851 with the arrival in Santa Fe of Jean-Baptiste Lamy, a native of France, who was to become New Mexico's first sitting bishop in the newly created Santa Fe diocese. The Frenchman was a humorless and strict disciplinarian where matters of the clergy were concerned, and he soon was shocked by what he considered the laxness of the Catholic Church in New Mexico and the transgressions of some of the priests.

Bishop (later Archbishop) Lamy warned Gallegos on several occasions that his outside activities were working to the detriment of his duties as a pastor. Gallegos answered that any claims of improprieties on his part were exaggerated.

In the later summer of 1852 Gallegos left Albuquerque with seven wagonloads of merchandise and headed for Mexico. Lamy, contending that Gallegos had left his pastorate without official permission, took immediate steps to replace him. Lamy sent to Albuquerque another Frenchman, Father Joseph Machebeuf, his vicar general, to take charge of the parish. Machebeuf informed the stunned congregation that he was their new pastor, and that Gallegos had been suspended from his priestly duties. He moved into the parish home that Gallegos had occupied.

Church members were not happy with the change, and 950 of them filed a protest with the bishop defending Gallegos and saying that they found Machebeuf's sermons "boring and annoying." Lamy was unmoved.

Gallegos returned to Albuquerque from his trip to Mexico early in 1853 and announced that he would conduct Sunday services in the church as usual. Machebeuf, who was visiting some nearby Indian missions, heard of Gallegos's plans and hurried back to Albuquerque. As he wrote later:

> I returned to Albuquerque on Saturday night, and on Sunday morning I went to the church an hour earlier than usual in order to be on the ground and ready for anything that might happen. What was my astonishment upon arriving there to find the Padre in the pulpit, and the church filled with people I knew to be his particular friends. These he had quietly gathered together, and now he was inciting them to revolt, or at least to resistance.
>
> I tried to enter the church through the sacristy, but this communicated with the presbytery, which he still occupied, and I found the doors locked. Going then to the main door

of the church I entered, and assuming an air of boldness I commanded the crowd to stand aside and make room for me to pass.

Then, as one having authority, I forced my way through the crowd and passed up by the pulpit just as the Padre pronounced the Bishop's name and mine in connection with the most atrocious accusations and insulting reflections. I went on until I reached the highest step of the sanctuary, and then turning I stood listening quietly until he had finished. Then all the people turned to me as if expecting an answer.

I replied, and in the clearest manner refuted all his accusations; and I showed, moreover, that he was guilty of the scandals that had brought on his punishment.

To finish, I called upon him to justify himself, or at least to answer, if he had any reply to make. But not a word; he went out as crestfallen as a trapped fox and left me in peaceful possession of the church. I sang the high mass as usual, and preached on the Gospel of the day without making the least allusion to the scene that had just taken place.

After a few unsuccessful efforts to regain control of the church, Gallegos embarked on a political career. As a Democrat, late in 1853, he was elected to the first of his several terms as New Mexico's delegate to Congress. This in spite of the fact that he did not speak English, and was not allowed to have an interpreter with him on the floor of the House.

Gallegos moved to Santa Fe in 1857 and established himself in a large home north of the plaza. In following years he served as speaker of the Territorial House of Representatives, territorial treasurer, and New Mexico superintendent of Indian Affairs.

In 1868, at age fifty-three, he married Candelaria Montoya, a thirty-one-year-old widow. The marriage took place in the Episcopal Church in Santa Fe. Gallegos died of a stroke in Santa Fe on April 21, 1875, at which time the *Daily New Mexican* in Santa Fe called him "the most universally known man in the Territory."

### A Camel Caravan, 1857

It was a most unusual survey expedition that arrived on the southern outskirts of Albuquerque on August 9, 1857. This one, among other things, included more than two dozen camels, of both the one-humped (dromedary) and two-humped (Bactrian) varieties, prodded along by

Greek, Turkish, Syrian, and Armenian camel drivers who cursed the large beasts in a variety of tongues.

This was the first and only U.S. Camel Brigade, an experiment to determine if camels from North Africa and the Near East were suitable for use as transportation and beasts of burden in the arid and desert lands of the American Southwest. They had been shipped to the United States from Mediterranean ports.

Leading the survey expedition, which also included wagons, soldiers, teamsters, horses, and mules, was Lieutenant Edward F. Beale, a Navy veteran of the Mexican War and superintendent of Indian Affairs in California and Nevada. His two-fold mission was to survey a wagon road across northern Arizona, then still a part of New Mexico, and to incorporate camels in the survey to test their ability to perform.

The camel experiment was the brainchild of Jefferson Davis, then U.S. secretary of war in the cabinet of President Franklin Pierce, and later president of the Confederate States of America. In a letter to President Pierce, he wrote:

> For military purposes, for expresses, and for reconnaissances, it is believed, the dromedary would supply a want now seriously felt in our service; and for transportation with troops rapidly moving across the country, the camel, it is believed, would remove an obstacle which now serves greatly to diminish the value and efficiency of our troops on the western frontier.

The military appropriation bill that was passed by Congress in 1855 contained an amendment that appropriated $30,000 "to be expended under the direction of the War Department in the purchase and importation of camels and dromedaries to be employed for military purposes."

Government agents purchased the camels and hired camel drivers at Mediterranean ports and the camels were shipped to the Texas gulf coast aboard two sailing ships. They were taken to a staging area near San Antonio, Texas. The expedition headed west out of San Antonio on June 25, 1857, and reached Fort Bliss, Texas, on July 27.

From Fort Bliss the caravan moved north up the Rio Grande Valley in New Mexico, passing through Las Cruces and moving up the flat and waterless Jornada del Muerto to the Socorro area. North of Socorro, the inhabitants of one village thought the caravan was a traveling circus, and when

Beale was asked what he had to offer besides camels, he jokingly replied, "We have a horse that can stand on his head and drink a glass of wine."

The expedition reached the Albuquerque vicinity on August 9 and camped on the east side of the river about two miles south of town. Beale always selected the campsites some distance from settlements to prevent his teamsters and camel drivers from partaking of the excesses of urban life.

But at Albuquerque, two miles proved to be less than a safe distance. Two of the civilian teamsters, Joe McFeeley and John Hoyne, got drunk at an Albuquerque fandango and in an ensuing brawl Hoyne shot McFeeley in the hand. Beale reported that he had to "administer copious supply of the oil of boot" to several camel drivers who had not found "even in the positive prohibitions of the prophet sufficient reason for temperance."

During his brief visit to Albuquerque, Beale stayed at the large adobe home of Major D. H. Rucker, the army quartermaster, who lived just off the southeast corner of the plaza. One of Rucker's daughters became the wife of General Philip H. Sheridan in 1879.

The expedition forded the Rio Grande on the afternoon of August 12, camped for the night about a mile west of the river, then continued on its journey to California the next day. It disbanded at Beale's Tejon Ranch near Bakersfield.

The camel experiment proved to be a success, the imported animals traveling long distances with heavy burdens without water, and even thriving on mesquite bushes and greasewood. "Although the mesquite bushes are covered with sharp thorns the camel seizes them in his mouth and draws the limbs through his teeth," Beale reported, "stripping off the leaves and briars and eating both greedily."

The outbreak of the Civil War in 1861 put an end to camel experiments, however. Some of the camels were sold to individuals and organizations at public auctions in California and Texas. Some escaped from, or were turned loose, by their owners, and were seen roaming sparsely settled sections of the Southwest for years to come. What was believed to be the last surviving camel of the U.S. Camel Brigade died in 1961 at a San Francisco zoo. It was estimated to be 125 years old.

### Albuquerque in 1860

Albuquerque was achieving a cosmopolitan atmosphere by 1860, according to the census report for that year, with new citizens from many states and foreign countries. Albuquerque had a population of about thirteen hundred persons, not including more than five hundred members of the

Fifth Regiment of Infantry stationed in the town, nor such adjacent communities as Atrisco, Alameda, and Corrales.

The inhabitants included the Swiss tavern owner Jacob Meyer, the Prussian grocer Morris Miller, the English tailor Edward J. Carter, the German beer-maker Earnest Kramer, and the French clergyman Father I. M. Coudert. Most of the laundresses at the Albuquerque military post listed their birthplaces as Ireland. Joseph Winnemon, a native of Bavaria, listed his occupation as physician, surgeon, and barber. His personal estate was valued at $500.

Other Albuquerque residents of 1860 included Green Wilson of Tennessee, auctioneer; Charles Page of Maine, druggist; Joseph Puma of Bavaria, baker; Lyman Jones of New York, cooper; Pedro Torres of New Mexico, constable; John Cady of Ireland, deputy sheriff; William Pool of Nova Scotia, grocer and tavern owner; C. P. Swan of Kentucky, cabinet-maker; and William H. Henrie of France, lawyer.

Dozens of Albuquerque residents merely listed their occupations as merchants. Prominent among them were members of the Armijo family, including Manuel, Salvador, Rafaél, and Ambrosio Armijo. There were two jewelers, Secundino Romero and Ramón Rodríguez, both from Mexico. Listed as musicians were José Pena, from Texas, and Juan Gutiérrez of New Mexico.

Frank Huning, thirty-four, and Charles Huning, twenty-seven, were listed as merchants from Hanover, Germany. Also from Hanover was another merchant, Simon Rosenstein. German immigrants Franz (Frank) and Charles Huning were brothers who operated the F. & C. Huning mercantile store in Albuquerque, while two of their brothers, Louis and Henry Huning, operated a mercantile and ranching business in Los Lunas about twenty miles south of Albuquerque.

Franz Huning, who was to leave his mark on Albuquerque for decades to come, arrived in the United States in 1848 and followed the Santa Fe Trail to New Mexico the following year as a bullwhacker with a wagon train. He settled in Albuquerque late in 1852 after a short career as a merchant in the village of San Miguel, about forty miles southeast of Santa Fe.

Huning was passing through Albuquerque while traveling to Mexico with a small wagon train owned by Gaspar Ortiz when Simon Rosenstein, owner of a store on the south side of the Albuquerque plaza, persuaded him to stay in Albuquerque and go to work for him in his store. He worked as a clerk for Rosenstein for several years before opening his first store in Albuquerque in 1857 with Charles as a partner. Charles later returned to Germany to live, the only Huning brother to do so.

Franz acquired wagons of his own and made frequent Santa Fe Trail trips to Missouri where he bought merchandise for the Albuquerque store, which was located at the northwest corner of the plaza. He bought from some Catholic priests a two-wing home, called La Glorieta, dating from at least 1803, on the eastern fringes of Albuquerque. He added two wings to the existing wings to form an enclosed patio. Nearby, he erected a flour mill and a sawmill.

In 1863, while returning home from a visit to his native Germany, he married Ernestine Franke, a German girl, at St. Louis, and they journeyed to Albuquerque by wagon train.

In his memoirs, written in 1894 but not published until 1973, Huning recalled his earliest years in Albuquerque when he said it was a prominent military post with a garrison of two companies of dragoons and generally two companies of infantry. The post also included the chief quartermaster, commissary and purveying departments, and a military hospital, he wrote.

The building next to the church on the east side housed a succession of post commanders, he continued, including Paris-born colonel Benjamin Louis Eulalie de Bonneville, "a plain, genial old gentleman without any military presumption or arrogance." Huning wrote that a fellow townsman, Melchior Werner, was sergeant major attached to the military band, which consisted of all German musicians with one or two exceptions.

Albuquerque had many gamblers and camp followers, he wrote, plenty of stores and saloons, "and all did well as money was plenty." There were few evenings without a fandango, and often two or three, he wrote, "and as a natural consequence quarrels and fights abounded, and killings were frequent."

The Albuquerque plaza was much larger and lower in those days, he wrote, extending to the south and east, and after every heavy rain a large pond would form on it, attracting wild ducks.

Huning and his wife lived in their La Glorieta home until 1883, when they moved a short distance east to a large and elaborate home Huning built to resemble castles in his native land. Called Castle Huning, the two-story home, topped by a square tower and including numerous second-floor balconies, was constructed of adobe faced with wood. It contained at least fourteen rooms, and was surrounded by elaborate gardens.

Castle Huning, commonly known as Huning Castle, was the elaborate home of German-born Franz Huning from 1883 until his death in 1905. Located on west Central Avenue at Fourteenth Street, the historic residence stood until 1955 when it was demolished. Courtesy the Albuquerque Museum Photoarchive, PA1980.154.25. Landis collection. Donated by Donald Landis.

Huning gave his former home to his daughter, Clara, when she married lawyer H. G. Fergusson in 1887. Their children, Erna, Harvey, Lina, and Francis, grew up there. Erna and Harvey Fergusson were destined to become well-known Southwestern writers.

Franz Huning died in 1905, and Castle Huning later housed a private school, but was standing vacant when it was demolished in 1955. La Glorieta remains intact into the twenty-first century, housing the private Manzano Day School.

## Chapter Five

# CONFEDERATE OCCUPATION OF ALBUQUERQUE, MARCH–APRIL 1862

## Triumphant Entry, Sorrowful Retreat

### Arrival of the Texas Brigade, March 2, 1862

Captain Herbert M. Enos, assistant quartermaster in charge of the U.S. government supplies at the Albuquerque military post, learned on the afternoon of March 1, 1862, that the vanguard of an advancing Confederate army of nearly twenty-five hundred Texas volunteers had reached the town of Belen, about thirty miles to the south. That evening, an express rider informed him that about fifty Texans had reached Los Lunas, twenty miles to the south, and had captured a citizen train carrying public stores.

Having under his command only twelve regular soldiers and some militiamen and volunteers, Captain Enos began making preparations to destroy all the quartermaster and subsistence supplies that could not be carried off to safety. Quantities of ammunition and ordnance stores were quickly loaded into wagons and started north for Santa Fe.

Enos also readied eight or nine other wagons, loaded with the baggage of the regulars, volunteers, and militia, for movement at a moment's notice. He had hoped that troops from Santa Fe would be sent south to reinforce him. Most Union troops in the territory, however, had earlier been sent to Fort Craig, on the Rio Grande about one hundred miles south of Albuquerque, to resist the anticipated Confederate advance up the Rio Grande Valley.

At six thirty the next morning, with no help in sight and the enemy fast approaching, Enos ordered that all buildings at the military post housing public stores be fired. Within minutes, the buildings were engulfed in flames, and thick columns of smoke billowed into the air. Many Albuquerque citizens, anticipating such a move, had gathered nearby in hopes of carrying off items that were not destroyed.

"The destruction of the stores involved the destruction of the buildings containing them," Enos reported later, "as it would have been impossible with the force and the short time at my disposal to have removed the property from the buildings in order that it might then be burned. Had I attempted to carry out this plan, I am of the opinion that the native population would have overpowered me and saved the property for the enemy." Enos reported that the only property that was not burned consisted of molasses, vinegar, soap, and candles in the subsistence department, and a few saddles, carpenter's tools, and office furniture in the quartermaster's department, and that these articles were carried off by the citizens.

The small Union garrison evacuated Albuquerque and soon learned that five of their provision-laden wagons were attacked by a band of robbers while camped near Sandia Pueblo and three of them carried off. The robbers were said to be deserters from New Mexico volunteer and militia companies.

Smoke from the burning buildings was still much in evidence that afternoon of March 2 when about four hundred members of the Second Regiment of Texas Mounted Rifles, commanded by Major Charles L. Pyron, entered and took possession of Albuquerque almost on the heels of the departing Federals. Some of the Texans thought to their dismay that their own men had torched the buildings.

The next morning, a small group of Southern sympathizers demanded and received the surrender of a small Union outpost at Cubero, about sixty miles west of Albuquerque, and obtained more than twenty wagonloads of military supplies including sixty small arms and three thousand rounds of ammunition. These were taken to the Confederate forces in Albuquerque. Later, a Confederate detachment in Tijeras Canyon, just east of Albuquerque, captured a train of twenty-three wagons carrying provisions from Fort Union south to Fort Craig.

General Henry Hopkins Sibley, whose official title was "Commander of the Army of the Confederate States of America in the Southwest," arrived in Albuquerque on March 7 with the remainder of his force, which was generally known as Sibley's Brigade. In formal ceremonies, he took possession of Albuquerque in the name of the Confederate States while a Confederate flag was hoisted over the plaza to the sounds of a thirteen-gun salute and a Texas band playing "Dixie" and "The Girl I Left Behind Me."

General Sibley established Albuquerque as his supply and hospital base, and took up residence in the spacious home of Rafaél and Manuel Armijo, brothers who owned a large mercantile firm in Albuquerque. They furnished him with money, and supplies from their store, actions that they later were to regret.

Texas cavalrymen began confiscating needed supplies from Albuquerque stores and the homes of private citizens. Some of the citizens, anticipating such a move, had moved their livestock to hiding places in the mountains. Among the stores losing goods was the sutler's store, owned by the Spiegelberg brothers of Santa Fe.

Sibley, seldom sober and referred to by his men as "a walking whisky keg," relaxed in the Armijo home and contemplated the next move in his New Mexico campaign.

The Civil War had come to New Mexico in July 1861 with the Confederate occupation and control of the southern reaches of the territory close to the Texas border. Many of the nonnative citizens here were from southern states and sympathetic to the Confederate cause.

Lieutenant Colonel John R. Baylor, commander of Fort Bliss at present-day El Paso, Texas, left the fort on the night of July 23 with 258 men of the Texas Second Regiment of Mounted Rifles and headed up the Rio Grande Valley to the New Mexico town of Mesilla, about forty miles to the north. They reached and occupied Mesilla on the afternoon of July 25, having passed Fort Fillmore, about six miles to the south, which was garrisoned by about seven hundred Union soldiers.

Major Isaac Lynde, commander of Fort Fillmore, led 380 men of the United States Seventh Infantry and Third Cavalry to the outskirts of Mesilla late that afternoon and engaged in a feeble attempt to oust the Texans. Failing to do so, he led his men back to the fort. Believing the fort to be indefensible, Lynde ordered that it be evacuated, and after burning some of the stores, the entire garrison moved out at one o'clock in the morning of July 27 and headed for Fort Stanton, about 150 miles to the northeast.

Baylor, with less than two hundred men, intercepted the retreating Union force that afternoon in the upper reaches of the Organ Mountains as they struggled in disarray, dehydrated, under the hot summer sun. Lynde surrendered his entire command to Baylor without firing a shot. The seven hundred Federal soldiers were later released on parole. Baylor proclaimed most of the southern third of New Mexico as the new Confederate Territory of Arizona, with Mesilla as its capital, and himself as military governor.

General Sibley, having recruited a brigade of about twenty-six hundred volunteers at San Antonio, Texas, led them on a long march west to Fort Bliss, arriving there in December 1861. Most of the volunteers were young men from east and south central Texas, and they had armed themselves with a variety of weapons, including hunting rifles and shotguns.

It was Sibley's grandiose plan to capture New Mexico for the Confederacy, take over the Colorado goldfields to the north, and to eventually extend the conquest to California, providing the Confederacy with Pacific seaports. This would have included a great deal of living off the land and local inhabitants flocking to the cause. Neither the land nor the citizens were to cooperate, however.

Sibley selected Fort Thorn, an abandoned United States military installation on the west bank of the Rio Grande about forty miles north of Mesilla, as his advance base of operations. His brigade assembled here in January 1862, and in early February the Confederate Army of New Mexico began moving north for its intended conquest of the region. The army, consisting of some twenty-six hundred men, included several regiments of Texas Mounted Volunteers, artillery pieces, and a wagon train carrying supplies.

The first major obstacle in the path of the Texans was Fort Craig, a Union stronghold on the west bank of the Rio Grande about seventy miles to the north. Assembled at the fort were about thirty-eight hundred Union regulars and volunteers under the command of Colonel Edward R. S. Canby, commander of the New Mexico Military Department.

Sibley, realizing that the fort was too strong to take by force, decided to bypass it on the opposite side of the Rio Grande. The Texans crossed to the east side of the river a short distance below the fort and continued north, planning to cross back to the west bank at Valverde, about four miles north of the fort. On the night of February 20, 1862, Union troops at the fort could see the Confederate campfires across the river to the east.

James "Paddy" Graydon, Irish-born captain of an Independent Spy Company for the federal forces, devised a plan he hoped would panic the Confederate encampment. He lashed two wooden boxes containing twenty-four-pounder howitzer shells to the backs of two old mules, and with four companions waded across the river with the mules under cover of darkness.

When the five men and two mules were about 150 yards from the slumbering Texans, the fuses were lit and the mules whipped forward toward the camp. Graydon and his men beat a hasty retreat back toward the river, only to be followed by the explosive-laden mules. The resulting explosions startled both the Union and Confederate troops, but the mules were the only casualties.

Early in the morning, a Union force of 850 regulars and New Mexico and Colorado volunteers left Fort Craig and marched north along the west bank of the river to the Valverde ford where the Confederate force was preparing to cross to the west bank. The Union troops crossed to the east bank, and in skirmishing managed to dislodge advance Confederate troops from their initial positions near the riverbank.

As the day progressed, however, with each side receiving reinforcements, the engagement developed into a fierce conflict that included deadly artillery duels, heavy small arms fire, cavalry charges, and savage hand-to-hand fighting. Sibley retired from the field early, saying he was ill, and Canby arrived later to assume command of his troops. Leading the First New Mexico Volunteers in the battle was the frontiersman Colonel Christopher "Kit" Carson.

The Union troops began to withdraw from the field and retreat to the fort late in the afternoon after a desperate Confederate charge captured the artillery battery commanded by Captain Alexander McRae, killing McRae in the process. Six of the eight Union cannons were captured during the battle, and one of the two remaining was damaged.

The Texans held the field, buried their dead, and prepared to move on north, leaving unconquered Fort Craig in their wake. Union casualties at the February 21 Battle of Valverde were given as 110 dead, 160 wounded, and 204 missing, while Confederate casualties were listed at 230, including 72 dead or mortally wounded.

Running short of supplies, the Confederate Army moved north through Socorro to Albuquerque, hoping to capture supplies at the U.S. quartermaster depot, only to find upon arrival that the stores had been reduced to ashes.

Needing more pasturage and firewood than Albuquerque had to offer, various units of the Confederate force camped at locations outside the town. Some camped at the Spruce Baird ranch south of town, where the former Texan had welcomed them with a Confederate flag over his house; some camped in Tijeras Canyon east of town; and others moved on through the canyon to camp at the eastern foot of the Sandia Mountains.

The Confederate occupation of Santa Fe began on March 13 when about seventy Texans under the command of Major Charles Pyron entered the city to find the streets nearly deserted. Territorial officials had packed their belongings and fled about sixty-five miles up the Santa Fe Trail to establish a temporary capital at Las Vegas.

About two hundred more members of Pyron's command arrived in Santa Fe on March 23. The Texans searched Santa Fe in vain for provisions, for the U.S. quartermaster stores had been loaded into more than one hundred wagons on March 4 and dispatched about ninety miles up the Santa Fe Trail to Fort Union. Government stores not shipped to Fort Union were either burned or distributed to local citizens.

Sibley, relaxing in Albuquerque, believed that he had captured and appropriated enough supplies to last his army another three months. In order to complete his conquest of the Southwest, he realized, it was necessary to capture Fort Union, the principal U.S. military supply depot in the region. Confederate troops began moving out of Albuquerque on March 20 when Major John S. Shropshire headed north with four companies to reinforce Pyron at Santa Fe. On the next day, Colonel William Scurry and Major Powhatan Jordan headed northeast with a larger force to Galisteo, a village about twenty miles south of Santa Fe.

The Confederate move up the Santa Fe Trail began on March 25 when about four hundred troops under Pyron and Shropshire left Santa Fe and proceeded about fifteen miles up the trail to the mouth of Apache Canyon at the western edge of Glorieta Pass. They camped for the night near Anthony Johnson's ranch, the present village of Cañoncito.

The Confederate force soon learned that they were on a collision course with a large Union force that had been hurrying down the Santa

Fe Trail from Colorado and Fort Union. The bulk of this force consisted of more than nine hundred men of the First Regiment of Colorado Volunteers, commanded by Colonel John P. Slough, a Denver lawyer. Upon reaching Fort Union, the Coloradans were joined by some U.S. regular infantry and cavalry and New Mexico volunteers, bringing the total Federal force to more than thirteen hundred men.

The initial clash occurred on the afternoon of March 26 when Pyron's force entered Apache Canyon and encountered an advance force of about four hundred Union troops commanded by Major John M. Chivington of the Colorado volunteers. Several hours of skirmishing resulted in few casualties, although the Colorado troops, known as Pike's Peakers, captured at least seventy-one Texans and started them under guard for Fort Union.

The Confederate force, gradually pushed back during the Battle of Apache Canyon, retreated to Johnson's Ranch. The Federal troops, instead of following up their initial success, withdrew about seven miles through Glorieta Pass to Pigeon's Ranch, a major trail hostelry and stage-coach stop operated by a Frenchman, Alexander "Pigeon" Valle, said to have earned his nickname by his peculiar style of dancing.

Pyron's small force at Johnson's Ranch was reinforced during the night by about six hundred troops under Colonel Scurry who had hurried north from Galisteo. Chivington's force was augmented by the arrival of Colonel Slough and the main body of the Federal force, bringing their number to about eleven hundred men.

The Confederate move up the Santa Fe Trail resumed on March 28 when Scurry led about 1,200 troops through Apache Canyon and Glorieta Pass and suddenly encountered about 850 Union troops under Slough relaxing at Pigeon's Ranch. Both sides sprang into action, and in a fierce battle that raged for hours in rugged, wooded, and rocky terrain, the Texans drove the Federals back from successive defensive positions and claimed a victory. Their jubilation was short-lived, however.

During the battle, a force of at least 450 Union troops, commanded by Chivington and guided by Lieutenant Colonel Manuel Chaves of the New Mexico volunteers, had skirted the battle lines by moving across the lofty top of Glorieta Mesa and had attacked and destroyed the lightly defended Confederate wagon train at Johnson's Ranch. About seventy supply-laden wagons were burned, and hundreds of draft animals and cavalry horses killed or scattered. With the burning of the wagons the Confederates lost great quantities of arms and ammunition, clothing, blankets, food, forage, and medical supplies. Left high and dry, the Texans realized that their hopes of conquest had come to an end.

Union casualties at the Battle of Glorieta were reported as forty-seven dead and seventy-eight wounded, while the Confederate losses were reported as forty-two dead and sixty-one wounded. Major Shropshire was among the Confederate officers killed. (The remains of thirty-one soldiers, identified as Confederate dead, were discovered in shallow graves at the Pigeon's Ranch battleground in 1987 and later reburied at the Veterans National Cemetery in Santa Fe.)

Valle, the Frenchman who operated Pigeon's Ranch, later gave his version of the battle:

> Government mans vas at my ranch and fill his canteens vis my
> whiskey, and government nevaire pay me for zat whiskey.
> Texas mans come up and surprise zem, and zey fought six
> hour by my vatch, and my vatch was slow.

The retreating Texans began arriving in Santa Fe on March 29. "Their appearance clearly manifested the severe usage to which they had been subjected," the *Santa Fe Gazette* reported on April 26, 1862. "Some rode, some walked, and some hobbled in. All were in a most destitute condition in regard to the most common necessities of life." Caring for the sick and wounded Confederate soldiers in Santa Fe were some of the city's most prominent women, including Louisa Canby, wife of the Union commander at Fort Craig.

The Texans, after confiscating some needed supplies from Santa Fe merchants, departed the city on March 7 and 8 and headed south for Albuquerque.

+≡ ≡+

Remaining in Albuquerque during the Apache Canyon and Glorieta battles was a force of about two hundred Confederates commanded by Captain William P. Hardeman. Sibley, who took no part in the battles, arrived in Santa Fe from Albuquerque in time to meet the main body of his troops retreating from Glorieta Pass.

Learning that a large Union force under Canby had left Fort Craig and was moving north up the Rio Grande Valley towards Albuquerque, Sibley sent reinforcements south from Santa Fe to help Hardeman defend Albuquerque and its supply depot. These reinforcements had not yet arrived in Albuquerque on April 8 when Canby's force of 860 regulars and 350 volunteers arrived that afternoon at a point about a mile east of Albuquerque and unlimbered a few pieces of artillery.

"I immediately made a demonstration upon the town, for the purpose of ascertaining its strength and the position of the enemy's batteries," Canby reported a few days later. "This demonstration was made by Captain Graydon's Spy Company, supported by the regular cavalry, and developed the position of the batteries. In the skirmish Major [Thomas] Duncan, Third Cavalry, was seriously but it is hoped not fatally wounded. No other casualties were sustained."

Canby's artillery, consisting of about four cannons, opened fire on the town, and the Confederate force responded with three or four pieces of artillery set up at the east edge of town, moving the cannons from place to place to create an illusion of greater strength.

The cannonading and skirmishing continued all afternoon and most of the next day without inflicting any casualties and little if any property damage. The so-called Battle of Albuquerque ceased on the afternoon of April 9 when some townspeople reportedly went to the Union lines and complained to Canby that his most likely victims would be women and children. That night, Canby abandoned his position and led his force east through Tijeras Canyon to the village of San Antonio, where he awaited reinforcement from Fort Union.

The main Confederate force began arriving in Albuquerque from Santa Fe on the morning of April 10. Sibley, realizing that his weary force was outnumbered and undersupplied, began making plans to evacuate Albuquerque and retreat back to Texas. Confederate burial details were busy at night interring comrades who had died of illnesses or wounds in Albuquerque, their burial places unknown to this day. Also buried at night were eight small cannon barrels, as their wheeled undercarriages were needed to transport supplies.

On April 12, the Confederate flag was lowered from the tall flagpole in the center of the plaza and the Confederate Army of New Mexico began retreating south along the banks of the Rio Grande. Joining the exodus were a number of civilians who had collaborated with the Texans, including Spruce Baird and his family, and the brothers Rafaél and Manuel Armijo, their New Mexico properties soon to be confiscated by the federal government.

Canby's command was joined in Tijeras Canyon on April 13 by reinforcements from Fort Union led by Colonel Gabriel Paul, swelling the

Union force to about twenty-five hundred regulars and volunteers. Receiving information that the Texans had abandoned Albuquerque and were moving downstream, the Federal force emerged from Tijeras Canyon on the morning of April 14 and hurried southwest towards the Rio Grande below Albuquerque to intercept the retreat.

The retreating Confederates, still divided by the Rio Grande, had established camps that evening on opposite sides of the river about twenty miles south of Albuquerque. Camped at the village of Peralta, on the east bank, were about eight hundred men commanded by Colonel Thomas Green, while the main force under Sibley was camped across the river at Los Lunas.

After a thirty-six-mile march, the Union force reached the outskirts of Peralta before dawn on April 15 and were greeted with the sounds of laughter and fiddle music. The Confederate officers, unaware of the Union approach, were holding a loud and boisterous party in the large home of Henry Connelly, a prominent local merchant who was serving as territorial governor of New Mexico in Santa Fe. Quietly, Canby set up artillery batteries close to the camp.

The Federal artillery opened fire on the Confederate camp at dawn, and the surprised Texans quickly responded with their own guns. The Battle of Peralta continued until mid-afternoon with artillery duels and skirmishing in and about the town, coming to a halt with the arrival of a tremendous sand and dust storm. Casualties were light, the Texans reporting four killed and eight wounded, the Federals reporting only one man killed.

The Peralta defenders crossed to the west bank of the Rio Grande at night to consolidate the entire Confederate force under Sibley at Los Lunas. They began retreating south along the west bank the next day, paralleled by the Union force moving south on the east bank. After a march downstream of about thirty miles, the Confederates camped on April 17 where the Rio Puerco flows into the Rio Grande from the northwest. They were in sight of the Union encampment across the river.

The Confederate Army was in a precarious position, with a superior and well-supplied Union force just across the river, while in its path downstream was the Union stronghold of Fort Craig, garrisoned by more than six hundred troops under Colonel Kit Carson. After some debate, the Confederate command decided that their only hope was to leave the Rio Grande Valley and detour around it through trackless mountain country miles to the west.

Union scouts who crossed the river in the morning found that the Confederate camp had been abandoned during the night, their camp-fires left burning to conceal their departure. Left behind were thirty-eight wagons filled with supplies, the burning remnants of other supplies, and a few sick, wounded, or disabled Texans who were unable to continue on. Canby decided not to follow the retreating Texans into the wilderness, and led his force south down the river to Fort Craig.

From their riverside encampment, the Confederate troops head-ed southwest on what proved to be an agonizing, ten-day trek across more than one hundred miles of rugged and nearly waterless ter-rain. Reaching the northern edge of the Magdalena Mountains, about twenty miles west of the Rio Grande, the Texans continued south along the western fringe of the range and through the eastern foothills of the San Mateo Mountains west of Fort Craig, returning to the Rio Grande along Cuchillo Negro Creek about forty miles south of Fort Craig. Left in their wake was a long trail of discarded equip-ment, buried cannons, dead horses and mules, and the shallow graves of those who died along the way.

The Confederate troops, reunited in southern New Mexico with comrades who had remained at Mesilla and Fort Thorn, made their way back to Texas, ending the Civil War campaign in New Mexico. Left behind were about one thousand of their original number in unmarked graves, in makeshift hospitals, as prisoners of war, or reported missing.

### The Man Who Buried Cannons

Trevanion T. Teel, who had served as a captain of light artillery with the Confederate Army in New Mexico, was practicing law in El Paso in 1889 when he received an urgent request. Would he go to Albuquerque and point out the place where he had buried some can-nons when the Confederates were evacuating the town twenty-seven years before?

Making the request was John W. Crawford, known as Captain Jack, the Poet Scout, a Civil War veteran and former Indian scout who was living at abandoned Fort Craig. Crawford told the sixty-seven-year-old Teel that he wanted some Civil War relics to take to the New Era Exposition at St. Joseph, Missouri.

Teel agreed to offer his assistance, and he and Crawford arrived in Albuquerque on the afternoon of August 17, 1889. They contacted Harry S. Whiting, a Union veteran and commander of G. K. Warren Post No. 1,

Grand Army of the Republic, and the three proceeded to this historic Albuquerque plaza.

Teel, after orienting himself, led his two companions to a garden, cultivated by Sofre Alexander, about five hundred feet northeast of the San Felipe de Neri Church. Entering the garden, which Teel said had been a walled corral in 1862, he pointed to a chile patch and said, "Dig here, and you will find them." Teel left for El Paso that evening.

Sofre Alexander, however, voiced strong objections to anyone digging up his chile patch, even turning down a $100 offer to let the digging proceed. Judge William D. Lee turned down his request for a preliminary injunction, saying, "Besides, Sofre, I am curious myself about those cannons. I'd like to see if those rebels really buried them there." Judge Lee was a Union veteran.

The excavating began on the morning of August 19 when Albuquerque resident George Lail wrote out a mining location notice, posted it in the chile patch, and told the workers, "Go ahead with your mineral prospecting."

It was late that afternoon before the cannons were uncovered, just a few feet north of the spot Teel had indicated. Eight brass cannon barrels were found at a depth of three feet in an area about five feet square. They were bright and shiny when first uncovered, but became tarnished shortly after they were exposed to the air. All were twelve-pounder mountain howitzers, equipped to fire twelve-pound balls. Their inscriptions revealed that they had been manufactured by Charles Ames and Company of Boston, two of them cast in 1847, one in 1849, one in 1850, and four in 1853.

A squabble ensued among several Civil War veterans' groups as to who should possess the cannons. Eventually, two of them remained in Albuquerque, and the others were sent to various organizations in Colorado and Texas.

Replicas of their undercarriages were made for the two that remained in Albuquerque, and they were displayed on the plaza for years until removed to the nearby Albuquerque Museum for safekeeping, at which time exact replicas were placed on the plaza.

✦ ✦

Trevanion Teel, who was promoted to major following the New Mexico campaign, was born in 1822 in Pittsburg, Pennsylvania, and moved with his parents to Texas in about 1838 where he lived until his death in 1899.

The finding of the cannons prompted some Civil War recollections in various published interviews and letters.

As the Confederates were evacuating Albuquerque, he recalled, Captain Thomas Ochiltree, Sibley's aide-de-camp, approached him with a large oil painting of Napoleon Bonaparte rolled under his arm, and offered it to him as security for a $110 loan. Teel said the painting, which was seven feet tall, had been hanging in one of Albuquerque's finer homes.

Teel, an art lover, handed over the money and took the painting, hoping that Ochiltree would never redeem it. He placed the painting, which was rolled in an oilcloth, between the canvas roof and a roof support of his ambulance, a military vehicle, which was being used to transport supplies.

Days later, during the difficult retreat through the rugged foothills of the San Mateo Mountains, Teel paused west of Fort Craig to bury four cannons that had become too burdensome to move. He left his ambulance, which was beginning to break down, over the spot where he buried the cannons, forgetting to retrieve the oil painting that was rolled up under the roof.

A quarter century later, during an 1887 visit to the Bullion newspaper office in El Paso, Teel was surprised to find his long-lost painting hanging on a wall. He asked Carl Longuemare, the editor, how he had come into possession of the painting.

Longuemare answered that he had found the Napoleon portrait hanging in the San Miguel Catholic Church in Socorro, where the parishioners believed it to be a representation of San Miguel (St. Michael), patron saint of the church. Somebody, perhaps a sheepherder, had found the painting in Teel's abandoned carriage and had taken it to the Socorro church where it was thought to be a picture of San Miguel, blessed with holy water, and given a place of prominence in the chapel.

Longuemare said he was given the painting after convincing those in charge that it was a picture of Napoleon, not San Miguel. Teel said that the painting mysteriously disappeared from the El Paso newspaper office the night he saw it there and that he never saw it again.

Shortly after the cannons were uncovered in Albuquerque, Elias S. Stover, Albuquerque merchant and former lieutenant governor of Kansas, wrote to Teel in El Paso requesting additional information about buried cannons. Teel's letter of reply was published in the *Albuquerque Daily Citizen* on August 26, 1887. It read:

Your letter of the 20th instant is at hand, and in reply to the questions asked, would say:

I do not now recollect whether there were more cannons buried at the place you found the eight; nor do I remember whether larger guns were buried in that place or not. There are a number still unearthed in New Mexico, some I think I could find, others I do not believe I could.

The pieces buried in the mountains opposite Fort Craig I think could be found; they are large pieces, field guns, 6s and 12s brass. Those near Santa Fe I do not believe I would be able to locate. My command entered Santa Fe at night, and while we were there the days were cloudy, and much snow fell, hence I did not notice the points of the compass. The pieces were interred in the night, I think about a mile north of the government corral, in an open place, such is my recollection. I regret exceedingly that I cannot point out the exact place.

You ask me to give you a short history of the transaction. So many years have passed since that eventful period that much of the history has passed beyond my recollection. Ordinarily I would have paid more attention to the surroundings, but at that time there was hardly any thought in the army but one to "get out of the country."

We were without food, clothing, and ammunitions of war, but little transportation, and between two columns of Federal troops. General Canby below us, Colonel Slough above us, each with an equal number of troops, and twice as many as we could muster. So you see but that little time was left for observation at that city.

All the guns we had were captured from the United States forces at one time or another, after hostilities had commenced, and at this day it would impossible for me to state to you when and where they were captured; but this I can say, that the Valverde battery captured at the battle of that name was not left in New Mexico, but was taken by us to Louisiana, and at the close of the war was at Red River in that state.

As to the officers of my command who assisted in hiding the guns in Albuquerque, Capt. J.W. Bennett (dead), Capt. Maginnis (dead), Lt. McFarland (dead), Lt. Bradford (dead) and Lt. Phil Fulcroid; the others I do not recollect; in all probability there may have been some non-commissioned officers and soldiers of my command also of the party, and there may have been some other officers of the army present.

I do not think there were any large guns buried at Albuquerque. I have been taxing my memory about the matter, and I have concluded that there were no large guns left there.

We lost by battle and disease nearly one-half our command; many died in Albuquerque. We had pneumonia, smallpox and measles. The deaths were so many there that the dead were buried in the night so that our loss could be kept from our own as well as the Federal army.

We left Albuquerque with a day and a half rations, three rounds of ammunitions to the man, and had about a quarter transportation for the long trip ahead.

When we left Puerco River, we had nothing to eat; traveled all that night, camped a short time about daybreak, rested our animals an hour or two, and then started our march. I lost ninety head of animals, this was the reason we left the pieces in the mountains. I left my ambulance by the roadside, having taken my four horses to hitch to the guns. Every horse and mule that was able to work was taken and hitched to the guns. The next night we camped without food or fuel, and the weather was intensely cold.

The next morning about 8 o'clock we found water at Alamosa Canyon. We rested most of the day, then took up our line of march for Fort Thorn. Our cannon were hauled up the mountainside by the troops. It was an almost impossible undertaking, but we succeeded.

That day we met General Steele with provisions, dried beef, some coffee, and a little flour; it makes my mouth water now to think how I relished that poor diet.

My heart bleeds when I think of the poor wounded and sick soldiers we left in the snow by the roadside; some with measles, others with pneumonia or smallpox; some were wounded. Captain Kirk was wounded at Glorieta, had his leg amputated while on the road through the mountains, a wagon for the hospital; with all this he recovered and lived for many years afterwards.

All these details, governor, are not pleasant reminisces. I pray your petition to the Secretary of War will be granted and that your city may be the depository of the guns which have lain so long in her soil.

God bless our united, prosperous and happy country, and may there never be another fratercidal war in this glorious land.

Fraternally yours,

***T. T. Teel***

# Chapter Six

# ALBUQUERQUE IN THE 1860s AND 1870s

## Visitor Impressions, River Problems, and a Few Lynchings

### Renewed Indian Campaigns

Life in Albuquerque returned to normal following the departure of Confederate troops from the territory. Once the Texans were gone, the military turned its attention to the nomadic Navajos and Apaches whose forays against settlements and ranches had increased during the conflict.

Devising a grandiose but ill-fated plan to "pacify and civilize" the Navajos and Apaches on a reservation away from their traditional homelands was Brigadier General James H. Carleton, who was named military commander of the Department of New Mexico in September 1862, succeeding the departing and recently promoted General Edward Canby.

General Carleton had arrived in New Mexico in August as leader of the California Column, a force of more than two thousand California volunteers who had marched about nine hundred miles from the West Coast to help expel the Confederates from New Mexico. By the time they arrived on the Rio Grande in the Mesilla Valley, however, the Texans had left the territory.

Carleton, no stranger to New Mexico, had served as a dragoon major at the Albuquerque Military Post in the 1850s and was acting commander of the post at intervals during the absences of General John Garland, his wife's uncle. During that time he was credited with a number of civic improvements in Albuquerque, including the draining of swamp areas, street construction, the erection of a 120-foot-high flagpole on the plaza, and the building of a ferry boat.

His wife Sophia had acquired some Albuquerque property in 1854, consisting of a dozen buildings, some corrals, and other improvements west of the plaza, which she rented to the army for $125 a month. She lost everything when this property was destroyed by fire as the Confederate troops were approaching Albuquerque.

Carleton believed that the Navajos and Apaches could be taught to become peaceful farmers after being rounded up and escorted to a reservation to be established on New Mexico's eastern and most uninhabited plains. Selected as the site of this reservation was a locale known as the Bosque Redondo, on the east bank of the Pecos River about 165 miles southeast of Albuquerque.

Units of the California Column went to the site during the winter of 1862–1863 and erected Fort Sumner to serve as military headquarters of the reservation. Given the task of rounding up the Navajos and Apaches were regiments of the New Mexico volunteers, assisted by members of the California Column.

Placed in command of the New Mexico volunteers was a reluctant Colonel Kit Carson, who did not fully agree with Carleton's Indian policy of unconditional surrender or extermination. Nevertheless, he quickly led forces that rounded up about five hundred Mescalero Apache men, women, and children in southeast New Mexico and escorted them to the Bosque Redondo Reservation.

Beginning in 1863, Carson's troops began rounding up thousands of Navajos in northwest New Mexico and northeast Arizona and escorting them more than three hundred miles to the new reservation. Many died along the way on what the Navajos always remembered as the Long Walk. Eventually, more than eight thousand Navajos and about five hundred Apaches were held under military guard at the Bosque Redondo under what proved to be deplorable conditions. The Apaches suddenly departed and headed for home, but the Navajos remained captive until 1868.

In the fall of 1863, Captain William Ayres of the First Infantry of New Mexico Volunteers began recruiting about one hundred able-bodied men from Albuquerque and vicinity to serve in a new regiment to campaign against hostile Indians in the Southwest. Recruitment notices offered pay from $13 to $30 a month plus subsistence and clothing.

Captain Ayres, a veteran of the regular army, had served as a New Mexico volunteers lieutenant during the recent Confederate invasion.

The regiment he raised in Albuquerque became known as Company D, and by mid-January of 1864 the new recruits were on their way south to Fort Craig for garrison duty.

In October, the men of Company D, along with eighty other infantry and cavalry soldiers, left Fort Craig and headed west on a scouting mission into the mountain wilderness of the recently created territory of Arizona. For nearly sixty days they struggled over difficult terrain in heavy rains and snow, living on scant rations, their paths often blocked by steep canyons and rushing streams. Exhausted, with their clothing and shoes in tatters, they returned to New Mexico late in November without having encountered any hostile Indians.

Although the Albuquerque volunteers proved to be tough and disciplined campaigners in the field, they became restless and undisciplined during routine and boring garrison duty at various forts. During these periods there was a high incidence of fighting, drunkenness, gambling, theft, and disobeying of orders.

Company D was sent to Fort Bascom, in eastern New Mexico, when Comanche and Kiowa Indians threatened to attack that post. The attack did not materialize, however, and the company was sent to Fort Union for garrison duty. Captain Ayres, having difficulty controlling his men, resigned in April 1866 and was replaced by a man from the ranks who was appointed second lieutenant.

The company was sent north to Fort Garland, Colorado, where Colonel Kit Carson, the post commander, anticipated an attack by Ute Indians. This attack also failed to materialize, and after two months at the Colorado fort, the men of Company D returned to Albuquerque and honorable discharges. Later, some of the men filed claims for battle wounds they had never received.

### Albuquerque's Early Newspapers

Continual newspaper publication in Albuquerque began in 1860 with a weekly called the *Albuquerque Review*, owned by Theodore S. Greiner. After about two years of operation, the paper was sold to Hezekiah S. Johnson, who early in 1863 began publication of the *Rio Abajo Weekly Press*.

Johnson, a native of Pennsylvania, was an Albuquerque lawyer and an ordained Episcopal deacon who had lived in New Mexico since 1849. As a lay missionary, he conducted Sunday services in the dining room of a local hotel between the breakfast and luncheon hours.

The first issue of the newspaper appeared on January 20, 1863, and in a front page "Salutatory" Johnson introduced himself to the readers and explained the purposes of his newspaper. His editorial said in part:

> We have named our paper the RIO ABAJO WEEKLY PRESS, partly in honor of the section in which we reside, and partly to indicate its periodical publication....
>
> We may not be inclined to wear out our Webster's unabridged searching polysyllable words wherewith to express our views on any subject. We make no pretensions to being a D.D., LL.D. or M.D., nor do we think the brilliancy of our style will throw any considerable numbers of readers into ecstatic raptures or set the Rio del Norte on fire. However, we can master enough simple English to manifest our meaning on the generality of the readers of the language.
>
> The subscriber pays us his subscription; we furnish him with the best and most accurate news that the market affords. The merchant, or other individual, pays us a certain price for a certain space in our columns for advertising, we publish his advertisement. These are plain business transactions, and we have not yet arrived at that state of beatified transcendentalism which produces repugnance to the "almighty dollar."

Advertisements in early issues of the *Rio Abajo Weekly Press* provide a partial picture of the business life in Albuquerque at the time. Located on the east side of the plaza was the Union Hotel, operated by Evan and Stone, who advertised that they had leased and refitted the house formerly kept by J. J. Hutchason. The Union, according to the ads, had well-supplied tables, foreign and domestic liquors, a well-ventilated billiards room, and polite and attentive waiters.

The U.S. Hotel, located on the southwest corner of the plaza, advertised that it accommodated both permanent and transient boarders and that the tables were supplied with the best the market could afford. Louis Bieler was listed as the proprietor, and the ads said that the rooms were large and well ventilated.

Jacob Meyer, a confectioner, ran advertisements for his business on the southeast corner of the plaza. His wares included ice cream, pies, cakes, coffee, chocolate, wine, and liquor served in cool and comfortable rooms. Henry August, a carpenter with a shop on the east side of the plaza, advertised that he was prepared upon short notice to do all kinds of carpentering, joining, and cabinet work. No location was given for the Sutler Store, operated by William T. Strachan, which dealt in fancy and staple dry goods, wines and brandies, miners' goods, canned fruit, and clothing.

A general store on the plaza was operated by A. and L. Zeckendorf, who advertised a large assortment of ready-made clothing, hats, caps, boots, shoes, groceries, hardware, wines, cigars, china, drugs, and medicines. Our House, operated by H. Miller, advertised that it had a good supply of Santa Fe Lager Beer always on hand, as well as other good liquors. Maurice Schwarzkopf, a bookkeeper and translator on the plaza, advertised that he translated to and from German, English, and Spanish.

Santiago L. Hubbell advertised that he was a U.S. Claims agent with offices in the residence of doña Mariana Sarracino. He said he would promptly attend to and adjust all claims against the government, including claims for back pay, bounty, and pension.

Born James. L. Hubbell in Connecticut in 1821, Hubbell settled in New Mexico in 1848 and soon adopted the first name Santiago, the Spanish equivalent of Saint James. He married Julianita Gutiérrez, whose family owned the Pajarito Land Grant a few miles south of Albuquerque, and they established an adobe hacienda at Pajarito that still stands today. Hubbell became a prominent freighter, cattle dealer, and merchant, and at one time operated a train of forty-eight ox-drawn wagons on the Santa Fe Trail. He was followed to New Mexico by a brother, Sidney Hubbell, who served as a district judge.

J. Lorenzo Hubbell, a son of James, left Albuquerque in the 1870s and founded the Hubbell Trading Post on the Navajo Reservation at Ganado, Arizona, a post later designated as a National Historic Site.

When Hezekiah Johnson was appointed judge of the Second Judicial District Court, he sold the *Rio Abajo Weekly Press* to Marshall Ashman "Ash" Upson, an itinerant journalist from Connecticut. The second judicial district not only included Bernalillo County, of which Albuquerque was designated the county seat in 1854, but all of the present-day Valencia, McKinley, Sandoval, and most of Torrance counties.

Upson, who changed the name of the weekly paper to the *New Mexico Press*, was forced to give the paper back to Johnson later when he failed to pay for it. Upson was associated with a number of New Mexico newspapers for a quarter century, and in 1882 was the ghostwriter for

Pat Garrett's book, *The Authentic Life of Billy the Kid*. Harry R. Whiting bought the paper in 1869, and it was sold a year later to William McGuinness, who published it until 1882 as the *Republic Review* and the *Albuquerque Review*.

### First Police Ordinances, 1863

Albuquerque's first police ordinances were adopted unanimously at a public meeting of citizens held at the Bernalillo County Courthouse on March 25, 1863. The ordinances had been drawn up by members of the town's first board of aldermen, who had been elected on March 2 when Albuquerque was incorporated as a town. The aldermen were W. H. Henrie, Salvador Armijo, Tomás Gonzáles, William T. Strachan, Moritz Miller, and Cristóbal Armijo. The ordinances were published in full in the May 5 and May 12 issues of the *Rio Abajo Weekly Press*.

Ordinance No. 1 provided that judicial authority be conferred on a police magistrate, to be appointed by the aldermen. The police magistrate was authorized to appoint a proper person to serve as police marshal, who in turn was authorized to appoint a deputy marshal. The marshal was authorized to call on sufficient people of the town to aid him in arresting any person.

The magistrate was authorized to call on every homeowner, family head, or other residents "to give their services, either in person, money, wagons, carts, mules, etc., for assisting and helping to clean the roads, streets and plaza, until there are funds in the treasury." Many of the ordinances were designed to keep Albuquerque in a clean and sanitary condition.

Residents were prohibited from "throwing or laying dirt, rock, bricks, adobes, logs, lumber, boxes, carriages, wagons, carts, or other obstructions of any kind or nature whatsoever" on the plaza or in the streets, roads, or alleyways. It was also against the law to make excavations in the plaza, streets, or roads.

One ordinance made it unlawful to place any obstruction or nuisance or to cast away filth in the *acequia madre* (main irrigation ditch) of the town. Homeowners were required to take special care that their servants did not cast dirty water, sweepings, or kitchen residue into the plaza or streets. According to another ordinance, "Any person or persons who may sell, or offer for sale, meat, vegetables, fruit, etc., are required to go to the public place behind the corral of Louis Bieler and in front of the house of Morris Miller."

Other ordinances included:

> Every person who shall enter or go, with any animal or animals, within the plaza, road or streets of the Town of Albuquerque, is prohibited to run them, or to tie them to any prop or pillar of any porch, or to put them into the porches or sidewalks of the said plaza, road or streets.
>
> All persons are prohibited to walk intoxicated in the plaza or streets within the limits of the aforesaid town, or to utter scandalous words or phrases containing obscene words.
>
> All person or persons are prohibited within the limits of the Town of Albuquerque to carry arms about their persons.
>
> Every person who shall keep a disorderly house within the limits of the Town of Albuquerque, or allow riots or other disorderly conduct within the limits of or in his or hers, or their premises, when convicted thereof before the Police Magistrate shall be fined not less than $50, or shall be sentenced to imprisonment and hard labor for a term not less than one day or more than 10 days.

The ordinances also provided a $3.50 license fee for staging concerts, theater, or circus performances in Albuquerque.

### Some Visitor Impressions, 1866–1867

A U.S. Army officer who visited Albuquerque in the summer of 1866 was not particularly impressed by the appearance of the town or the beauty of its women. He also complained about the flies and the heat, which he said was 83 degrees in the shade and 125 degrees in the sun.

Colonel James F. Meline, a fifty-four-year-old bachelor, visited Albuquerque late in July during a horseback journey from Leavenworth, Kansas, to New Mexico and back, accompanied by a small military escort. He wrote of his experiences in an 1868 book titled *Two Thousand Miles on Horseback*.

A New Yorker and the son of a French officer in the U.S. Army, Meline was educated in the law and served as a U.S. consul in Europe and a journalist before entering the Union Army during the Civil War. "Albuquerque is an uninteresting village of some 1,000 inhabitants," he wrote. "A few nice adobe buildings and the old church in the Plaza with its modern façade form the sum total of its architectural interest. This church—above other Mexican churches—is quite aristocratic in having a board floor. Some half-dozen long kneeling benches used for pews at the upper end show the extent of American innovation."

Meline said he entered the church with the expectation of hearing a sermon in Spanish, but that the padre, Father Augustine Truchard, after reading the gospel of the day in Spanish and making a few remarks upon it, announced that there would be no sermon because of the extreme heat.

Portions of the service were sung to the accompaniment of a scratchy violin and two guitars, played by three gray-haired old men bending under the weight of years. The guitars were monumental in size, he added, and contained enough wood to make a table. "The guitars, who were opposite each other, played as to tune and time as if each one wished it distinctly to be understood that he had no connection with the establishment over the way," he wrote.

The brass band of the Fifth U.S. Infantry was present and performed some solemn airs, Meline continued, and played again that evening in the plaza. He was impressed that the program included a selection from the Donizetti opera, *Lucia di Lammermoor*. The band members included five Frenchmen who were deserters from the French Army in Mexico, he wrote, who had made their way out of that country with the help of native citizens who were strong supporters of Benito Juárez.

Meline wrote that he saw a band of thirty-seven starving Navajos arrive in Albuquerque and surrender to military authorities. They were kindly treated, he wrote, and arrangements were made to move them southeast to the Bosque Redondo Reservation at Fort Sumner.

Meline left Albuquerque on the night of July 30, 1866, after attending a grand ball at the home of Salvador Armijo honoring Brigadier General John Pope who was visiting the town. The bachelor officer wrote that he was disappointed in not finding such beautiful women in Albuquerque as those described by Zebulon Pike in 1807 and George Kendall in 1841, writing:

> Kendall, in his Santa Fe Expedition, speaking of the entry into
> Albuquerque of the procession formed by his fellow prison-
> ers and their guard, describes the population of the place
> flocking out, and among the rest, a beautiful girl of fifteen
> standing on an adobe wall to look at them pass by, the taper
> fingers of her right hand supporting a huge pumpkin upon
> her head, while her left was gracefully resting upon her hip.

The description of her peerless beauty, I recollect, occupied some three pages—one of those little impromptus labored at leisure—and closes by saying that the prettiest girl he ever saw was selling woolen socks at twenty-five cents a pair at Holmes Hole, and her twin sister in beauty was standing in her bare feet on a mud wall in Albuquerque.

I have only to remark that I, also, twenty-five years later, on the same spot, saw the population of Albuquerque swarm out on a more attractive occasion; and if that young lady of the pumpkin, bare feet, taper fingers, hip, and all that sort of that thing, left daughters resembling herself, I certainly did not see them.

An Englishman who visited Albuquerque in 1867 described it as a pleasant little community, filled with gardens and orchards, in which the town butcher doubled as editor of the local newspaper.

The visitor was William A. Bell, a fellow of the Royal Geographical Society and Geological Society of London, who at the time was attached to a Kansas Pacific Railway Company surveying expedition to determine the best route for a southern railroad to the Pacific Coast. His experiences and observations on the five-thousand-mile trip were published in London in 1870 under the title *New Tracks in North America—A Journal of Travel and Adventure.*

Bell arrived in Albuquerque in early October 1867 not long after the August 23 closing of the Albuquerque Military Post. "Albuquerque, the second town in rank to Santa Fe, does not present an imposing appearance," he wrote. "It is a straggling collection of adobe houses, scattered among innumerable acequias or irrigation ditches, in the perfectly flat lowlands of the Rio Grande Valley. In a direct line it is 63 miles from Santa Fe. A few groves and solitary cottonwood trees give a degree of shade to the place, but beyond this it might be a brickyard as seen at a distance," he continued.

> Distance here certainly does not lend enchantment to the view, for on close inspection every house is found to possess a garden well filled with peaches, apples, plums of every description, and vines bearing most delicious grapes. Then, as one approaches, fields of Indian corn pop up on all sides, having been hidden from view by the lowness of their position,

and, lastly, in the center of town, a very inviting church, with
twin spires, adds greatly to the appearance of the plaza.

The Englishman wrote that he was received most hospitably by the little "American Colony" in Albuquerque, adding that they all sat together in
the evening, a party of nearly a dozen, in a large, cool room of one of the
resident merchants. The most entertaining man of the evening, Bell wrote,
was a young Southerner, who kept the party in roars of laughter with his
droll stories. He was the town butcher, he added, and he found him hard
at work the next morning butchering some slaughtered sheep.

"Two hours later, on our return to the hotel, we stopped at the office
of the Albuquerque Chronicle," he wrote. "At the door we met the editor
and proprietor who, to our great amusement, was no other than our
facetious host of the night before, the butcher of Albuquerque, and now,
bereft of blouse, the energetic editor of the daily paper." Since there was
no daily paper called the "Albuquerque Chronicle" in 1867, Bell apparently was referring to the *Albuquerque Press*, a weekly paper edited by the
colorful M. A. "Ash" Upson, who was not a Southerner but a Connecticut
Yankee.

The closing of the Albuquerque Military Post in 1867 caused an eco-
nomic depression in the town, which caused some of the prominent
merchants to close their doors and move to more profitable locales.

### The Long Walk Home, 1868

General Carleton's project of settling thousands of nomadic Navajos at
the Bosque Redondo on New Mexico's eastern plains, and teaching them
to become sedentary farmers, proved to be a dismal failure. Crops failed
year after year, livestock was lost due to insufficient grazing, fuel for
warmth was scarce, and deaths were many.

General William Tecumseh Sherman, accompanied by Colonel
Samuel F. Tappan, arrived at Fort Sumner on May 28, 1868, armed with the
authority to negotiate a peace treaty with the Navajos there and to determine their fate. Noting that the reservation had cost the military more
than $1 million in eighteen months, Sherman remarked that it would be
cheaper to put the Indians up at the Fifth Avenue Hotel in New York.

By June 1 a treaty had been drafted and signed, allowing the Navajos
to return at once to their traditional homelands in northwest New
Mexico and northeast Arizona. The government had considered moving
them on east to Oklahoma, but the Navajos persuaded Sherman to let
them go home.

On June 15, about seven thousand Navajo men, women, and children left the reservation at Fort Sumner on the long walk home, accompanied by a military escort, more than one hundred supply wagons, and about five thousand head of livestock.

It took the ten-mile-long procession twenty-one days to reach the mouth of Tijeras Canyon, about a dozen miles east of Albuquerque, and it was here that the Navajos caught sight of a familiar landmark, their sacred Mount Taylor, on the far western horizon. One Navajo man, it was reported, became temporarily deranged upon recognizing the landmark, and soldiers had to quiet him down by tying his hands to the endgate of a wagon.

The long procession arrived in Albuquerque on Sunday, July 5, and the Navajos were free to wander about the plaza and mingle with native citizens who had been their enemies. For many of them, it was the first time they had ever heard the ringing of church bells, and it was to make a lasting impression on them.

The Indians camped on the east bank of the Rio Grande that night, some of them chanting and singing, and they began fording the river to the west bank the next morning, holding on to a rope that had been stretched across the river. Soon they were back in the country they loved. Thereafter, Navajos referred to Albuquerque in their native language as *pe-el-de-1-tah-sinil*, in English "place where the sounding things are suspended," or "place where the bells ring."

Italian Jesuits, led by Father Donato Maria Gasparri, who was fluent in Spanish, took charge of the church on the plaza in 1868, replacing the French priests sent there by Bishop Lamy. They remodeled parts of the church, established large gardens, orchards, and vineyards, and began sponsoring church schools for boys.

### River Crossings, 1870s

Ferryboat service across the Rio Grande, conducted for years by Juan Chávez and his son under a military contract, continued as a private enterprise following the closing of the military base in 1867. A Santa Fe newspaper reported on April 20, 1869, that a new ferryboat was being built in Albuquerque by Juan Chávez, the old ferryman, and some others.

The new ferryboat apparently was not yet completed eighteen months later when an unidentified traveler described the river crossing in an article appearing in the *Santa Fe Weekly Post* on November 5, 1870.

Telling of a stagecoach journey from Santa Fe south to Fort Craig, he wrote:

> We pass Albuquerque at about 10 o'clock and a short drive brings us to the ferry, three miles beyond, where we are to cross the Rio Grande. We find the ferryboat an extremely primitive craft, being a low, narrow barge, evidently of considerable age, and somewhat shaky as to its deck timbers.
>
> The motive power was in full accord with the general character of the establishment, and consisted of two brunettish individuals, who, after depositing their garments upon the prow of the craft, took to the water, rope in hand, and drew us across by main force. The Rio Grande is nearly a hundred yards wide at this point, but the average depth does not exceed three feet during this season of the year.

General Oliver O. Howard was a passenger on the ferryboat in June of 1872 and recalled the experience later in his book *My Life and Experiences Among Our Hostile Indians.* At the time, he was en route to the East Coast with ten Apache, Pima, and Papago Indians from Arizona with the object of showing them "the hopelessness of resisting a government as powerful as ours."

The eastbound caravan included a six-mule wagon, a six-mule ambulance as an escort carriage, some teamsters, and a few soldiers. It reached the west bank of the Rio Grande below Albuquerque during a late spring runoff. "The river had risen over its banks and was as swift in its flow as the Mississippi in flood time," General Howard wrote. "The Indians were full of wonderment and gazed up and down the fierce waters."

Soon the group caught sight of a large flatboat coming toward them across the Rio Grande from a point farther north on the opposite bank. The swift current swept the boat past the waiting party and it struck the shore far below them. Howard and his party walked down to the ferryboat, and the general wrote that "it took close packing to get our party, wagons, ambulance, animals and all else on board."

As the boat was shoving off, he continued, one of the mules kicked a wagon driver in the stomach, causing him to somersault overboard into the water. He was pulled back onboard, and the Indians thought the incident quite humorous, clapping their hands and shouting with glee. "The flatboat, shooting across the torrent, brought us up against an island," Howard wrote. "Here we had to disembark and wade to the eastern shore. Our mules wallowed in the muddy bottom, and now and then sank in quicksand, so that we had trouble to save them, and our staunch army wagon was so broken and mired that it had to be abandoned."

An Albuquerque ferryboat story that may or not be true was told in 1896 by Lute Wilcox, editor of a weekly publication in Denver called *Field and Farm*. A former New Mexico newspaperman, Wilcox published several stories in his periodical about life in Albuquerque in the 1870s, which were reprinted in the *Albuquerque Citizen* with the expressed opinion that Wilcox exaggerated quite a bit.

Five cowboys, according to the story, rode up to the ferryboat landing in the 1870s and hailed the ferryman, who was sitting on the flat-bottomed barge on the opposite bank of the Rio Grande, sunning himself and dangling his bare feet in the water.

"Say, you," called one of the cowboys.

"Well, what is it?" asked the ferryman.

"We want to cross over," answered the cowboy.

"Maybe you ain't heard the news," said the ferryman after a long pause.

"What is it?" asked the cowboy.

"The price for getting over used to be a quarter, but it has riz."

"What is it now?"

"Half a dollar."

"Well, I have some news for you," said the cowboy. "The price of cartridges used to be fifty cents a box, but they's come down to a quarter, and I can afford to waste a dozen or so."

"Shooting at what?" asked the ferryman.

"At you," responded the cowboy. "I'll give you five minutes to make a start."

The ferryman took off his hat, put it on the end of a stick, and held it up in the air.

"Can you plunk that?" he asked.

"You bet," answered the cowboy, drawing his six-shooter and sending two quick bullets through the hat.

"Mighty peculiar how the price of cartridges fell down just as my price riz up," the ferryman muttered as he poled his boat across the river to his waiting customers.

A second river crossing became available to Albuquerque residents in the summer of 1876 when a wooden toll bridge was opened that spanned the Rio Grande west of the plaza and north of the ferry crossing. No part of Albuquerque, other than grazing lands, existed on the west bank of the river at the time.

Building the bridge as a private enterprise was Thomas D. Post, a former stagecoach driver who arrived in Albuquerque from Kansas in the 1860s and opened a butcher shop on the plaza. He became a successful hotel owner in the 1870s, operating two successive hotels he called the Exchange, often referred to as Post's Exchange and the Post Exchange, the second hotel located a short distance south of the plaza. Prices were $1.50 a day for transient boarders, and $7.00 a week room and board for regular boarders.

Tom Post's toll bridge, said to have been built on pontoons, included his home, a grocery, and toll station (charging 10¢) on or adjacent to the east end of the bridge. The bridge and home were washed away by Rio Grande floodwaters a few years later.

A second toll bridge, financed by private citizens, was built on the site in 1882, and the Rio Grande washed it away in 1891.

### The 1874 Flood

"From parties from below we hear that the Rio Grande is rising rapidly." This item, appearing in the *Daily New Mexican* at Santa Fe on May 23, 1864, proved to be the first in a series of dispatches telling of a disastrous Rio Grande flood that almost inundated Albuquerque and left the town stranded on an island. The swollen river left its channel north of Albuquerque and sent gushing streams of water on a southward course both east and west of the town.

On May 26, the Santa Fe newspaper reported that Albuquerque was almost deserted "on account of everybody and the cook having gone to Alameda to aid in the stoppage of the present overflow of the river." Their efforts were in vain, as can be seen from a news article of May 27:

> The town of Albuquerque is an island, the river crossing on both sides of town. Many people have left the town already and are living on the hills east of town. Hundreds of people are without homes, and thousands of dollars of property have been destroyed.

An unidentified Albuquerque resident furnished more details on May 29:

> I am now living on the west instead of the east side of the river. The greatest channel runs at the foot of the hills on the east side of the valley, and has washed away a great many houses and fields.
>
> The town is nearly deserted, and we are working day and night to keep the water from coming into the plaza. Nearly all of the families are encamped on the sandhills in dread of the river coming in and washing down the town. Too much praise cannot be given to Don Salvador Armijo and Mr. F. Huning for the efforts they are making to save the town and people.

Don Ambrosio Armijo of Albuquerque provided an account of the flood in a letter dated May 28 and published in the Santa Fe paper on May 30:

> I write a line to say that the county of Bernalillo is being annihilated by the rushing waters. A body of land 12 miles long by two miles wide, embracing the fields and houses from Alameda above to Los Barelas below, is a watery waste and the loss must be at least two million dollars, for all the towns and settlements within that area must be swept away.
>
> We are now isolated here in the midst of the waters. Ruin seems inevitable, and God only knows where it will stop. All seems lost—lands and houses and much property of all kinds.
>
> The people are leaving day and night for the adjacent hills, and still the river rises. Albuquerque proper the river had not yet reached, but the place must be abandoned. The merchants are packing their effects and leaving. The hammer is heard everywhere in the packing of goods for transportation, and terror reigns among the people.
>
> I shall not leave myself yet, but have erected a platform whereon to place my goods, and if I cannot get away in wagon will leave in boats.

Southbound stagecoaches from Santa Fe could not cross the river at Albuquerque, the newspaper reported, and mail and passengers were being ferried across the floodwaters to coaches waiting on the west bank.

"No mail from Albuquerque for the past two days," the newspaper reported on June 2. "The last buckboard down from here attempted to get into the town, but the driver had all he could do to save himself and the animal."

The *New Mexican* reported on June 4 that Albuquerque, except for its suburbs, had escaped the wrath of the floodwaters:

> Accounts from the Rio Abajo state that the river is falling slowly and that Albuquerque will not be inundated, but the damage to the eastern suburbs of the town and Los Ranchos and Alameda is very great. The river still continues to run a swift and rapid current east of Alameda, Los Ranchos and Albuquerque.
>
> The church and all the buildings at Alameda have been swept away, and where a few weeks ago were comfortable residences, extensive vineyards and fields of grain now flow the turbid waters of the Rio Grande.

The newspaper added that Albuquerque would have been swept away were it not for the efforts of such citizens as Salvador Armijo, Santiago Baca, Franz and Charles Huning, Diego and Manuel Armijo, and money contributed by H. Springer, Ambrosio Armijo, and a few others. The newspaper reported on June 5 that the river was still falling slowly at Albuquerque, and it reported on June 9 that the Rio Grande was back in its old channel at Albuquerque and that people were returning from the hills.

Late spring floods, caused principally by the runoff from melting mountain snows, created havoc at intervals along the length of the Rio Grande in New Mexico, washing away many small river communities. Alameda, once close to the east bank of the river north of Albuquerque, was reestablished about two miles east at its present location. An 1886 flood destroyed part of Santo Domingo Pueblo, between Albuquerque and Santa Fe, and washed away its mission church that dated from the early 1600s.

## The Hanging Trees

The *Albuquerque Review* reported on June 3, 1876, that Antonio Lerma, owner of a small store in the village of Alameda north of town, had been brutally murdered in his store by three robbers. Lerma was alone in his store on a Friday afternoon, according to the recollections of some Albuquerque pioneers, when three intoxicated young men entered the store.

"Look up my account and see how much I owe you," one of the men told Lerma. "I am ready to pay." Lerma turned to his desk and began shuffling through some papers. As he was searching for the account, one of the men came up behind him with an axe and sank it into his skull, killing him instantly. The store safe was opened, and the three men disappeared after taking all the money they found in it. Lerma's daughter estimated the amount as about $7,000 in gold coins.

The three robbers, soon apprehended, were identified as Meliton Cordova and the brothers Juan and Gregorio Miera, the latter's first name also given as José. They were said to be members of a gang of robbers and murderers led by Sostenes Archibeque and Pantaleón Miera of Bernalillo and vicinity. The three men were placed in the Albuquerque jail, where they reportedly confessed to Lerma's murder.

About three weeks after the crime, according to the pioneer recollections, a group of men removed the accused murderers from the jail and took them north to the home of Guadalupe Chávez, a justice of the peace in the small settlement of Los Poblanos in Los Ranchos de Albuquerque. Here they were found guilty after what was described as a brief "trial." The three condemned men were led immediately to a row of three cottonwood trees that lined the edge of the road, and at dusk each was hanged, one by one, from separate trees. Friends removed the bodies from the trees the next morning and hauled them off in a wagon.

Known thereafter as "the hanging trees," the three cottonwoods stood for decades along the east edge of what later was known as Rio Grande Boulevard. By 1956 only a section of the trunk of the southernmost tree, the one Juan Miera was hanged from, remained in place on property then owned by Albert G. Simms. It crumbled to the ground in October of that year and was hauled away. The lynching of the three men was confirmed by the *Albuquerque Review* on June 24, 1876.

## Albuquerque Business Life, 1876–1879

Melchior Werner helped celebrate the nation's centennial observance in 1876 by opening a hotel west of the plaza he called the Centennial. The German-born Werner had been the Albuquerque postmaster since 1867, and the post office became a part of his new hotel. It was in 1876, too, that Albuquerque received its first telegraph line. The telegraph office, like the post office, was located in the Centennial, and the line went into operation on February 12 when a message was tapped out to Santa Fe.

Albuquerque's economy improved in the late 1870s as an approaching railroad line brought the promise of prosperity usually associated with new railroad towns. The Atchison, Topeka and Santa Fe Railroad (AT&SF), building down the Santa Fe Trail from Kansas, reached Las Vegas, New Mexico, in the summer of 1879, and the tracks were expected to reach Albuquerque in the spring of 1880.

The *Albuquerque Review*, on July 16, 1879, published a list of business establishments in Albuquerque. The list included four large and seven smaller mercantile houses, three butcher shops, three blacksmiths, two bakeries, two carpenter shops, two hardware stores, two cobblers, three doctors, three lawyers, one barber, and one saloon. Among the prominent merchants who had stores on and off the plaza were Franz Huning, Salvador Armijo, Elias S. Stover, the Ilfeld brothers, the Rosenwald brothers, and the Spiegelberg brothers, the latter operating a branch of their Santa Fe business.

The lawyers included William C. Hazeldine, a former Arkansas state legislator and district judge, and William H. Henrie, a native of France. One of the butcher shops was owned by Joseph Pohmer, a native of Bavaria, whose daughter, Francisquita, later was to marry the legendary Elfego Baca. The only barber was William Brown, a former soldier from Pennsylvania who set up shop in a small, fortresslike building in the center of the plaza that had once served as a jail or guardhouse, and from the roof of which extended the towering flagpole. Brown, who also offered his services as a dentist and podiatrist, called his place of business the Flag Staff Barber Shop.

The lone saloon was the Mint, owned by Henry Springer, located a block west of the southwest corner of the plaza. As the only saloon in town, it was known to attract some pretty rough customers. The perhaps exaggerated story of a young Englishman who encountered serious trouble in the Mint was related in 1896 by Lute Wilcox, the Denver editor and former New Mexico journalist.

The Englishman, new to America's western frontier, arrived in Albuquerque one summer day in 1878, and after resting up at a local hotel, entered the Mint and handed a letter of introduction to the proprietor. At about that time, according to the account, a man identified by Wilcox as "a typical bad man," walked into the saloon and offered to

Pioneer Albuquerque merchant Franz Huning (center) stands in front of one of his many enterprises, the Molina Glorieta Flour Mill, which stood a few blocks southeast of the Old Town Plaza until destroyed by fire in 1904. Courtesy UNM Center for Southwest Research, the Albuquerque Museum Photoarchive, PA1978.50.59.

buy a round of drinks. The Englishman stepped up to the bar, accepted his free drink, and proceeded to cut it with some water, which made the bad man mad.

"Who in hell are you drinking with?" the bad man asked.

"At your invitation, sir," the Englishman replied.

"Not by a darned sight," the bad man exclaimed, picking up the drink and tossing it in the Englishman's face.

When the Englishman reached into his right hip pocket for a handkerchief to wipe his face, his antagonist thought he was reaching for a gun, drew his own revolver, and shot him, and as he went down the bartender cracked him on the head with a bottle. The proprietor rushed in from the back room, knocked the bad man out, and disarmed him.

The Englishman recovered from his bullet wound, Wilcox wrote, and in 1896 was managing a large ranch within fifty miles of Denver. "But he never forgot the lesson that he learned at The Mint in Albuquerque," he wrote. "He never cares to drink with strangers, carries his handkerchief in plain view in a top flap pocket, and never puts water in whisky as was his custom previous to the year 1878."

Another disturbance at the Mint in 1879, this one verified by contemporary newspaper accounts, resulted in dire circumstances for the perpetrator.

J. P. Fish, an itinerant gambler, who was said to have killed six men at different times and places, was arrested after creating a disturbance at the Mint on Sunday night, November 9, 1879. Fish had arrived in Albuquerque recently from Arizona, the *Albuquerque Citizen* reported, and during the short time he was in town his violence showed itself on several occasions, as he shot at and threatened to shoot several people.

"On the slightest pretext he drew his revolver and in short seemed determined to 'run' the town," the newspaper reported, "and although he was lame in the left arm and right leg, the result of former wounds, yet he exhibited such strength and dexterity with his sound limbs, added to which was an apparent fearlessness, that it made him an extremely ugly customer to deal with."

Charged with being drunk and disorderly at the saloon, and threatening to kill various persons, Fish was taken before a justice of the peace on the morning of November 10 where his bail was set at $20,000. He was lodged in jail, heavily manacled. On the night of November 12, a group of men in disguise entered the jail, overpowered the guards, shot Fish in the head, and dragged his lifeless body outside and hanged it in front of the jail door. A coroner's jury ruled that "J. P. Fish came to his death by a gunshot wound inflicted by unknown parties."

### Approach of the Railroad

In spite of its name, the Atchison, Topeka and Santa Fe Railroad did not extend its main line into Santa Fe, but bypassed it at the village of Lamy, about fourteen miles to the south, and from there built a spur line into the New Mexico capital. From Lamy the main line was built west into the Rio Grande Valley, then south along the eastern edge of the valley.

Railroad officials had selected the town of Bernalillo, on the east bank of the Rio Grande, to be the chief division point on the line, with offices, a roundhouse, and extensive railroad yards. First, it was necessary to purchase the needed land.

Owner of much of the land in and about Bernalillo was José Leandro Perea, millionaire sheep rancher, merchant, and freighter. He listened to the railroad's offer of from $2 to $3 an acre, and countered with a request for $425 an acre. The railroad land buyers hurried eighteen miles south to Albuquerque where the land was cheaper.

A site on level and vacant land about one and one-half miles east of Albuquerque was selected by the railroad for its depot and rail yards. A railroad subsidiary, the New Mexico Town Company, was given the task of obtaining land at low prices for the proposed railroad property and an adjoining town site.

Three Albuquerque residents, Franz Huning, E. S. Stover, and William Hazeldine, working silently as agents for the Town Company, bought up the needed land and deeded it to the company for $1, plus a share in the profits of the company's sale of town building lots. It proved to be a profitable venture for the three men. However Albuquerque merchants, some with freight wagon operations that might be doomed by the railroad, awaited the coming of the railroad with mixed reactions.

*Chapter Seven*

# THE TURBULENT 1880s

## The Railroad Creates a New and Boisterous Albuquerque

### Welcoming the Railroad

Albuquerque celebrated the coming of the railroad on April 22, 1880, about two weeks after the steel rails of the Atchison, Topeka and Santa Fe Railroad reached the new depot grounds and town site east of town. The celebration was held in conjunction with the arrival of the first passenger train that brought about three hundred guests from Santa Fe and vicinity to join in the festivities.

Arriving from Santa Fe in advance of the excursion train was the U.S. Ninth Cavalry band, composed of black "buffalo soldiers," which presented a concert on the afternoon of April 21 on a temporary bandstand that had been erected on the town plaza. The plaza presented a festive atmosphere, with business houses decorated with flags and streamers.

Crowds began to gather on the plaza the next morning, including civic dignitaries sporting sashes and badges of authority. At 11 A.M., the crowd fell in behind the military band for a procession to the railroad along newly designated Railroad Avenue, a dirt thoroughfare that years later was to be renamed Central Avenue.

"A little after 12 the train from Santa Fe rolled in and was received with long and continued cheers," the *Advance*, an Albuquerque weekly newspaper, reported. The excursionists piled off the train to greet and shake hands with the waiting crowd at the depot and railroad offices, housed temporarily in railroad boxcars. A railroad flatcar had been placed nearby to serve as a speakers' platform.

The principal speaker, introduced by Franz Huning, was William C. Hazeldine, Albuquerque lawyer and promoter. Other talks in English were given by William B. Childers, also an Albuquerque lawyer, and Miguel A. Otero, a railroad vice president. Responses were given in Spanish by Santiago Baca and Ambrosio Armijo of Albuquerque.

The leader of the Ninth Cavalry Band did not understand Spanish, and when one of the Spanish orators paused near the beginning of his speech, the bandmaster thought he was finished and struck up the band. The surprised orator sat down without finishing his speech.

When the speechmaking was over, the Santa Fe excursionists boarded the train for the backward trip home, pausing in Bernalillo for some more celebrating. The Albuquerque celebrants returned to the plaza where festivities continued well into the night with more band music and speeches. The *Advance* reported that the town was illuminated with bonfires and the glare of rockets. Open wine barrels were placed at strategic locations for those wishing a free drink.

Speakers on the plaza that night included Judge L. S. Trimble, Colonel J. Francisco Chaves, Tranquilino Luna, and Father Donato Gasparri, pastor of the San Felipe de Neri Church. Judge L. Bradford Prince of Santa Fe spoke on behalf of the residents of his community.

Track laying by the AT&SF did not pause at Albuquerque but continued south at a rapid pace for an eventual link with the Southern Pacific Railroad, which was building east across southern New Mexico from California towards El Paso, Texas. The link, which occurred on March 8, 1881, at the new railroad town of Deming, New Mexico, created the nation's second transcontinental rail service.

The Atlantic and Pacific (A&P) Railroad Company, owned jointly by the AT&SF and the St. Louis and San Francisco Railway, established headquarters in Albuquerque in 1880 and began building west to California from a point fifteen miles south of Albuquerque, creating the New Mexico towns of Grants and Gallup along the way. It became a part of the AT&SF main line to Los Angeles.

### Developing the Town Site

Walter G. Marmon, a civil engineer from Ohio, was selected to survey, mark, and name the streets in the new Albuquerque town site adjacent to the railroad. He had arrived in New Mexico in 1872, and was living at Laguna Pueblo, west of Albuquerque, at the time.

From the railroad to the west he named the north–south streets in numerical order, beginning with First Street, also called Front Street, west to Sixteenth Street, which marked the dividing line between the original and new towns. For the principal cross streets, Marmon selected the names of New Mexico's mineral resources, including Gold, Silver, Copper, Lead, and Coal. Such town boosters as Hazeldine, Stover, and Huning also had streets named after them. The new town should have a Broadway Avenue, Marmon concluded, and this was the name he gave the main north–south street east of the railroad tracks. It was reached by Tijeras Canyon Road, the only street crossing the railroad tracks at the time.

Franz Huning, with the lawyer Thomas F. Phelan as a junior partner, developed the Huning-Highland neighborhood addition east of the tracks. One of the streets was named Arno Avenue for Huning's only son, Arno Huning.

New Albuquerque was surprisingly slow in getting started, however. A predicted early boom failed to materialize, and some had little faith in the new town site. Henry H. Tice, a railroad surveyor who was an early arrival on the scene, wrote that the railroad depot was an aggregation of old boxcars, and there was not a building on the town site. "There were numerous small signs scattered over the sandy waste where now is Albuquerque," he wrote later, "and these signs conveyed the information that lots were for sale at ten dollars each, make your own selections. No lots had yet been sold."

The only businessman on the scene was Peter "Shorty" Parker, who squatted on six square feet of ground by the tracks and opened a roofless saloon, turning a barrel end up for his bar, and selling drinks for two bits each. He went out of business when a saloon known as the Concannon House, housed in two tents, was erected nearby.

The first building contractor on the scene was J. S. Brownewell, who from a tent office accepted contracts for erecting wooden buildings. Business was slow, however, and at least one merchant gave up even before his store was completed and moved on in search of a more prosperous settlement. Potential businessmen and land speculators who journeyed to Albuquerque were not impressed with what they saw and moved on, complaining that the town site didn't even have any rooming houses and that they had to sleep in boxcars with railroad crews.

Elwood Maden, one of the few optimists, hired a hall on the plaza to give a speech promoting New Albuquerque as a town with a bright future. After waiting a half hour for somebody to show up, he snuffed out the lamps and went home. Merchants on the plaza were reluctant to move their businesses east to the sand hills.

The first wood building erected in the new town was a small restaurant, operated by Charlie Stein. It was located on the bank of an irrigation ditch about one block west of the railroad tracks. Among other wood buildings soon to be erected in the new town were two prefabricated structures that had followed the railroad to New Mexico, being assembled and later dismantled at various railroad towns along the way. The sections were shipped from town to town on railroad flatcars.

One was a two-story hotel, assembled on the southwest corner of Railroad Avenue and First Street, which had seen service in Topeka and Dodge City, Kansas, and Trinidad, Colorado. Owned by James G. Hope, it was known as Hope's Corner until 1893 when it was sold to J. F. Luthy. He leased it to Frank E. Sturges, who operated it as the Sturges European Hotel, complete with a restaurant, bar, and gambling room. The building remained intact until demolished in 1956.

L. G. Putney, a former Lawrence, Kansas, retailer, assembled a pine panel grocery and mercantile store on the northeast corner of Railroad Avenue and First Street. It had seen service at Trinidad, Colorado, and Las Vegas, New Mexico.

Oliver E. Cromwell, a financier from Long Island, New York, provided the first public transportation between the plaza and the railroad by means of mule- and horse-drawn streetcars. As president of the Albuquerque Street Railway Company, he financed the shipment by railroad of three twelve-passenger streetcars to Albuquerque, along with steel rails and spikes needed for construction of a narrow-gauge track.

The track was put down along the center of Railroad Avenue, and by the end of 1880 passengers could ride the small trolley cars upon payment of a 10¢ fare. A section of double-track was put down midway between the plaza and the railroad so that east- and westbound cars could pass one another.

Some of the drivers left passengers stranded on their cars while they visited a local bar for a drink. The drivers, in turn, were often harassed by boys who placed small obstacles on the tracks, or who jumped on the sides of the fragile cars and rocked them off the tracks. The mule- and horse-drawn streetcars remained in operation until the advent of electric streetcars in 1904.

An 1881 street scene in New Albuquerque, looking south along the west side of the 100 block of First Street from the northeast corner of Railroad Avenue. Occupying the corner building was Hope's European Hotel, later the Sturges European Hotel. Courtesy the Albuquerque Museum Photoarchive, PA1990.13.2. Cobb Studio collection. Museum purchase from G. O. Bonds.

Albuquerque's first daily newspaper, the *Golden Gate*, began publication on June 5, 1880, but ceased publication a short while later when the editor, E. W. Deer, was stricken with a fatal illness. The paper was purchased a few months later by the newly organized Albuquerque Publishing Company, which began publication of the *Albuquerque Journal* as a daily and a weekly on October 4, 1880.

The Albuquerque Publishing Company had been organized by a group of Albuquerque businessmen, including Franz Huning and William Hazeldine. Chosen as the first editor was W. S. Burke, a former Kansas newspaper editor, who later was to serve as Bernalillo County's first schools superintendent. The *Albuquerque Journal*, originally located at the southeast corner of Second Street and Silver Avenue, continues in publication to this day.

An earlier Albuquerque weekly paper, the *Advance*, had published only a few issues in the spring of 1880 when the editor, A. M. Conklin, closed shop and floated the press south to Socorro on a Rio Grande flatboat and began publication of the *Socorro Sun*. The Ohio native was murdered on Christmas Eve in 1880 outside a Socorro church by some young men he had had an altercation with during the church services.

New Albuquerque began experiencing a building boom late in 1880 that was to continue unabated for years to come. With two Albuquerques now in existence, local newspapers used various designations for the new railroad town and the original settlement to the west, using East End and West End, New Albuquerque and Old Albuquerque, New Town and Old Town, Albuquerque and Old Town, the latter remaining outside the Albuquerque city limits until annexed in 1949 by the city that surrounded it.

## Sheriff Perfecto Armijo

Serving as Bernalillo County sheriff during New Albuquerque's formative period was Perfecto Armijo, member of a prominent Albuquerque family, who achieved a reputation as one of the most courageous and efficient lawmen on the western frontier.

The Las Vegas (New Mexico) *Optic*, in reference to him in 1881, said his name "casts a chill to the heart of every criminal in New Mexico." An Albuquerque newspaper, upon his death in 1913, said the former sheriff was "absolutely without fear," and that a biography of him would rival the biographies of Kit Carson for thrills and excitement. Unfortunately, no biography of Armijo was ever written. Sheriff Armijo's reputation was such that lawbreakers surrendered to him peacefully and he never had an occasion to shoot one. On several occasions, he dispersed angry lynch mobs by mere words or the shaking of a cane.

Born on February 10, 1845, Perfecto was the son of the elder Ambrosio Armijo, wealthy Albuquerque merchant and freighter, who also had a son named Ambrosio. After some schooling in Albuquerque, Perfecto was sent by his family to Missouri where he was a four-year student at St. Louis University.

Armijo returned to New Mexico in the early 1860s and began operating wagon trains up the Santa Fe Trail to Missouri, south into Mexico, and west into Arizona. On occasion he helped fight off Comanche and Kiowa attackers on the Kansas plains, and Apache attackers in New Mexico.

Perfecto and a brother, Jesús Armijo, were operating a mercantile business in the southern town of Las Cruces in 1869 when Perfecto narrowly escaped death at the hands of hostile Indians. In May of that year, while returning to Las Cruces from Tularosa, he was stopped by a U.S.

Cavalry troop in the Organ Mountains east of Las Cruces and warned that there were some Apaches on the warpath in the vicinity. He insisted on traveling on west to Las Cruces, and a cavalry escort was sent with him. What happened next was told in the *Weekly New Mexican* at Santa Fe on May 25, 1869:

> On the 7th instant four soldiers, in company with Don Perfecto Armijo, while coming through San Augustin Pass, were attacked by a party of fifty Indians. A desperate fight ensued in which Corporal Young was killed and Don Perfecto and two soldiers wounded. Corporal Young fought bravely to the last and fell with fifteen mortal wounds in his body. The party succeeded in getting back to Shedd's Ranch, the Indians pursuing them closely and keeping up rapid fire for three miles.

Armijo, suffering from a severe arrow wound in his thigh, pulled a wounded soldier up on his horse with him and delivered him safely to Fort Selden, north of Las Cruces.

Armijo moved back to Albuquerque in the 1870s, and in addition to the years he served as sheriff, he operated a mercantile business, managed the family ranch at Los Poblanos in Los Ranchos de Albuquerque, and invested in real estate. He served almost continuously as Bernalillo County sheriff from 1879 to 1886, and again from 1906 to 1908. However it was early in his law career that Armijo spent much time solving a sensational murder mystery and bringing the culprits to justice.

Some Albuquerque residents began receiving letters and telegrams late in November of 1880 asking for any information regarding the whereabouts of Colonel Charles Potter, member of a prominent Rhode Island family who was last seen leaving Albuquerque on horseback on or about October 11 of that year. The inquiries brought no response.

Colonel Potter had been a visitor at the Albuquerque home of Edward Branford in October while employed by the U.S. Geological Survey to gather material on New Mexico's mining districts for the forthcoming U.S. Census. The thirty-year-old visitor, who lived with his wife in a fashionable home in Newport, Rhode Island, was a stepson of Charles C. Van Zandt, governor of that state. Potter had been given the honorary title of colonel while serving on the staffs of his stepfather and a previous governor.

Ferdinand S. Van Zandt, a Leadville, Colorado, businessman and a relative of Potter's stepfather, arrived in Albuquerque in December to assist in the search for the missing man. He traced Potter's movements east to the Sandia Mountain village of Tijeras, where he was told that Potter was last seen riding north from that village on October 14 along the eastern foot of the mountain range towards the mining village of Golden in the New Placers district. Here his trail vanished.

Late in January 1881 Sheriff Armijo learned that an open-faced gold watch and chain, answering the description of one carried by Potter, had been left in pawn on November 3 at the J. K. Basye jewelry store in Albuquerque by Pantaleón Miera, leader of an outlaw gang that had been operating out of Bernalillo and nearby Algodones north of Albuquerque. Although Basye had melted down the gold case and chain, the remains were identified as Potter's watch. It was too late for Armijo to arrest Miera, however, as he and a companion, Santos Benavidez, had been hanged by a lynch mob in Bernalillo on December 28 after being arrested for stealing horses.

Armijo learned that a man loitering around Isleta Pueblo south of Albuquerque was said to know something about Potter's disappearance. Brought in for questioning, Escolástico Perea revealed that Potter had been ambushed and killed by robbers about a dozen miles north of Tijeras. Although admitting that he was present, Perea claimed he had nothing to do with the killing. Perea identified the other members of the gang as Pantaleón Miera, Marino Leyba, Miguel Barrera, Faustino Gutiérrez, and a man identified only as California Joe. He said Potter had fought valiantly for his life against overwhelming odds, firing a shot with his revolver that struck Leyba in the arm.

Perea led Armijo and others to the murder scene on January 31, where the partially decomposed bodies of Potter and his horse, which also had been shot, were found in a dry stream bed near the Chimal Spring. Since two of the alleged robbers, Barrera and California Joe, lived near the murder scene, Armijo arrested them and took them to Albuquerque. Perea, Barrera, and California Joe were placed in the county jail in Albuquerque's Old Town that night, but their stay was a short one. All three were found hanging from a beam in front of the jail the next morning, having been dragged from the jail during the night by a lynch mob.

A short while later, another of the alleged robbers, Faustino Gutiérrez, was captured by a sheriff's posse near the village of Chilili, southeast of Albuquerque, and lodged in the Old Town jail. He claimed that he knew nothing about Potter's murder, other than what Marino Leyba had told him. Nevertheless, his lifeless body was found hanging in front of the jail on the morning of February 25, 1881, with a note attached to his clothing that read, "Hanged by the 601—Assassin of Col. Potter." The meaning of "601" was not made clear.

Of the six alleged gang members, only Marino Leyba remained alive and at large. Although there was speculation that he had fled to Mexico, Armijo was not convinced, and turned his attention to Leyba's home base, the Pecos River village of Puerto de Luna more than one hundred miles east of Albuquerque, where he had a wife and a four-year-old son. The sheriff sent a deputy on a secret mission to the town in an effort to locate the wanted man.

A posse of local townspeople, including the Albuquerque deputy, captured Leyba on about March 15 after a long chase, and escorted him north to the San Miguel County jail at Las Vegas. Leyba reportedly had told sheepherders that he had killed Potter. Armijo went to Las Vegas, intending to take custody of Leyba and remove him to Bernalillo County to face murder charges. He was prevented from doing so, however, as the grand jury could not indict Leyba because the only witnesses who could testify against him had been hanged.

Leyba, known as the Sandia Mountain Desperado, was instead sentenced in Las Vegas to seven years in prison on a charge of horse stealing, serving most of his sentence in the prison at Leavenworth, Kansas. Following his release in 1886, he was shot and killed in 1887 near Golden by two Santa Fe deputy sheriffs, Joaquín Montoya and Carlos Jácome.

Sheriff Armijo, meanwhile, was to have the unpleasant duty of executing a fellow lawman.

### The Trigger-Happy Marshal

Selected as New Albuquerque's first police officer in 1880 was an illiterate gunman from Arkansas who went by the assumed name of Milton J. Yarberry. Although his official title was constable of newly organized Precinct 12, he was generally known as the Albuquerque town marshal.

Little was known about Yarberry's background when the Bernalillo County Commission appointed him constable and when he was later elected to the job. It was said that he was involved in a number of shooting scrapes while wandering around Texas, Kansas, and Colorado; had used the assumed name of Johnson in Texas; and with partners had operated several short-lived saloons, variety theaters, and dance halls.

Albuquerque newspapers described him as being about thirty-four years old, tall and lean with slightly stooped shoulders, having steel gray eyes and a small black moustache, and walking "in a shambling sort of gait." The *Albuquerque Journal* said that while Yarberry was serving as Albuquerque constable "he carried things with a high hand and had the reputation of being a bully."

Yarberry's Albuquerque troubles began in 1881 when many citizens believed that he had used his badge to eliminate a rival for the affections of Sadie Preston, a young divorced woman. His alleged rival was Harry Brown, about twenty-four years of age, an express messenger for the Adams Express Company, and the son of Neil S. Brown, former governor of Tennessee and U.S. minister to Russia.

On the evening of March 27, 1881, Brown and Mrs. Preston, riding in a hired hack, drew up in front of Girard's restaurant on the northeast corner of Railroad Avenue and Second Street. Mrs. Preston entered the restaurant, and Brown waited outside the door. Moments later, Yarberry approached the restaurant on foot, leading Mrs. Preston's four-year-old daughter by the hand. He took her into the restaurant, then walked back outside where Brown was standing.

The waiting hack driver, John Clark, was the only witness to what happened next. He said he heard Brown say, "Milt, I want to talk to you," and after some conversation he heard him say, "I want you to understand that I am not afraid of you and would not be even if you were marshal of the United States." At that moment, Clark continued, he heard shots, and turned to see Brown reeling and Yarberry shooting him in the chest. He said Yarberry fired two more shots into Brown as he lay on the sidewalk.

Yarberry, charged with murder, was released on his plea of self-defense, testifying that Brown was reaching for his gun when he shot him, and producing witnesses who testified that Brown had sworn to kill Yarberry on sight. The *Journal* said that Brown had made "numerous bad gun plays" in Albuquerque, but that his friends had always kept him out of trouble, adding that he was a perfect gentleman when sober and well liked by all.

Less than twelve weeks after he shot Brown to death, Yarberry gunned down yet another man in his role as constable. This time, a jury didn't buy his self-defense plea.

On the evening of June 18, 1881, Yarberry and a friend, Albuquerque gambler Frank Boyd, were at the corner of Railroad Avenue and First Street when a shot was fired in the crowded R. H. Greenleaf Restaurant on First Street a short distance to the south. Yarberry and Boyd hurried south down the street to investigate the matter, and as they approached the restaurant, a bystander pointed to a man crossing the street and said, "There goes the man."

Witnesses said Yarberry approached the man from behind, called "throw up your hands," and immediately began shooting at him, firing more shots into him as he lay in the street, and saying to Boyd, "I've downed the son of a bitch." Some said Boyd fired at the man, too. The victim, Charles D. Campbell, a thirty-two-year-old Atlantic and Pacific Railroad carpenter, died with three bullet wounds, two in his back. No gun was found on or near his body, and it was not determined that he was the one who fired a shot in the restaurant.

Sheriff Perfecto Armijo arrested and jailed Yarberry, protecting him in the process from a mob that wanted to hang the policeman on the spot. A coroner's jury ruled that Campbell was killed "by Yarberry and another person whose name is unknown." The unknown person apparently was Boyd, who hurried west out of town the next day, soon to be killed by Navajo Indians in Arizona after killing a Navajo and stealing his horse.

At a preliminary hearing on July 5, Yarberry was ordered held to await action by the grand jury, and was taken north to a Santa Fe jail for safekeeping, as the Old Town jail was not considered escape proof. He remained in the Santa Fe jail for months before a Bernalillo County grand jury returned a murder indictment against him.

After a long delay, Yarberry's murder trial began in Albuquerque on May 18, 1882, with District Judge Joseph Bell presiding. Attorneys William Breeden and Arnet O. Owen appeared for the prosecution, and attorneys L. S. Trimble and Colonel J. Francisco Chaves for the defense. The trial lasted three days, with Yarberry insisting that he had shot Campbell in self-defense, and prosecution witnesses testifying that he had shot down an unarmed and innocent man. The jury, after a short deliberation on May 20, returned a guilty verdict, and Judge Bell sentenced Yarberry to death by hanging.

Yarberry was taken back to the Santa Fe jail, where he languished for months during a series of unsuccessful appeals and clemency requests. He and three other prisoners escaped from jail in September, but he was captured and taken back three days later. When the New Mexico Territorial Supreme Court upheld Yarberry's murder conviction and death sentence, Governor Lionel Sheldon refused a request to commute the sentence and ordered that Yarberry be hanged at Albuquerque on February 9, 1883.

When the day of execution arrived, Yarberry was taken from the Santa Fe jail early in the morning and placed aboard a one-passenger-car train for the trip to Albuquerque. His escort on the trip included Romulo Martínez, sheriff of Santa Fe County; Mace Bowman, sheriff of Colfax County; and Colonel Max Frost with nineteen uniformed members of the Governor's Rifles.

When the train arrived in Albuquerque shortly before ten thirty that morning it was greeted at the depot by a crowd of at least two thousand persons, including Captain John Borrodaile and the Albuquerque Guards, a militia organization, attired in colorful uniforms and plumed helmets. Yarberry and his escorts boarded horse-drawn streetcars for the short trip west to Old Town, where the execution was scheduled for three o'clock that afternoon at the county courthouse and jail.

The *Albuquerque Morning Journal*, in anticipation of the execution, said of Yarberry:

> Naturally a man of less than ordinary intelligence,
> Yarberry's education had not tended to improve the work of
> nature. Every instinct of his narrow brain has been fostered
> and nursed from childhood until now, upon his last day on
> earth, he will mount the scaffold and die the death of a
> felon, never having known the pleasures and comforts of
> home, always an outcast from society, from childhood a
> refugee from justice, and at last dispatched by his fellow
> men to a tribunal higher than any in existence on this earth.
> May the All-powerful Judge have mercy on him.

Sheriff Perfecto Armijo, whose duty it was to dispatch the former fellow lawman, had ordered the construction of a special hanging device from plans he reportedly had seen in a recent issue of *Scientific American*. It consisted of two upright poles, supporting a crossbeam, together with a system of ropes, pulleys, and a heavy weight, which caused death by jerking the victim upward when a rope was cut that caused the four-hundred-pound lead weight to drop.

The gallows had been erected in the courtyard of the courthouse and jail, a U-shaped, one-story adobe building that stood a short distance east of the northeast corner of the town plaza. For the purpose of the execution, a board fence, about eight feet tall, had been erected across the open side of the courthouse, providing a square enclosure. Admission to the enclosure was limited to one hundred guests who had been given special invitations to witness the hanging.

At the jail, Yarberry was served his last meal at noon, a meal, which at his request, consisted of cranberry pie, a pint of whisky, and a bottle of ale.

Among friends who visited Yarberry at the jail was Elwood Maden, owner of a New Albuquerque hotel called the Maden House, to whom the condemned man revealed his life story. He told Maden that his true name was not Yarberry, nor Johnson, the name he had used in Texas, but that he had changed his name to protect his respectable parents, although he did not know if they were still alive. He said he had three cousins living at Walnut Ridge, Arkansas. He gave his true name to Maden, who was sworn not to reveal it. Yarberry admitted to Maden that he had been involved in some shooting scrapes over the years, but denied that he killed anybody other than the two men he shot in Albuquerque.

Several of Yarberry's friends brought him a new suit of black clothes to wear, which he put on, discarding what the *Journal* described as "a brown, seedy looking suit of clothes and clean white shirt without any collar."

Two priests from the San Felipe de Neri Church across the street visited Yarberry in jail, and when he expressed a desire to join the Catholic Church, they baptized him.

At 2:40 P.M., Sheriff Armijo led Yarberry out into the enclosed courtyard, which was crowded with the invited guests. Uninvited guests, meanwhile, had sought vantage points from nearby trees and rooftops, some home owners offering vantage points on their flat roofs for $1 a head.

Placed under the scaffold, with a noose around his neck, Yarberry was asked if he had anything to say. Quiet until now, he talked for fifteen minutes, his voice loud and firm, telling of his killings of both Brown and Campbell and claiming that he was justified in both instances. "You are going to hang Milt Yarberry," he said. "You are going to hang him not for the murder of Campbell, but for the killing of Brown."

Armijo, looking at his watch, admonished Yarberry several times that his time was growing short, but Yarberry interrupted him each time with "let me finish this." He kept talking until Archie Hilton placed a black hood over his head.

"How near is the time, Perfecto?" Yarberry asked the sheriff. Armijo replied that his last moment had come. "Gentlemen, you are hanging an innocent man," Yarberry said. At that moment, Armijo snapped shut his watchcase, and Count Epur, identified in the newspapers as a Polish nobleman living in Albuquerque, cut the rope with an axe and Yarberry was yanked upward into eternity. Yarberry's remains were taken across the street to the Catholic Church for services, then transported east to Santa Barbara Cemetery and buried, the rope still around his neck.

### A Wild and Woolly Town

A Vermont newspaper editor who visited New Albuquerque late in 1881 was impressed by the rapid growth of the new railroad town, but expressed shock at what he called a serious lack of moral standards.

C. M. Chase, editor of the *Vermont Union* at Lyndon, Vermont, paused in Albuquerque on November 30, 1881, during a tour of New Mexico and Colorado. He published his travel observations in a series of letters to his newspaper, and compiled them in 1882 in a booklet entitled *The Editor's Run*. (He misspelled Albuquerque's name as "Alberquerque," and on at least one occasion referred to a citizen of the town as an "Alberquerquite.")

Chase wrote that Railroad Avenue, the main thoroughfare to Old Town, was nearly solid with business houses for five blocks, or about west to Sixth Street, and that buildings were springing into existence all over the platted part of the new town. Building lots, depending upon location, were selling from $200 to $2,000 each.

The town had two daily papers, he continued, one bank, two churches, a small schoolhouse, a foundry, a grist mill, a planing mill, four hotels, and saloons too numerous to count. Railroad repair yards and roundhouses were under construction south of the depot, and the sound of the hammer and the trowel was heard on every corner.

As for New Albuquerque's social atmosphere, however, the New England editor wrote:

> The social atmosphere of Alberquerque is no more pleasing
> than at Socorro. A standard of morals has not yet been

erected. Scripture is not floating around loose in the streets. The devil seems to be in command of enterprises and principles intended for human elevation.

The saloons, with three to ten gambling tables each, are in the lead, and the ring of bottles, the rattle of high ball, the click of billiards and the shake of dice, accompanied by the roundest and loudest profanity, fill the air.

Set down in Vermont any of the business streets of Alberquerque for just one evening and the governor, with all his staff and all the sheriffs, would take to the woods under the impression that hell had broken loose, and that any attempt at legal restraint would be suicidal.

The omnipresent revolver seems to be the only law of the town, and strapped to the belts of men full of rum, the law is not altogether a conservator of the peace.

While Albuquerque may have seemed wild and woolly in comparison with Vermont towns, it never achieved the "wild west" notoriety attached to many new railroad, mining, and cattle towns on the western frontier. While the new town attracted its share or more of gamblers, prostitutes, confidence men, thieves, and drifters, newspapers of the period do not reflect a great deal of violence or homicidal activity.

The *Evening Review*, an Albuquerque daily newspaper, launched a campaign early in 1882 to remove the brothels and an opium den that lined Railroad Avenue west of Fourth Street. The newspapers did not ask that these places be closed, only that they be moved off the main street. "All Western towns are vicious," the newspaper said, "but none of them flaunt their vice so openly in the faces of strangers as does Albuquerque."

B. F. Saunders, the crusading editor of the newspaper, wrote that there were seven houses of prostitution and an opium den on that part of Railroad Avenue, halting all business building in that vicinity. Three more were going up in the neighborhood, he added, and "lewdness has claimed that part of town as its own." "Remove the prostitutes from Railroad Avenue" became a daily reminder in the newspaper.

"Pull that opium joint," the editor wrote on February 25, 1882. "It is a corrupting agency too potent to be ignored." Saunders expressed shock at an article in a Bernalillo newspaper that said in part:

But as far as our individual experience has gone, which is not inconsiderable in our own estimation, we have found the use of opium to be as harmless as the habit of cigarette smoking.

The Albuquerque editor responded that the Bernalillo editor had no respect for the truth.

Opium dens, as well as brothels, continued to flourish in Albuquerque for years to come, although eventually at locations off the main street. The *Albuquerque Journal*, on August 15, 1883, reported that there were four opium dens in Albuquerque and doing a thriving business. "There appears to be no law to reach them, and they are permitted to go on ruining mind, soul and body without any molestation," the article said. "In the open light of day the hop smoker may be seen on his way to the joint to hit the pipe a lick, as it is expressed in the vernacular manner of the victim."

The *Journal* said that the doors of the opium dens stood wide open and that anybody could walk in. Inside the dimly lit rooms, patrons could be seen lying on double-deck bunks smoking the pipes, their heads held firmly in head rests. Frequently the smoker became crazed, the article continued, and had to be held down by force. A "fallen woman" told the newspaper that she smoked from ten to as many as one hundred pipes each afternoon, and that it cost her about $2 per afternoon.

Months later, on April 9, 1884, the *Journal* published an interview with a stagecoach driver who said he had been an opium addict but had managed to kick the habit. The driver, known as Buckboard Bill, said he had decided to kick the habit one morning when he woke up and found that he could not open his right eye. He said he was cured by a long treatment at the Sisters Hospital in Santa Fe. "My eye is all right again and I am a free man," he said. "You don't know how good I feel."

Albuquerque newspapers of the period indicate that most "wild west" episodes in the new town created more noise than damage, and that Sam Blonger, who had succeeded Yarberry as town marshal, was kept busy arresting people on such minor charges as disturbing the peace. Typical was the case of Tom Kennedy, proprietor of a livery stable and the proud owner of a racehorse named Daisy Price.

On the afternoon of July 24, 1882, according to the newspapers, an "insane desire" took possession of Kennedy to ride his horse into the various saloons and order drinks at the bars without dismounting. He rode his horse through the doors and up to the bars of the St. Julien, White House, and several other saloons without encountering any problems.

It was a different story, however, when he arrived at the door of the Elite Saloon. The bartender, Jack Stoner, stopped Kennedy at the door and told him horses were not allowed in the saloon. Kennedy shoved him aside, rode his horse up to the bar, and ordered a drink.

Stoner, instead of reaching for a bottle, reached for a .41 caliber revolver and began blasting away at man and horse. The horse, frightened by the gunfire, sped out the door, with Kennedy hanging on tight. The angry bartender fired several more shots at the rapidly departing horse and rider, one of the bullets passing through Kennedy's vest and just grazing his skin. Both Kennedy and the bartender were arrested for disturbing the peace.

Another man, according to the newspapers, devised a novel way to obtain free drinks at the saloons. Placing a dark colored bottle on the bar, he would ask the bartender to fill it with 50¢ worth of whisky. Once this was done, he would say he forgot to bring any money, whereupon the bartender would pour the whisky back into his own bottle.

Once outside the saloon, the man would take from his pocket a piece of wire with a hook on the end, hook it to a sponge that was concealed in the bottom of the bottle, and pull it through the narrow neck, squeezing enough whisky into the bottom of the bottle for a drink or two. Then he would proceed on to the next saloon and repeat the process.

The *Albuquerque Evening Review*, on September 30, 1882, told of a trio of men who decided to "hurrah" the town:

> Yesterday morning, about one o'clock, the residents of Albuquerque were startled by the wildest uproar in the streets, pistol shots, swearing and yelling, all tending to make the night hideous and to arouse the inhabitants from their slumbers. The racket was caused by three men from a mining camp in Coyote Canyon, named Johnny Sullivan, Charles Hulse and "Tex."
>
> After riding about the east end for some time and drinking in every saloon in the city, they rode to the west end and did pretty much the same way. Returning to the east end, they rode down Railroad Avenue, firing their

revolvers, and when reaching First Street proceeded to the Chicago Saloon, run by Ike Blondin, and awakening him, shoved their guns in his face and demanded whisky, which was furnished to them. As it was now getting daylight, they started to return to the mountains, which they reached in due time.

A sheriff's posse trailed the three east into the mountains, the newspaper added, but returned to town empty-handed.

Harry Montague, a New York actor, brought a controversial variety show to Albuquerque in 1883 for a two-week engagement at the recently opened Albuquerque Opera House, operated by Charlie Boyd and Tom Wade. Some of Montague's skits, such as "The Bachelor's Bedroom" and "Bashful Venus," were considered so indecent that authorities had clamped down on him in New York, San Francisco, Denver, Newark, and Pueblo, Colorado.

"Verily a play that cannot be tolerated in Pueblo or Newark must be pretty tough," the *Albuquerque Evening Review* commented as the Montague troupe opened its Albuquerque engagement on February 24, 1883. Among the entertainers appearing with Montague were James Reilly, a vocalist, Harry Leavitt, a comedian who doubled as stage manager, the Duncan sisters, and Minnie Branscombe. The variety show was presented without serious incident until the final performance on Sunday evening, March 11.

Being Sunday, the skits presented that evening were rather conservative. Montague, however, ran up a $7 bar bill during the course of the evening, "keeping his spirits up by pouring others down," as the *Albuquerque Daily Democrat* put it. Near the end of the performance, Montague, wearing a red wig, appeared on stage and announced that the final skit of the evening would be a much requested play that was considered quite vulgar in some quarters.

Tom Wade, co-owner of the opera house, ordered Leavitt to go on stage and tell Montague that such a play would not be appropriate for a Sunday audience in Albuquerque. Leavitt walked out on the stage and told Montague that he would either have to cut the vulgar parts out of the skit or present a more decent play. This made the actor furious. "I am Harry Montague, and my reputation is at stake," he shouted.

"I own a $65,000 home near the Vanderbilt residence in New York, and I made my money putting on this type of play."

Angered by this outburst, Leavitt hit Montague in the jaw, sending him to the floor. Reilly, the vocalist, who was standing in the wings, picked up a club, rushed out on stage and whacked Leavitt, sending him to the floor. Wade rushed out on stage to help Leavitt and was immediately attacked by the Duncan Sisters and Minnie Branscombe, who kicked him, scratched him, and knocked him down.

All this excitement on stage was too much for the audience, and patrons began leaving their seats to climb up on the stage to join the melee. The entire stage was the scene of a free-for-all when somebody rang down the curtain, much to the disappointment of the patrons who were enjoying the impromptu show.

Most of the participants were nursing cuts and bruises the next morning, and there was talk of lawsuits, but the Montague troupe left town peacefully and the whole thing was forgotten.

### Early Territorial Fairs

Some prominent Albuquerque citizens began meeting early in 1881 to study the possibility of holding annual New Mexico territorial fairs in the community. The idea was not too popular with citizens of Santa Fe and a few other New Mexico towns who thought it was presumptuous of Albuquerque to organize such expositions without any legislative authority.

Nevertheless, the Albuquerqueans went ahead with their plans, incorporating the New Mexico Agricultural, Mineral and Industrial Exposition and Driving Park Association for the purpose of staging territorial fairs each October. Elias S. Stover was elected association president, and Franz Huning first vice president.

Other association officers included vice presidents José L. Perea, Ambrosio Armijo, M. A. Otero, and Thomas Post. Named to the executive committee were William Hazeldine, Santiago Baca, Nicolas Armijo, Thomas Hughes, and Elwood Maden. Hughes recently had purchased the *Albuquerque Journal*.

A site selection committee obtained twenty acres for the exposition grounds immediately west of Old Town through contracts with L. S. Trimble, Perfecto Armijo, and the Street Railway Company. A racetrack with grandstands was erected on the grounds, and construction started on an exhibition building.

Heavy and continuing rains practically washed out the First Annual New Mexico Territorial Fair, which began on October 3, 1881. Most of the outdoor events were cancelled, and many exhibits that had been brought to the fair to be displayed in tents never left their packing boxes.

An earlier starting date was set for the second annual territorial fair, which opened on Monday afternoon, September 18, 1882, with the weather cooperating. Horse races were run during the afternoon, and a trained bear performed next to a long saloon bar under the grandstands. The exhibition building was filled with agricultural and mineral displays, and music was provided by the U.S. Thirteenth Cavalry band from Fort Wingate.

A highlight of the second day of the 1882 fair was a baseball game between the San Marcial Rio Grandes and the Carbonateville Mountain Boys. Newspapers said the Rio Grandes did not play the latter part of the ninth inning as they had already won the game 33–6.

Park Van Tassel, Albuquerque saloon owner and balloon enthusiast who had accomplished Albuquerque's first balloon ascension earlier that year, was invited to repeat the performance on Thursday, fourth day of the exposition. Like some early balloonists, he was called Professor Van Tassel.

The earlier ascension had occurred on July 4 with Van Tassel piloting a large hydrogen balloon he called the "City of Albuquerque," which held thirty thousand cubic feet of gas. The *Albuquerque Evening Review* told its readers on July 3, 1882, that it would take all night to fill the balloon with gas, and that the ascension would take place the next day between 10 and 11 A.M. from a vacant lot on Gold Avenue between Second and Third streets.

Supervising the inflation job was C. W. Talbott, manager of the new Albuquerque Gas Works. By ten o'clock on the morning of July 4, however, there was still not enough gas in the balloon to get it airborne, and a crowd that had gathered at the launch site began to grow impatient. The crowd had dwindled by two o'clock, convinced that the balloon would not go up.

The crowd returned to the launch site late in the afternoon when word got around that the ascension was about to take place. Van Tassel and a passenger, J. Moore, boarded the balloon, but Moore got out when it was found that the load had to be lightened. The ascension was described the next day by the *Evening Review*:

> It was exactly at 6:15 p.m. when the balloon quit the earth
> and it rose rapidly, floating gently to the south, the crowds
> cheering themselves hoarse while Van Tassel waved the stars
> and stripes as she went up. It was truly a grand spectacle,
> and aroused the enthusiasm of the multitude to the highest
> pitch. At an altitude of about 10,000 feet, Van Tassel dropped
> one of his flags overboard and it came down like an arrow.

The balloon rose to an altitude of 14,207 feet, according to Van Tassel's barometer, and he began his descent over the territorial fairgrounds. Finding that he was descending too fast, Van Tassel threw overboard his coat, lunch basket, and water bottle to lighten the load. He landed in a cornfield north of the fairgrounds.

For the scheduled repeat performance at the 1882 fair the gas balloon once again was inflated at the vacant lot in New Albuquerque, the inflation taking more than twenty-four hours. Once inflated, on the afternoon of September 21, about one hundred men and boys, holding the balloon with ropes, walked it west on Railroad Avenue to the fairgrounds.

As Van Tassel was preparing for the ascent, the balloon got away from its handlers and went up without him. The unoccupied balloon reached a height of about a mile over the fairgrounds when it burst and began falling to earth, sending fairgoers scampering for cover. Van Tassel picked up the pieces and walked away, but balloon ascensions were to be popular features at the fairs for years to come.

Officials of the 1882 fair apparently forgot that they had invited Judge Warren Bristol of Mesilla to deliver the closing address on Saturday, September 23, closing day of the exposition. Judge Bristol, who had sentenced Billy the Kid to death the previous year, failed to find any reception or greeters when he arrived at the railroad depot that morning. Finding his way alone to the fairgrounds, he was at the appointed place at the appointed time, but nobody paid any attention to him. He took the next train home with his speech still in his pocket.

Cowboy tournaments, an early version of rodeo shows, were a feature of the 1885 territorial fair and successive expositions. In these tournaments, the cowboys not only had to ride the bucking broncos, but first had to lasso, tie, saddle, and mount them. The *Albuquerque Daily Democrat* told how the October 1 tournament got off to an exciting start:

> Francis Martin gathered up the slack of his rope, and sin-
> gling out a brown bronco, started for his victim. The bronco
> also started, and despite the efforts of all the cowboys,
> jumped the enclosure, dashed through the cordon of car-
> riages about the main entrance, and dashed into the exhibi-
> tion hall which was filled with men, women and children.

The horse caused no injury or damage in the crowded hall, the newspaper added, and was finally caught in a bazaar booth. The 1885 cowboy
tournaments also included steer-roping contests. "In this contest, man
after man failed, in one case taking five punchers to tie one slow-moving
bovine," the *Democrat* reported. "Jimmie Jones, the boys called him, did
finally tie a steer—did it in a magnificent manner in 5 1/4 minutes—and
it was believed that he was the only man in New Mexico who could rope
a steer until Joseph B. Lovario came to the scratch, roping and tying his
animal in just four minutes, thus winning the contest."

Among the visitors at the 1885 fair was Bob Ford, notorious as the
killer of Jesse James. Ford was operating a saloon in Cerrillos, south of
Santa Fe, at the time. "After talking a while with Bob," a *Democrat*
reporter noted, "one is impressed with the idea that he is not half as bad
as he is painted. On the contrary, he is a nice, gentlemanly appearing
young man, and is far from the desperado-looking person you would
expect to meet."

The newspaper enjoyed poking fun at fair visitors: "Las Vegas has
sent us some of the prettiest ladies and homeliest men that were ever
frightened at electric lights and dumfounded at things in general." A visitor from Arizona may have considered this a compliment:

> Joe Milner, one of the best boys that Prescott turns out, is
> here to pass judgement on the territorial fair. He could not
> be passed off as a professional beauty, nor does he want to
> enter in that class of exhibits, but for good, square, moderate
> looking people, Milner will stand his show.

Although Old Town lost some of its major mercantile businesses to New
Albuquerque in the early 1880s, it continued to thrive as an entertainment center, influenced by the adjacent territorial fairgrounds and the
streetcar line that connected the two towns. A sketchy picture of the

plaza area as it appeared in 1881 can be drawn from newspaper advertisements paid for by some of the Old Town merchants.

Located on the west side of the plaza was the Old Town Music Hall, operated by S. M. Ovelin. He advertised that he had "the best wine and liquors" and that there was dancing every other evening, with a piano and full band of musicians. Also on the west side of the plaza was the Cabinet Saloon.

The Monarch Saloon and Billiard Hall was located on the south side of the plaza. Brown and Winn, the proprietors, advertised that "this popular resort is supplied with a 15-ball pool table and the best liquors in the city." Also on the south side of the plaza was the Retreat, operated by W. S. Munroe, which advertised free lunches every morning and night, and, strangely enough, "the only 15-ball pool table in the city."

Located on or near the southwest corner of the plaza was the clothing store of T. Romero and Son, Staple and Fancy Groceries, operated by Mrs. M. Holdoway, and the Aberdeen Hotel, operated by Mrs. A. C. Fisher. Henry Springer's Mint Saloon stood a short distance to the west.

Located on the southeast corner of the plaza was the Plaza Restaurant, operated by Mrs. M. C. Gibbens. Advertised as "on the plaza" was the New Mexico Emporium, operated by Captain Sweeney, which specialized in fresh imported and domestic fruits and candies, news periodicals, cigars and tobacco, guns, pistols, and cartridges.

Wainey's Turf Exchange Saloon, located "opposite the post office," advertised the finest line of liquor and cigars ever brought to the city. Thomas Post's Exchange Hotel, south of the plaza, advertised that "a coach leaves the hotel every Tuesday morning for the New Placers," the mining district at Golden.

Completed in Old Town in 1881 was a two-story convent adjacent to the west side of the San Felipe de Neri Church, said to have been the first two-story adobe structure built in the town. Erected for the Sisters of Charity, who had been brought by the church to Albuquerque to open schools, much of the construction was supervised by the energetic Sister Blandina Segale, a native of Italy. Sister Blandina later was named mother superior of Our Lady of the Angels School, located directly behind the convent.

### Some Famous and Legendary Visitors, 1882–1885

Keeping a low profile in Albuquerque for a week or more in the spring of 1882 were seven noted gunmen who were facing murder charges in

Arizona. Most Albuquerque residents were unaware of their presence until after they had left town.

Arriving on a northbound train on April 15 were the brothers Wyatt and Warren Earp, John H. "Doc" Holliday, Sherman McMasters, Dan Tipton, John "Turkey Creek Jack" Johnson, and Jack "Texas Jack" Vermillion. Wyatt Earp and Doc Holliday had been participants in the legendary O.K. Corral gunfight at Tombstone, Arizona, on the previous October 26.

The seven who arrived in Albuquerque had fled from Arizona on horseback after tracking down and killing several men Wyatt believed were responsible for the death of his brother, Morgan, who had been gunned down March 18 by unseen assassins while playing pool in a Tombstone saloon.

The morning after their arrival in Albuquerque, Wyatt visited the offices of the *Albuquerque Evening Review* and requested that their "temporary sojourn" in the city remain unnoticed by the press. The evening paper honored his request. It was not until May 13, after the Earp party had left town, that the newspaper revealed that they had been hiding out in Albuquerque. The occasion was a news report, which proved to be false, that Wyatt had been killed in Arizona. The *Review* article said:

> On the morning after their arrival and before more than one or two knew of their presence, Wyatt Earp called at the Review and Journal offices and had an interview with the reporters of both papers. He stated that they had come to Albuquerque to escape persecution while awaiting the result of an effort being made by Governor [Frederick] Tritle [of Arizona] to secure their pardon from the president; that they were then being sought by their foes, and that they would not give themselves up to Arizona officers without resistance.
>
> In view of both of these facts, Earp requested of both papers that their temporary sojourn in Albuquerque should remain unnoticed until they could be assured that the knowledge of their whereabouts would not bring a party of cowboy avengers down upon them. To back his assertions, Earp presented the Review several convincing documents, and his request was accordingly granted by this paper, as it was by the *Journal*.

Albuquerque's first luxury hotel, the Armijo House, was opened in 1881 on the southwest corner of Railroad (now Central) Avenue and south Third Street and played host to many noted visitors including Wyatt Earp and Pat Garrett. The thirty-five-room hotel, shown here in about 1895, was destroyed by fire in 1897. Courtesy the Albuquerque Museum Photoarchive, PA1990.13.68. Cobb Studio collection. Museum purchase from G. O. Bonds.

> The party remained in Albuquerque for a week or more, their identity being well known to fifty people or more, leaving the city nearly two weeks ago. During their stay here Doc Holliday and Wyatt Earp quarreled, and when Albuquerque was left the party disbanded, Holliday going with Tipton.

The *Albuquerque Journal,* on May 18, denied statements in the evening paper that Earp had also visited the morning paper, saying: "At no time in their lives did Earp desperadoes call at the Journal office. They seem to have consorted with the sandy sorehead at the sundown sheet while they remained in hiding in this city."

While it was not publicized where members of the Earp party found lodging in Albuquerque in 1882, a good possibility was the Armijo House, a new three-story hotel on the southwest corner of Railroad Avenue and Third Street in New Albuquerque. It was considered the only first-class hotel in Albuquerque at the time, and was popular with visitors and as a social center. Later, an Albuquerque newspaper reported on November 12, 1884, that Wyatt Earp and his wife were guests at the Armijo House. (There appears to be some question as to whether Wyatt and his longtime companion, Josephine Marcus, were ever married.)

Mariano Armijo, son of Ambrosio Armijo, began construction of the hotel late in 1880 at a reported cost of $25,000. Built of frame and adobe, with a long portal along the front, the Armijo House contained thirty-five guest rooms, a restaurant and bar, a billiards room, and a ballroom.

Armijo leased the hotel to W. Scott Moore, a retired railroad freight conductor, who previously had owned and operated a health spa at the Montezuma hot springs near Las Vegas, New Mexico. While operating the spa, Moore played host to Jesse James, who used the name Mr. Howard while a guest at the spa in July 1879. Moore said that he grew up with the brothers Jesse and Frank James in Missouri.

Moore opened the Armijo House in the spring of 1881 with a champagne supper, attended by guests from Albuquerque, Santa Fe, Las Vegas, and Denver. Guests danced to the music of a military band from Santa Fe following the feast.

Sheriff Pat Garrett of Lincoln County checked in at the Armijo House on August 2, 1882, for an overnight stay. He was basking in the limelight as the lawman who shot and killed Billy the Kid at the village of Fort Sumner on the night of July 14, 1881.

Garrett was standing in the hotel's billiard room that evening when Joseph Antrim, Billy the Kid's only brother, entered the room. Antrim had arrived in Albuquerque several days before from his home in Trinidad, Colorado, where he was a professional gambler. There was a tense moment in the billiards room when Garrett and Antrim came face-to-face, as a Trinidad newspaper earlier had reported that Antrim threatened to shoot Garrett on sight in revenge for his brother's death. Those in the room familiar with Antrim's threat either froze in their tracks or began edging towards the nearest exit.

Instead of reaching for a gun, however, Antrim walked over to Garrett and began conversing with him in low tones, much to the disappointment of bystanders who could not hear what was being said. A reporter for the *Albuquerque Evening Review*, who heard of the incident, approached Garrett the next morning and asked him what he and Antrim talked about. Garrett replied that Antrim wanted to talk about the killing of his brother, and that he denied that he harbored any ill feelings against the lawman. Garrett said that he told Antrim that he had only done his duty, and should not be hated for it. "We parted the best of friends," Garrett told the reporter.

+≕ ≕+

Frances E. Willard, national president of the Women's Christian Temperance Union (WCTU), arrived in Albuquerque by train on the evening of March 22, 1883, during a lecture tour through western states and territories. She was accompanied by her private secretary, Anne Gordon, a young lady from Boston.

Miss Willard told a reporter for the *Albuquerque Journal* on the night of her arrival that the WCTU was composed of fifty thousand members and was the largest society ever composed exclusively of women and conducted entirely by them. She said she paid all her expenses on her lecture tours to reform the drinking classes and accepted nothing for any of her talks. She said one of the purposes of her visit to Albuquerque was to form a local auxiliary of the WCTU. "Miss Willard talks like a woman who had undertaken a life work, and who has the determination to come as near making so gigantic a venture successful as any living being," the *Journal* said.

A large crowd gathered at the new Presbyterian Church at Fifth Street and Silver Avenue the next afternoon to hear the lecture. The room was filled with one of the most intelligent and fashionable audiences that had assembled in Albuquerque for many months, the newspaper reported, adding: "It was noticeable, however, that there was but a small portion of men in the room, nine-tenths of the large audience being women and children."

At the close of her hour-long lecture, Miss Willard conducted the organization of an Albuquerque WCTU, and boarded a train that night for her next speaking engagement at Tombstone, Arizona. "It was our purpose to give Miss Willard's lecture in full," the newspaper said, "but our space is too limited, and attempt at condensation would mar the whole beauty of an eloquent discourse, therefore we will report nothing said by Miss Willard."

+≕ ≕+

General William Tecumseh Sherman, a frequent visitor to New Mexico both before and after his Union leadership during the Civil War, made no secret of the fact that he was no admirer of the region. In fact, the

Ohio native once suggested that the United States go to war with Mexico again to make Mexico take back New Mexico.

Nevertheless, the general received what amounted to a red carpet reception when he visited Albuquerque in the fall of 1883 while on a rail tour of western states and territories before retiring from the military service. Accompanying him on the tour were General J. C. Tidball, his aide-de-camp; Colonel R. I. Dodge of the Eleventh Infantry; and Associate Justice Horace Gray of the United States Supreme Court.

General Sherman and his party, after visiting California, headed east on a special Atlantic and Pacific Railroad passenger car. They paused at Fort Wingate, New Mexico, on September 13, 1883, where they spent the night and the general reviewed the troops.

The visitors arrived in Albuquerque the next afternoon, September 14, where they were greeted by members of the Board of Trade and a delegation of leading citizens. They were immediately placed in three horse-drawn carriages for a tour of the city. After visiting the San Felipe de Neri Church in Old Town, they returned to New Albuquerque and paused at the homes of Elias Stover and William Hazeldine, and the A&P shops.

A reception and supper followed at the Armijo House, after which the crowd adjourned to the Aztec Club where champagne was served and speeches given. Colonel Molyneaux Bell of Albuquerque introduced Sherman, who according to the *Albuquerque Journal*, "arose and began his address in an easy conversational way which at once elicited the sympathy of everyone in the room."

These are some excerpts from Sherman's speech, as published in the newspapers:

> Gentlemen of Albuquerque: I speak on behalf of my fellow travelers as well as myself when I say we thank you for the gracious receptions we have received.
>
> I am no stranger in this territory. I visited Albuquerque many years ago when the chief matter of interest about the place was merely of a traditionary character, and had to do with Aztec romances only. I thought this at the time to be the dreariest part of the continent of America I had ever traveled. The fact is, no part of God's footstool seemed to present a more forbidding aspect.
>
> I had heard, prior even to my first visit here, of a railroad which had, amongst the prominent points it was to touch, a

place called Anton Chico, which my imagination pictured as quite a metropolis, or at least, an incipient community of some pretensions. When I visited Anton Chico, over the range, down southeast of here, I thought it about the most desolate, miserable substitute for a civilized village I had ever seen.

Well, all that is past now, only that this very Albuquerque that you young men take such pride in appeared to me then to be not much more promising than poor, old, decrepit Anton Chico.

And it is not a matter that you can well reproach one for, since out here to the west you have nothing but sand and volcanic scoria apparently, and it is almost as much as a man's life is worth, even today, to cross this river. He don't know at what moment he is going to sink out of sight and meet eternal oblivion in the quicksand.

Such a development as you have attained in this young city you call New Town in a period of two years is almost unparalleled in the history of the world, and all indications point to the conclusion that it is substantial and enduring.

There is a certain region called the Southwest which demands a center of population, of wealth and of commercial industry, which shall be sufficient for the demands of thousands of square miles of tributary country.

Now, my dear young friends, I don't want to flatter you, but I think that the town of Albuquerque has everything in favor to become such a center or supply point.

I will go even farther than that, and say that I believe Albuquerque likely will become the great interior city of the United States, that is between the Mississippi River and the Pacific Coast, Denver, perhaps, alone excepted.

Now, in conclusion, I am willing to confess to you that I never have had very favorable notions in regard to New Mexico, but the results and observations of this present trip will go far toward correcting all that.

General Sherman and his party spent the night in Albuquerque and left for Santa Fe the next morning.

General Philip H. Sheridan, who like General Sherman was on a western tour prior to his retirement, paused in Albuquerque on December 3, 1885, with just one goal in mind. He wanted to visit the Old Town house where his wife was born, saying that he had promised her that he would visit it and give her a first-hand report of its appearance.

His wife, whom he had married in 1879, was the former Irene Rucker, daughter of General D. H. Rucker, who had served as a major and quartermaster at the Albuquerque Military Post in the 1850s. He and his family lived in a private home just off the town plaza at the time.

Upon his arrival at the Albuquerque railroad depot, Sheridan was driven to Old Town in a horse-drawn carriage, accompanied by Franz Huning, William Brown, and several other pioneer residents who said that they remembered where the Rucker family had lived.

When they reached Old Town, the pioneers escorted Sheridan to a large, one-story adobe home that faced west a short distance south of the southeast corner of the plaza. The home was owned by Cristóbal Armijo at the time, and was occupied by E. Spitz. Newspapers said that the house, believed to have been the home of Governor Manuel Armijo during Mexican rule, had a long portal along the front, and contained a large *placita*, or "inner courtyard."

Sheridan was shown a large room in the house, and was told that his wife was born in that very room. The pioneers even described the room as it had appeared in the 1850s when the Rucker family lived there. They said the room had one small window, a mud chimney place in one corner, and a heavy door hanging on wood hinges. Hanging on the wall, they said, was a picture of General Winfield Scott, as well as a map of the Southwest region.

Sheridan was quite moved by it all, the newspapers said, and upon completing his tour of the house he walked outside and began climbing back into the carriage. At that moment, he was approached by another Albuquerque pioneer, John A. Hill, who identified himself as "one of the oldest and most authentic residents of Albuquerque." "Your wife wasn't born in Albuquerque at all, but at Fort Union," Hill told Sheridan. "Her two younger sisters were born at this place." Crestfallen, Sheridan rode off, muttering to himself. The historic home later was demolished.

The *Albuquerque Evening Democrat*, on March 21, 1885, launched a vicious attack against a young newspaperman who visited Albuquerque while walking from Ohio to California to accept a job as city editor of the

*Los Angeles Times.* Under a headline reading "A Talented Young Liar," the article said:

> A young newspaper tramp named C.F. Lummis who came to this city about two months ago on his way to California from Ohio has turned up in Los Angeles, California, and has written a long letter to one of the papers there in which he abuses and satirizes this city just as any scrub kid would be likely to do who thought he was saying something smart.
>
> Young Lummis made his headquarters at The Democrat office while here and was treated with the greatest kindness, and while he seemed to have lots of energy and not much brains, he met with no less consideration on that account. He is an ungrateful, conscienceless little scrub, and it can be truthfully said of him that he has traveled farther, seen less and lied more than any youth of his age and inches in the country.
>
> Young Lummis impressed a Democrat reporter while here as being a habitual and stalwart liar who relied mainly on imagination for the facts of his long and nonsensical tramp across the continent, and his newspaper letters bristling with falsehoods have confirmed this impression.
>
> He is a shallow, flippant, and cold blooded little Yankee who could tell a lie for fifty cents at any time, and while he has lots of the spirit of vagrant adventure in him and plenty of muscular energy, his sense of truth and right is so feebly developed that he ought not be allowed to write for a newspaper.

All this about Charles F. Lummis, who by the time of his death in 1928 was highly regarded as a Southwest author and historian, anthropologist, naturalist, newspaper and magazine editor, and founder of the Southwest Museum in Los Angeles. He was knighted by the King of Spain as a leading advocate of Spanish culture in America.

A native of Massachusetts and a Harvard graduate, Lummis was editor of the *Scioto Gazette* in Chillicothe, Ohio, when he decided to walk to California to accept the Los Angeles newspaper job. He compiled his experiences along the way in a book, *A Tramp Across the Continent*, published in 1892, in which he ignored his visit to

Albuquerque. He apparently had read the *Democrat* article, as it seems to have furnished him with the title of his book.

### Some Determined Women

There was an Albuquerque barber on Railroad Avenue in the early 1880s who entertained his customers by gossiping about everybody in town. While shaving a local man on the morning of December 26, 1883, according to newspaper accounts, he told his customer some choice bits of gossip about the man's estranged wife. When the customer left the shop, he went straight to his estranged wife and told her what the barber had said about her.

The woman, her honor at stake, proceeded at once to William Trimble's livery stables on north Second Street, borrowed a buggy whip, and strode to the barbershop with fire in her eyes, her husband following close behind. She entered the shop as the barber was cutting a customer's hair.

"When will you be at leisure?" she asked the barber, tapping the whip against her heels.

"I don't know," the barber replied, "and I don't know what business it is of yours, anyway."

With that, the woman attacked the barber with her whip, his customer fleeing into the street with a sheet still tied around his neck. The barber managed to grab the woman, but was floored by her husband who came up behind him and hit him on the head with his revolver. While her husband held the barber down, she lashed him with the whip until he begged for mercy. The two then left the shop, she contending that justice had been done.

Later, a newspaper reporter went to the barbershop and asked the barber what he had to say about the incident. "I could have gotten a razor and cut them all to pieces if I had tried," was his only comment.

The *Albuquerque Daily Democrat* provoked the wrath of another woman when it published the following article on January 23, 1885:

> A professional female tramp named Margaret Wheeler is
> now "doing" Las Vegas. She is a systematic and highly suc-
> cessful beggar and averages $8 per day, which beats the best
> salary that New Mexico newspapermen can get.

> She is accompanied by her kid, born a few years ago on a railroad train in the east, on which she was working in her professional way. She is a little off in her upper story, but is said to deserve the sympathetic consideration of the public. She has a pass to Deming.

The consequences of this article were revealed by the *Democrat* on the following day, January 24, with an article under the headline, "That Female Tramp." The article said:

> She came into the editorial sanctum at 10 o'clock this morning, swinging a wicked looking rawhide, and holding her year-old child on her left arm; plumped the baby down in the editor's chair, and turning around, surveyed the winsome scene with the look of a lioness.
>
> "Where's the man who wrote that item?" was her first question, and by the way in which she twirled that rawhide carelessly about she evidently wanted an answer.
>
> Two Missouri cattlemen happened to be sitting at the local editor's table at the time, and the visitor was at once referred to them, while the editor-in-chief, who is also the fighting editor, carelessly walked out the back door. It took just six stalwart men to hold that woman while it was explained to her that the item in question was copied from the [Las Vegas] Optic.
>
> "My name is Mrs. Wheeler, I am 21 years of age; was born in the county seat of Poweshiek, Iowa. I'm a married woman, but my husband is in jail or the penitentiary."
>
> At this rate she carried on a monopoly of the conversation for 23 minutes (actual time), when she stopped to take a breath before ending up with the statement that "newspapermen are the biggest liars on earth."
>
> Mrs. Wheeler took the southbound train for Deming, having a pass in her possession for the latter place. She did not know where she was going, and said she cared less.

The *Albuquerque Democrat* had another encounter with an angry woman seven months later, this time with one wanting something kept out of the newspaper. The episode was described in the newspaper on August 29, 1885, under a headline reading "Watch Out for Sairy."

The *Democrat* described the office visitor as being six feet tall and muscled like a hired hand, adding that "her teeth were set like the jaws of a bear trap, and the gleam of her cold, gray eyes meant mischief to anyone who should rile her." Her voice, the article continued, was built on the same plan as a sandhill crane.

"Which one of you fellers do the printin' bout the goin's on up the Rio Grande bottom?" she asked as she walked into the newspaper office. Referred to the city editor, she walked over to his desk.

"Young man," she told him, "I came in here to put a healthy old flea in this ear o' yours. My name's Sairy Davis, wider of Joshua Davis, deceased, which he was my seventh husband, but thank God all of 'em died natural deaths. Night afore last, my daughter Mandy run off with a man, and I don't perpose to have it printed in the paper."

"But my dear madame," the city editor said, "this is an item of news, and this is a newspaper. We can't allow..."

His sentence was cut short by the thump of a ponderous fist on his desk, the newspaper reported, and the woman shouted:

> Don't make a durn bit of difference what you kin allow or what you can't. I've been married seven times, and I never got hold of a man yet I couldn't wallop the socks off in a fair fight, and I say that piece ain't a goin' in the paper.
>
> I'm goin' on 42 years old, stand six feet high, and I'm built from the ground up, and if I see a word in the paper about me or Mandy, I'm comin' back here, and then thar'll be weepin' and whalin' and smashin' of teeth, as the scriptures says.
>
> When anybody treads on Sairy Davis's petticoats thar's goin' to be war, and Sairy will be the one that will jump up on the fence and do the crowin' after it's over. Good day, and look out for a cyclone and thunderbolt trimmin's if you hear Sairy's warlike tread on the sidewalk after she reads your paper.

The *Democrat* article ended with a sentence reading: "In respect for the good old lady's feeling, a graphic report of the elopement is omitted."

A highly imaginative story about a "matrimonial post" that supposedly stood in Old Town for years was published in the *Albuquerque Democrat*

on August 29, 1885. According to tradition, the article said, an unmarried woman would soon obtain a husband and be settled for life if she could hit the wooden post squarely with a rock from a distance of ten paces.

Whenever a band of yearning women took the notion to throw rocks at the target for husbands, the newspaper said, the barrage was something to behold. Few of the rocks ever hit the matrimonial post, and bystanders soon learned that the post was the safest place to be when the rock throwing started and they crowded around it. The article continued:

> Tradition tells us that the spot where the post now stands used to be the center of Old Town, but that so many windows were broken and there was so much personal danger from flying missiles that, as an act of self defense, the people all moved off to a safe distance and pitched their adobes on the present site of the ancient village.

One pioneer Albuquerque resident, Joe Dixon, was quoted as saying that he was still carrying the scar from a rock that had hit him while he was standing twenty yards southeast of the post many years before.

The *Democrat* claimed that the matrimonial post had become one of Old Town's prime tourist attractions:

> The place has become a great resort for female tourists from the East. Old maids who have been fishing for husbands for years without getting even a nibble hear of this tradition and come out here, each with two return tickets, expecting to take husbands home with them.
>
> On some days a perfect fusillade of rocks aimed at the post can be seen flying in other directions, while the dear old girls stand there and grit their custom-made teeth and stamp holes in the ground and swear in French so that the recording angel can't understand them.
>
> Up to last Saturday the face of the post was unmarred, and the old stock of husbands on hand when it was first planted were yet on the shelves, and were getting musty, and beginning to be regarded as a drug on the market.

The article could be regarded as a prime example of newspaper humor on the western frontier.

### Incorporation of New Albuquerque, 1885

New Albuquerque was five years old in 1885 when its citizens decided to incorporate it as a town and elect a governing body. The population, according to a special census, was 3,045, not including the adjoining communities of Old Town on the west and Barelas on the south.

The new town by the railroad had experienced tremendous growth during its first five years, with many substantial buildings replacing the frame and tent structures that originally dotted the landscape. Utilities, such as electric light, natural gas, water, and telephone services made their initial appearances on a limited basis.

The Central Bank, founded in Old Town in 1878 by the brothers Jefferson, Joshua, and Frederick Raynolds, relocated from a small building at the southwest corner of the Old Town Plaza to a two-story brick building on the northwest corner of Second Street and Gold Avenue in the new town.

Oliver Cromwell, with profits from his streetcar operation, erected a two-story office building on the northeast corner of Second Street and Gold Avenue in 1882. Years later, the Cromwell Building was inherited by his daughter, Louise Cromwell MacArthur, and her husband, General Douglas MacArthur. They transferred the property to P. F. McCanna, a real estate agent, in 1922. Several Old Town mercantile businesses, including those operated by the Rosenwalds and Ilfelds, relocated to the new town.

Angus A. Grant, a Canadian-born railroad contractor, erected a two-story building in 1883 on the northwest corner of Railroad Avenue and Third Street, which was known as the Grant Opera House, the opera house occupying the second floor and the Ilfeld Company the first. Grant also owned the Albuquerque Electric Light Company and the Albuquerque Water Works.

Angus, with his brothers John and Lewis Grant, had done contract work on both the Santa Fe and Atlantic and Pacific railroads as they built through New Mexico. While helping to build the A&P they established a construction site about seventy-five miles west of Albuquerque that was known as Grant's Camp, which later became the town of Grants.

The first Albuquerque businessman to trade in his gas lights for the new incandescent electric lamps was W. E. Talbott, proprietor of the popular Montezuma Saloon on Second Street. The switch-over occurred before a large crowd of spectators at 7:30 P.M. on October 31,

The San Felipe Hotel, erected in 1883–1884 on the southwest corner of west Gold Avenue and south Fifth Street, was a three-story structure containing eighty guest rooms. Shown here as it appeared in about 1892, the luxury hotel was destroyed by fire in 1899. Courtesy the Albuquerque Museum Photoarchive, PA1976.61.29. Seis collection. Donated by August Seis.

1883. Many Albuquerque residents had already seen demonstrations of the Brush electric lights, which gave off a glarish stream of unsteady illumination. Few thought they were a worthy successor to gas lamps.

The San Felipe Hotel, erected in 1884 on the southwest corner of Gold Avenue and Fifth Street, surpassed the Armijo House in size, luxury, and comfort. Built at a cost of $103,000, the three-story brick structure contained eighty guest rooms, including ornate bridal parlors, and sample rooms for salesmen. Liquor was banned from the premises, and a library was installed in what normally would have been a hotel bar or saloon.

Designed for the carriage trade, the San Felipe was financed by a group of Albuquerque business and professional men who organized the Albuquerque Hotel Company. The contractor was Albuquerque contractor Ed Medler. The room rates, $2.50 and $3.00 a day, were considered rather expensive at the time.

Henry Jaffa, a German-Jewish merchant, was elected the first mayor of Albuquerque when the city was incorporated in 1885. He served one term. Courtesy UNM Center for Southwest Research, the Albuquerque Museum Photoarchive, PA1978.50.281.

Taking shape in 1884 was the Albuquerque Indian School, on vacant land more than a mile northwest of the new town. The school was operated for the federal government by the Home Board of Presbyterian Missions.

New Albuquerque, however, was still regarded as a Bernalillo County precinct, and to remedy the situation a drive for incorporation was launched by lawyers William Hazeldine and Harvey B. Fergusson and merchant Santiago Baca. Incorporation was approved by voters on June 4, 1885, and the voters went back to the polls on July 4 to elect the first town officials. The Democratic Party and the nonpartisan Peoples Ticket both entered candidates for the positions of mayor, town recorder, and four seats on a board of trustees. The Peoples Ticket swept the field.

Elected Albuquerque's first mayor was Henry N. Jaffa, a German-Jewish immigrant who operated a grocery and dry goods business with his brothers Samuel and Sol Jaffa. They previously had operated a large mercantile business in Trinidad, Colorado.

Jesse Wheelock, a real estate developer, architect, and insurance agent, was elected town recorder. He served as acting mayor in the absence of Henry Jaffa. Elected to the board of trustees were William McClellan, member of the Borradaile and McClellan real estate firm; A. M. Whitcomb, a building contractor; Z. T. Phillips, an accountant for the A&P; and Charles P. Jones, operator of the Albuquerque Dairy north of town.

The mayor and the trustees appointed Tom Phelan as town attorney, and drew up the first ordinances. The ordinances included regulation measures for dance and gambling halls and opium dens. Municipal funds were obtained through the sale of business licenses and bond issues. The police force was allotted $4,000, ending the practice of paying town marshals with funds donated by local merchants. Another $1,000 went to a fire department.

Albuquerque's mayor-trustee form of government lasted only until 1891, when Albuquerque was reincorporated as a city, with trustees replaced by two aldermen elected from each of four wards.

### A Police Tragedy

Among the first police officers hired by the newly incorporated town of Albuquerque was Michael Robert "Bob" McGuire, a native of Oswego, New York. He joined the force on July 18, 1885, and was named town marshal on April 13, 1886.

Marshal McGuire learned on Saturday, November 20, 1886, that two wanted cowboy desperadoes, Charlie Ross and John "Kid" Johnson, had been seen loitering around Pasqual Cutinola's dance hall in Martineztown, at the northern edge of Albuquerque. Armed with warrants for the arrest of the two men, McGuire proceeded to Martineztown with Officer E. D. Henry, the assistant town marshal. They comprised most of what was Albuquerque's police force at the time.

Not finding Ross or Johnson at the dance hall, the two officers began searching the vicinity. Glancing in the window of a small adobe house about twenty feet south of the dance hall, McGuire and Henry saw the two desperadoes seated at a supper table inside with two young women, Simona Moya and Terecita Trujillo. The officers walked to the closed door of the home and decided that they would throw the door open and rush into the room with drawn guns, taking the outlaws by surprise.

Ross and Johnson had just finished eating, and Johnson asked for a glass of water. Miss Moya was cleaning off the table, and Miss Trujillo got a water pitcher and started for the door to obtain water from a well.

Miss Trujillo opened the door just as the two officers were rushing in, and all three went down in a heap in the doorway. McGuire quickly untangled himself and rushed Johnson, and Henry got to his feet and started for Ross as the two girls dived under a bed. Guns blazed, the light went out, and the guns kept blazing. Then all was quiet again.

When the light went on again, Henry was dead on the floor with two bullets in his chest and one in his leg. McGuire was also down, mortally wounded, with two bullets in his side and one in his arm. The two desperadoes had disappeared in the darkness outside, Johnson unharmed, and Ross suffering from a slight bullet wound in his back.

Ross found a horse hitched to a fence nearby and began riding it slowly west towards Old Town. Weakened from loss of blood, he fell from the horse but managed to drag himself to the home of some friends in a neighborhood known as Hell's Half Acre. He was found and arrested at the house the next morning and was taken to the county jail in Old Town. No trace was found of Johnson, who was described by the *Albuquerque Democrat* as "full of cowboy swagger, wears a Chihuahua hat and wears his pants in his boots."

Officer Henry, a thirty-eight-year-old native of Henry County, Ohio, was buried in the new Fairview Cemetery on the mesa east of Albuquerque. Marshal McGuire, also thirty-eight, lingered until November 26 before dying of his wounds. Flags in Albuquerque were lowered to half-staff, and black mourning crepe was placed on business houses. His remains were taken to his hometown in New York for burial.

Charlie Ross remained in the county jail until the night of January 17, 1887, when he and another prisoner, Peter Trinkaus of Gallup, New Mexico, escaped through an unbarred window. There was some evidence that the jailer had been bribed to assist them in their escape.

Upon leaving the jail, which Ross referred to as the county hotel, he left a note for the editor of the *Albuquerque Daily Democrat* that read:

> Please say in your paper that hearing there is a reward offered for my partner Johnson that I have gone to find him. Tell the boys not to feel uneasy about my absence, and as the weather is such that they might take cold, it may be better for their health to stay at home. We'll turn up in time, and don't you forget it. [Signed] C. Henry Ross with his hair parted in the middle.

Neither Ross nor Johnson were ever brought to justice for killing the two Albuquerque police officers.

### End of a Decade

Horses and riders were lining up for a race at the 1888 New Mexico Territorial Fair when a spectator shouted "Go!" And off they went, all the way around the track. The race had to be rerun with a more official start.

The territorial fairs in Old Town proved to be Albuquerque's greatest annual entertainment features, drawing visitors from all parts of the territory and beyond. Each fair included horse races, baseball games, cowboy tournaments, and band concerts.

The *Albuquerque Democrat*, describing opening day activities at the 1888 fair on September 24, reported that "a beautiful sunshiny day attracted a great number of persons who paid for admission at the gates and a less number who climbed over the wooden fences and so escaped relieving their pockets of fifty cents charged for admission."

A troupe of Comanche Indians entertained visitors "with feats of daring, mostly done on horseback at speed," and by staging a mock war dance and battle. A New Mexico group staged a traditional Matachines dance, which the newspaper described as "the national game of Mexico." "Football, which with cricket and horse racing may be classed as the great national games of Great Britain, also was played," the *Democrat* reported, without going into any details.

Floral Hall was filled with fruits and vegetables, including thirty-seven varieties from the Hubbell Ranch at Pajarito, and the A&P displayed New Mexico crops from along its line that included corn that was twelve feet six inches high, wheat that was seven feet high, and pumpkins that weighed forty-five pounds, all grown without irrigation.

Delivering the welcoming address at the 1888 fair was New Mexico governor Edmund G. Ross, who had settled in Albuquerque in 1882 as a political refugee from Kansas. A printer by trade, he joined the editorial staff of the *Albuquerque Journal* upon his arrival in Albuquerque.

As a Republican senator from Kansas in 1868, Ross had cast the deciding "not guilty" vote in the Republican-backed impeachment of President Andrew Johnson, a Southern Democrat. Although eventually vindicated as a courageous defender of the Constitution, Ross was politically and socially ostracized by Republicans and his fellow Kansans alike.

Ross became a Democrat in New Mexico, and in 1885 was appointed territorial governor of New Mexico by President Grover Cleveland, serving until 1889. One of his last acts as governor was his signing of a bill, on February 28, 1889, that "created and established within and for the Territory of New Mexico an institution of higher learning to be known as

Built in 1892, Hodgin Hall was the first classroom building erected on the University of New Mexico campus. It is shown here before it was remodeled into a Pueblo Revival style in 1908–1909. Courtesy UNM Center for Southwest Research, the Albuquerque Museum Photoarchive, PA1978.50.700.

the University of New Mexico near the town of Albuquerque." The same act also created the School of Mines at Socorro and the New Mexico College of Agriculture and Mechanical Arts at Las Cruces.

The bill creating the University of New Mexico had been pushed through the territorial legislature by Bernard S. Rodey, an Albuquerque lawyer and Bernalillo County senator. The bill provided that the university be situated on donated land about two miles east of New Albuquerque on the elevated East Mesa. Classes began in 1892 with the completion of a three-story brick building on the isolated campus and the hiring of faculty members.

Meanwhile, the appearance of Old Town was changing with the construction of two substantial county buildings and the loss of some of the historic structures. Erected in 1886 a short distance southeast of the plaza, and facing Railroad Avenue, was a new Bernalillo County Courthouse, a three-story building and tower of cast stone masonry construction. Built of the same material was a two-story county jail, a

Serving as the Bernalillo County Courthouse from 1886 to 1924 was this cast stone building on west Central Avenue southeast of the Old Town Plaza. It later housed the San Felipe School, and was unused when demolished in 1959. Courtesy the Albuquerque Museum Photoarchive, PA1990.13.55. Cobb Studio collection. Museum purchase from G. O. Bonds.

short distance southwest of the plaza near the entrance to the territorial fairgrounds.

Herman Blueher, a former Illinois gardener, had developed an extensive truck farm and nursery on fields a short distance northeast of the plaza.

The *Albuquerque Democrat*, on June 13, 1889, lamented the loss of some of Old Town's historic structures under a headline reading "Old Landmarks Going." The article said:

> Among other old buildings now dismantled that were formerly places of great business resort is the old store of Manuel and Rafael Armijo, where 40 years ago the largest stock of goods in the southwest was kept.
>
> The old McPheron cottage is a mass of ruins, and the gigantic cottonwood trees that were such a source of pride

147

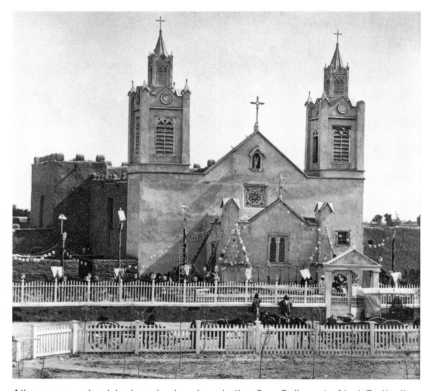

Albuquerque's oldest major landmark, the San Felipe de Neri Catholic Church on the Old Town Plaza, is shown here as it appeared in about 1885. The historic church has been in continuous use since the 1790s. Courtesy UNM Center for Southwest Research, the Albuquerque Museum Photoarchive, PA1978.50.37.

and pleasure to their owner have long since passed away in smoke and ashes.

The old government dispensary is now used as a corral and the graves of those who were buried here are obliterated, and fruit trees and splendid gardens are now the only monuments that exist to the memory of many a brave man who yielded up his life after a long and lingering sickness in which death becomes a master.

The home of Joseph Pohmer is closed, yet within its walls hangs a frame that adorned the picture of General Longstreet in 1850.

The march of progress and civilization is resistless as well as relentless, and a visit to West Albuquerque but attests to this statement.

The old landmarks are going, but in their stead new and commodious structures are to be reared, and less than a decade of years will roll by before these places so desolate will blossom with the flowers of prosperity and happiness. Schools and education are taking the place of the former darkness and soon a new people will fill the places of the past decade and happiness will reign supreme throughout the land.

# Chapter Eight

# ALBUQUERQUE IN THE 1890s

## Assuming Some Degree of Normalcy

### A Visitor in a Hurry

Nellie Bly, twenty-three-year-old reporter for the *New York World*, paused in Albuquerque for two minutes early in 1890 during the last leg of her record-breaking race around the world. Her newspaper assignment was to circle the globe in less time than it took the fictional Phineas Fogg in the Jules Verne novel, *Around the World in Eighty Days*.

Miss Bly's eastward journey had started in New York City in November 1889 and after traveling most of the way around the world by ship and train she reached San Francisco on January 21, 1890, five days ahead of the schedule of Mr. Fogg. Officials of the AT&SF placed a special train at her disposal, consisting of a locomotive-drawn Pullman and baggage car, and agreed to transport her to Chicago in the shortest time possible. The train, given the right-of-way over all scheduled AT&SF trains, raced eastward into New Mexico on the A&P tracks. The engineers were told to forget all speed limits.

Miss Bly's special train pulled up to the Albuquerque depot at ten o'clock on the evening of January 22, 1890. Waiting on the platform to greet the attractive young journalist were Albuquerque mayor Gurdon W. Mylert, city councilmen, some railroad officials, and a few curious citizens.

When the two-car train came to a halt, part of the welcoming delegation climbed aboard to greet Miss Bly and wish her luck. Thomas Fair, a railroad official, presented her with a wreath of flowers, in the center of which the words "Atlantic and Pacific" were worked in satin.

Before the Albuquerque delegation could disembark from the train, the conductor ordered the engineer to pull out for the next stop. "The train left the depot at lightning speed," the *Albuquerque Citizen* reported the next day. "Two miles above the city, someone pulled the bell cord, and the mighty iron horse suddenly came to a standstill. Those caught filed off the train and had to foot it back to the city."

The train, which reached speeds of up to ninety miles an hour on the Kansas plains, carried the reporter the 2,577 miles from San Francisco to Chicago in a record time of sixty-nine hours. Another train rushed her from Chicago to New York, and she arrived back at her office just seventy-two days, six hours, and eleven minutes from the time she had left—a world record.

"Where the hell have you been?" the city editor growled as she walked into the newspaper office. History does not record her answer.

### Promoting Albuquerque

About two hundred of Albuquerque's leading business and professional men, wishing to promote the new town to the outside world, met in the spring of 1890 and founded the Albuquerque Commercial Club, forerunner of the Chamber of Commerce. One of the first items on the agenda was to erect a building that would serve as the center of Albuquerque's business and social life.

Completed in 1892 on the southwest corner of Fourth Street and Gold Avenue, the $70,000 Commercial Club building was an ornate structure of red sandstone that contained three floors, a garret, and a tower. The sandstone, from near Flagstaff, Arizona, was shipped to Albuquerque free of charge by the A&P.

The ground floor was rented to business firms, and the second floor included the Commercial Club offices, card parlors, a billiards room, a ballroom, and a bar. The third floor consisted of bachelor suites for unmarried club members. Albuquerque's first public library, organized by a group of women volunteers, was housed in the building's reading room.

Club members sent out numerous booklets and brochures boosting Albuquerque's business and investment opportunities, often painting a rather idealistic picture of the new city. Typical was a folder issued in 1893 by club member Jesse M. Wheelock, who identified himself a "the

The Commercial Club building, which stood on the southwest corner of south Fourth Street and west Gold Avenue from 1892 until the 1950s, was erected by Albuquerque boosters and for years was the center of the city's business and social life. It was demolished to make way for the high-rise Simms office building. The historic building is shown here as it appeared in about 1890. Courtesy the Albuquerque Museum Photoarchive, PA1990.13.57. Cobb Studio collection. Museum purchase from G. O. Bonds.

leading architect of New Mexico and the real estate and insurance man of the Rio Grande Valley."

Wheelock's folder gave Albuquerque's population as about twelve thousand, which actually was the population of Bernalillo County. It said the city had twenty-five miles of graded streets, forty miles of good sidewalks, an excellent fire department, public water works, a thorough sewer system, electric light works, gas works, and a telephone system.

The folder said that Albuquerque also had a streetcar line, three daily newspapers, three weekly newspapers, good hotels and restaurants, a university, a college, and four elegant public school buildings. "Albuquerque is the only place in New Mexico that has letter carriers and the free delivery system," the 1893 folder stated.

The A&P Railroad shops employed 500 men, it said, and two foundries and machine shops employed another 150. Mechanics' wages ranged from $2.50 to $4.00 a day, common labor cost $1 a day, public school teachers made from $40 to $70 a month, bricks were $12 per thousand in the wall, and native lumber was $18 per thousand board feet.

One could rent a good four-room house in the best section of town for $18 to $20 a month. Downtown business space rented from $75 to $150 a month, and second-floor office space rented from $12 to $20 a month. "Good, unimproved land near Albuquerque, subject to irrigation, can be bought at $25 to $100 per acre," the folder said. "The mountains east of Albuquerque abound in the most delightful resorts for summer tourists. An Albuquerque man can send his family to the mountains for their summer outing and visit them every Sunday without losing any time from business."

The folder stressed that cyclones and destructive windstorms were unknown, thunderstorms were very rare, and that "there are more sunny days every year in the Rio Grande Valley than in any other quarter of the world." The efficient fire department noted in the folder consisted of three volunteer fire companies, the Albuquerque Hook and Ladder Company, the Scott Moore Hose Company, and the Angus A. Grant Hose Company.

The Commercial Club's promotional material did not mention that Albuquerque also had a thriving red light district. The brothels, originally located on Railroad Avenue west of Fourth Street, were soon relocated to an area a block north of that main thoroughfare. Most of the brothels, in what was known as Hell's Half Acre, were located on north Third, and on Copper Avenue between Third and Fourth streets. There also were a number of other brothels in Old Town.

The most elaborate brothels, often called "parlours," "cottages," or "wine rooms," were richly furnished and catered to businessmen. "Cribs," on the other hand, offered quick service to low income customers, and consisted of a series of tiny and dingy rooms, under a common roof, facing a street or alley.

Albuquerque's best known madam for years was Lizzie McGrath, known as the Lily of Copper Avenue, who operated the Vine Cottage at 312 West Copper Avenue. A Kentucky native, she arrived in Albuquerque in about 1882 and worked at several brothels before opening her own in about 1885. Other well known madams included Minnie Carroll and Nellie Driscoll.

The customers of one establishment presented the madam with a birthday present consisting of a silver loving cup with the names of all her best customers engraved on it. She displayed it on a mantel in her house of ill repute, and there it remained until the day she died, at which time it disappeared, never to surface again. It was said to contain the names of many prominent Albuquerque citizens. Albuquerque's downtown red light district remained in operation until closed by the city in 1914.

## A Bloodless Bullfight

Promising that no bulls would be hurt, a troupe of professional bull-fighters from Mexico and Spain erected an arena in Old Town and announced that a genuine but "bloodless" bullfight would be staged there on Sunday afternoon, January 21, 1894. Albuquerque citizens greeted the announcement with mixed reactions.

The *Albuquerque Daily Citizen* refused to carry any advertising or publicity about the planned event, fearing that even bloodless bull-fighting might be illegal in New Mexico. The *Albuquerque Journal* sent a reporter to Old Town to interview the leader of the troupe, don Antonio Fuentes, a matador from Durango, Mexico. He assured the newspaper that no bulls would be harmed, no horses would be used, and "there will be no more wounds than in the theater when a man is shot with a blank cartridge."

Many Albuquerque residents were not satisfied with this explanation, however, and they demanded that New Mexico governor William Thornton put a stop to it. The governor searched the New Mexico statutes in vain for any law prohibiting bullfighting in the territory.

Under increasing pressure and in desperation, Governor Thornton sent a telegram on January 19 to W. H. Whiteman, the district attorney in Albuquerque, which read: "Bullfights in violation of Sunday law and cruelty to animal law. Prepare writs and have parties put under bond. Stop it. Have wired the sheriff."

The district attorney, after conferring with the Bernalillo County sheriff Jacobo Yrissari, sent a telegram to the governor reading: "I will probably prosecute all violations of law referred to, but until some overt act has been committed, I know of no legal steps that can be taken. Kindly refer me to the statute under which you think I have the power to act."

The governor couldn't produce such a statute, however, so the bull-fight went on as scheduled that Sunday afternoon in the makeshift arena a short distance southeast of the Old Town Plaza. Just before the festivities began, Sheriff Yrissari climbed up on a railing and announced to the bullfighters that if any law was violated or any blood drawn, he would be compelled to halt the exhibition and arrest all parties concerned.

The bullfights were staged before nearly two thousand spectators who shouted their approval of the pageantry, the brass band music, the clowns, and the graceful skills of the bullfighters. As promised, no blood was shed, as the bullfighters wore protective bundles of straw strapped to their bodies and stuck their sharp banderillas into bales of hay that were strapped to the backs of the bulls. Everybody had a good time, although some spectators remarked upon leaving that they didn't think bullfighting was as dangerous or as exciting as football.

## Visit of the Healer

His name was Francis Schlatter, and he was a shoemaker by trade, but by the time he arrived in New Mexico in the summer of 1895 he was known far and wide as the Healer, a simple and soft-spoken man who was believed by many to possess miraculous healing powers. Few visitors to Albuquerque ever created as much excitement and curiosity as did this so-called messiah, who with his shoulder length brown hair and beard bore a striking resemblance to traditional representations of Jesus Christ.

Born in 1856 of German parents in the French region of Alsace-Lorraine, Schlatter attended school there until the age of fourteen when he decided to become a cobbler. He immigrated to the United States in about 1884 following the deaths of his parents, and worked as a shoemaker in New York until 1892 when he moved to Denver and set up shop there.

It was while he was working in his Denver shoe shop, Schlatter said, that a voice came to him, the voice of what he called his Master. He said the Master told him that a friend living in Long Island had a paralyzed right arm, and that if he would write to him, he would be healed. Schlatter said that he wrote to his friend, and that he was immediately healed. "For eight months, I kept at work, but during all that time I healed the sick," he said. "Then one day the Master told me to go out whither he sent me to comfort the inflicted."

Schlatter left Denver in the summer of 1893 and began wandering alone through western states and territories. Wearing a robe, with a small conical-shaped tent strapped to his back, he walked barefoot across the land, steadying his steps with a long metal rod. His wanderings took him as far east as Arkansas, and west to California. From

Francis Schlatter, a lone wanderer known as the Healer, attracted large throngs of curious and ailing visitors when he paused in Albuquerque in 1895. Author's collection.

California he followed the A&P line east into New Mexico and arrived in the Rio Grande Valley south of Albuquerque in early July 1895.

Two boys from the village of Peralta, while climbing up a nearby hill, found Schlatter lying on his back on the summit, his arms stretched up toward the heavens, his little tent pitched nearby. They took him down to the village, where he took up temporary residence at the home of Mrs. Juliana Sedillo. Within a short time, his reputation as a miracle worker spread like wildfire through Rio Grande villages. Spanish speakers called him El Sanador, Spanish for "the Healer," and crowds followed him from village to village.

His Peralta host, Mrs. Sedillo, said that both her arms had been paralyzed for sixteen years, and that when the Healer took her hands in his, the paralysis was gone, and that within a few days she was out working in the fields.

Juan Vásquez of Peralta, who had been blind for three years, said the Healer brought back the sight to his eyes. "He took my hands in his and said something which I could not understand," he said. "Almost immediately, I felt my sight coming back." Grateful Peralta residents gave Schlatter a pair of blue jeans and a calico shirt that he wore in place of the robe.

"Imitator of Christ in New Mexico" exclaimed a front-page headline in the *Albuquerque Morning Democrat* as Schlatter approached Albuquerque on foot, followed by throngs of admirers. He reached Albuquerque on the morning of July 20, 1895, and took up temporary residence in the Werner family home in Old Town. By that afternoon, streets in the vicinity were crowded with lines of carriages, wagons, and horseback riders as people from miles around flocked to see the Healer.

Schlatter announced that he had started a forty-day fast, but agreed to receive visitors, and long lines of men, women, and children filed into the Werner home for days to find him seated in a small room where he received one and all with kindness and compassion. The ailing whom he touched reported that they felt an electric shock in their bodies and immediately began to feel better.

A few denounced him as a fraud, even though he refused to accept any money for his services. When one man shoved some coins into his hand, he shoved them back, saying "I have no use for money." When another refused to take back some offered money, Schlatter turned and distributed it to some poor who were standing close to him.

Testimonials to Schlatter's healing powers were offered by a number of Albuquerque residents whom he touched. Charles Stamp said he could suddenly walk again on his crushed foot, Peter Maguire said he found himself cured of rheumatism, Mrs. C. J. Roentgen said she could hear better, and C. G. Lott said he could suddenly move a paralyzed arm.

Schlatter moved to the home of James A. Sommers at the corner of Sixth Street and west Roma Avenue in New Albuquerque where he continued to receive visitors and where he completed his forty-day fast on August 15. He then sat down and ate a dinner that included chicken, pork, eggs, chile, and wine. The long fast had left him weak and exhausted, and when he announced that he planned to leave for Denver, some Albuquerque citizens purchased him a train ticket, took him to the depot, and helped him board a Pullman car.

Schlatter created a sensation in Denver as the Healer, and thousands of men, women, and children began filing by him each day merely to feel his touch. He disappeared suddenly from Denver on November 14, 1895, and weeks later he was seen in a number of New Mexico villages near Santa Fe riding a big white horse called Butte.

Bypassing Albuquerque, Schlatter appeared early in January 1896 at the Morley Ranch at Datil, New Mexico, a village in western Socorro County. He was taken in and given an upstairs room by Mrs. Ada Morley. "My father had directed me to a safe retreat," he told Mrs. Morley. "I must restore my spiritual powers in seclusion and prayer." After remaining in seclusion at the ranch for several months, and saying that Datil had been chosen as the site of the New Jerusalem, Schlatter mounted his horse and rode south into Mexico, never to be heard from again.

In 1897 some Mexicans in Chihuahua discovered a man's body under a tree, a large white horse grazing nearby. Found among the possessions of the deceased man were a Spanish-English dictionary, an address book, a metal rod, and a Bible with the name Francis Schlatter written on the flyleaf. "When the day of judgment comes you shall know who I am," the Healer had said in New Mexico. "I shall return some day, but not in my present form." Schlatter's metal rod eventually was donated to the Museum of New Mexico, where it remains today.

### A Festive Hanging

Legal hangings, when carried out in public, were often considered a source of prime entertainment in New Mexico during its territorial period. Such was the case when Dionicio Sandoval, a thirty-seven-year-old sheepherder, was hanged in Albuquerque in 1896.

Sandoval, a resident of Trinidad, Colorado, had been working as a sheepherder for J. M. Sandoval at San Ysidro, about forty miles northwest of Albuquerque, when he was charged with murder in the fatal shooting of Victoriano Tenorio, a fellow sheepherder, on July 29, 1895.

According to trial testimony, Sandoval walked over to where Tenorio was herding a flock of sheep, sat down on a keg, and the two began to argue. The argument ended with a scuffle over a rifle that discharged, causing Tenorio to fall over dead. Sandoval said he was guilty of murder, but insisted that it was an accident. His murder conviction was upheld by the New Mexico Supreme Court, and he was sentenced to be hanged at Albuquerque.

Nearly two thousand spectators witnessed Sandoval's execution on the morning of September 24, 1896. The hanging took place on a gallows that had been erected about a half mile behind the Bernalillo County jail, which stood at what is now the southwest corner of Central (then Railroad) Avenue and Rio Grande Boulevard. The spectators converged on the scene from miles around, in wagons, on horseback, and on foot.

Some arrived on the eve of the hanging and camped out overnight near the gallows, thus assuring themselves of good vantage points. Some brought picnic lunches.

Sandoval was presented with a complete new outfit of clothing, including a hat, for his trip to the gallows. He discarded the new hat, saying that his old sombrero was more comfortable. "I'm going out of here mighty high toned," he said as he admired himself in his new suit. These apparently were his last words, and he went to his death quietly. Survivors included his wife in Trinidad, who, understandably, did not attend the hanging.

### An Albuquerque Hero

"A veritable scene of enchantment." That's how the *Albuquerque Democrat* described the Panoramic Procession of floats and marching bands that paraded along Albuquerque streets on Friday evening, October 16, 1896. The glittering procession, highlight of the week-long Carnival of Sports at the New Mexico Territorial Fairgrounds, was witnessed by thousands of men, women, and children who lined streets in New Albuquerque's downtown business district.

Downtown Albuquerque was lit up like a Christmas tree for the occasion, with brilliant displays of electric lamps, moving lights, and brightly colored torches. Skyrockets were fired from various parade units as the procession moved west on Copper Avenue and turned south on Fifth Street.

Near the rear of the procession, between the Old Town Band and the Flambeau Club, was a horse-drawn ammunition wagon loaded with fireworks. Driving the wagon was seventy-four-year-old John Braden, who had spent much of his life on the western plains as a stagecoach driver, wagon master, express messenger, and Indian scout. During his long career, Braden had guided many stagecoaches safely through hostile Indian country. But the Panoramic Procession in Albuquerque was to prove to be his greatest challenge.

The *Albuquerque Daily Citizen* described what happened with these words:

> Just as the parade turned the corner of Copper Avenue, coming south on Fifth Street, the Flambeau Club started the fireworks and sparks flew back into the ammunition wagon. Immediately an explosion occurred, shaking the earth's

foundations and scattering sparks and dangerous missiles in all directions.

Several rockets shot out of the wagon and struck the horses, and they, terror stricken, dashed away on a dead run between the Flambeau Club and the band boys, running over and knocking two band players to the ground.

By this time the wagon was a mass of flames, but Braden stayed at his post, trying to stop the horses and save the crowd that lined the streets. At the intersection of Railroad Avenue, the horses turned east on the avenue, but came to a standstill by running into the Scott Moore Hose Company cart, the wheels locking together.

Braden still had hold of the reins, his body enveloped in flames, and overcome with exhaustion he fell from his seat to the ground, calling out to take off his clothes, and holding his hands to his mouth to prevent suffocation. Several of the fire boys rushed to his assistance and smothered the flames with their jackets. Marshal Fornoff and Policeman Young responded and rendered valuable assistance.

A hack, with a half dozen little girls, was in front of the Scott Moore hose cart, and some of the boys rushed to their assistance, getting them out just in time, while others tenderly lifted poor Braden into the hack and took him to the city hospital. The Atlantic and Pacific hose company unreeled and put out the burning wagon.

Fred Fornoff, the Albuquerque town marshal, said that evening that he had never read of such personal heroism as displayed by John Braden. "He could have jumped off the wagon when the explosion occurred and saved himself," Fornoff said, "but he stayed at his post and prevented the thoroughly frightened horses from running away and doubtless killing a number of people."

Braden, burned severely from head to toe, died in the hospital at two fifteen the next afternoon, throwing Albuquerque into a state of mourning. Undertaker Montfort said that the penniless pioneer would not be buried in a pauper's grave, and Albuquerque citizens immediately began contributing money to give the pioneer a hero's funeral.

Albuquerque newspapers, meanwhile, were trying without much success to piece together the story of the pioneer's life. Those who knew him described him as a big, genial, generous man who seldom spoke about his life and career. They did not know if he had ever been married, or if he had any living relatives. One friend said he thought Braden was originally from Pennsylvania or Ohio.

J. B. Campbell said he first met Braden many years before in Hamilton, Ohio, and that the next time he saw him, in the 1860s, he was employed by the Ben Holladay Stage Company on the Platte River in Colorado. Jack Harris said he knew Braden as a driver for Ben Holladay on the Bitter Creek Division in Colorado and he believed that he was a driver for the Northwest Stage Company in Iowa and Minnesota before going to Colorado. "When Wells Fargo bought Holladay I think Braden worked for the express company for a few years," Harris added.

Other pioneers said they remembered Braden as a stagecoach driver between Denver and Salt Lake City, and between Fort Bridger and Fort Kearny. Some recalled that he had once been city marshal of Pueblo, Colorado.

Braden arrived in Albuquerque in the 1880s and was employed for six years by W. L. Trimble and Company as a driver in the Cochiti mining district north of Albuquerque. He spent the last four years of his life as a driver for Olmstead and Dixon of Albuquerque, and at the time of his death he was driving Olmstead and Dixon horses attached to a wagon owned by Herman Blueher, the Old Town gardener.

John Braden's funeral was held on the afternoon of October 20 at the Grant Opera House in Albuquerque's business district. All businesses, schools, and the university were closed for two hours in response to a proclamation by Mayor J. C. Baldridge. Reverends T. C. Beattie and James Menaul delivered the sermons in the packed opera house, and fire bells tolled as the long funeral procession made its way up the East Mesa to Fairview Cemetery where the pioneer was buried with full honors.

Albuquerque citizens donated money to erect a memorial honoring Braden for his heroism, and the memorial, consisting of a metal water fountain, was unveiled and dedicated on November 14, 1897, in Robinson Park, on Railroad Avenue at the west edge of Albuquerque's business district. The *Albuquerque Citizen* called the memorial "a beautiful and artistic piece of work," adding that "the upper part is a figure of a woman with a water jar on her shoulder, and the lower portion consists of dragons through whose mouths the water pours into the basin beneath." Albuquerque attorney Frank W. Clancy gave the dedication address, which the newspaper said included "a complete and thrilling account of the events of the day on which John Braden sacrificed his life."

The metal fountain had fallen into a state of neglect and disrepair by 1974 when it was refurbished and rededicated by the New Mexico chapter of the Daughters of the Founders and Patriots of America. A bronze plaque also was installed telling of Braden's heroism.

Robinson Park, Albuquerque's oldest public park, was established when New Albuquerque was platted in 1880. Later, it was named for Lena Robinson, daughter of a Santa Fe Railway official, who sold the most tickets in a popularity contest to raise funds to develop the park. Her father, Albert A. Robinson, general superintendent and chief engineer of the railroad, bought most of her tickets.

### Three Major Fires

Three prominent New Albuquerque landmarks, the Armijo House, the Grant Building with its opera house, and the San Felipe Hotel, were destroyed by fires during the closing years of the nineteenth century.

Destroyed by fire early in 1897 was the Armijo House, which recently had been renamed the Armijo-Lockhart House, the three-story hotel on the southwest corner of Railroad Avenue and Third Street that Mariano Armijo had built in 1880–1881. His father, Ambrosio Armijo, purchased the hotel soon after it was opened and built an addition to it, known as Ambrosio Hall, which was occupied for some years by the Albuquerque Athletic Club.

Originally leased to W. Scott Moore, other proprietors who leased the hotel in following years included P. B. Sherman, James G. Hope, W. E. Talbott, G. H. Miles, Perfecto Armijo, J. Arment, George W. Stubbs, and F. Valentine.

Sofre Alexander leased the Armijo House from the heirs of the Ambrosio Armijo estate in 1896 and subleased it to Mrs. Ellen Lockhart, who changed the name to the Armijo-Lockhart House. Alexander stored paint and wallpaper in a small room adjoining the hotel, and Mrs. Lockhart's son, Harry, operated a bicycle shop in another adjoining room. Mrs. Lockhart and her three daughters, Ida, Frankie, and Lizzie, occupied rooms on the third floor of the hotel. Girard's Café, operated by Joseph Girard, occupied a corner of the first floor.

At about two o'clock on the morning of February 10, 1897, William O'Brien, the night porter, left the hotel and walked to the railroad depot to meet a passenger train and to escort any prospective guests to the hotel. Finding that the train was running late, he returned to the hotel to find flames issuing from the paint room and the bicycle shop and the hotel filling with smoke.

O'Brien roused the sleeping guests by running up the stairs shouting "Fire!" The flames already were spreading quickly through the building, and the guests had time to escape only with their clothes and what possessions they could pick up on the run. Mrs. Lockhart's eyebrows and hair were singed as she struggled to get a large trunk down the back stairs, the only thing she saved. Her three daughters lost everything but the robes they had slipped on in a hurry.

A volunteer fire company under Chief Charles Bernard Ruppe poured streams of water into the burning building. Crowds attracted to the scene were held back as burning timbers crashed into the debris and the walls began to collapse. The firefighters managed to save some of the furniture in Girard's Café by dragging it into the street. The hotel, once considered Albuquerque's finest, was not rebuilt.

The Grant Building, on the northwest corner of Railroad Avenue and Third Street, was destroyed by fire in June 1898. The entire first floor of the building was occupied by the Ilfeld Brothers mercantile store at the time, and the opera house occupied the second floor. The building later was rebuilt, but without the opera house.

The once proud San Felipe Hotel, on the southwest corner of Gold Avenue and Fifth Street, had ceased operation and was being reno- vated when it was destroyed by fire in 1899. Built in 1884 at a cost of more than $100,000, the luxury hotel was never a financial success and closed its doors in 1895.

Frank A. Sturges, proprietor of the Sturges European Hotel on the southwest corner of Railroad Avenue and First Street, bought the vacant San Felipe Hotel in 1897 for about $18,000 and began restoring it to its former glory. He installed electrical and steam heating sys- tems, repainted and repapered the rooms, purchased new furniture and furnishings, and installed new sidewalks. After sinking about $40,000 into the venture, Sturges announced in the summer of 1899 that the San Felipe Hotel would open for business on September 1 in time for the territorial fair. It was not to happen.

On the afternoon of August 18, 1899, some pedestrians noticed some wisps of smoke issuing from the cupola atop the three-story building, which was occupied only by some plumbers in the basement. Turning in the alarm at a nearby fire alarm box was twelve-year-old

William Keleher, who later in life was to become a prominent and distinguished Albuquerque attorney and New Mexico historian.

Volunteer firefighters rushed to the scene led by Ruppe, the former chief, acting for Chief Pete Isherwood who was recovering from an injury. The fire was limited to the roof area at first, and firemen entered the building and managed to remove two pianos and some furniture and furnishings before being forced out by the fire's growing momentum.

The upper walls of the hotel began to cave in at dusk, and huge flames soared high into the air, creating an orange glow over the business district. By morning, only the empty shell of the hotel was left standing. The ruins of the San Felipe Hotel stood until 1902 when the Albuquerque Elks Lodge purchased the property for $7,500, tore down the walls, and erected the Elks Club and Opera House on the site.

### End of Century Fairs

Cakewalk dancing contests were one of the main attractions at the Eighteenth Annual New Mexico Territorial Fair that opened at the fairgrounds in Old Town on September 27, 1898. "Cakewalks are all the rage in eastern cities now, and whenever a first class cakewalk is advertised, hundreds of people have to be turned away to accommodate the immense crowd that gathers to witness it," the *Albuquerque Citizen* reported.

The 1898 fair, in addition to the cakewalk contests that were held each afternoon on a wooden floor in front of the racetrack grandstand, included horse and bicycle races, baseball games, and a Peace Jubilee celebrating the close of the Spanish-American War.

The *Citizen* urged visitors arriving by train to spend the entire week in Albuquerque. "Visitors can get good accommodations, room and board, for $1 a day and up, which will make the necessary expenses for one week very reasonable," the newspaper said.

Among visitors to the fair were Mr. and Mrs. A. H. Hilton and their son of San Antonio, New Mexico, who checked into the Hotel Highland. Their young son Conrad didn't own any hotels at the time. Also checking into the Highland was P. F. Garrett of Las Cruces, who had made headlines seventeen years before when he shot and killed Billy the Kid. New Mexico's Rough Riders, who were just returning home from the Cuba campaign, were given free passes to the exposition.

One of the major attractions of the 1898 fair was a series of afternoon baseball games between the Albuquerque Browns and the

Leadville Blues, champions of the Colorado State League. The Browns, founded and managed by W. T. McCreight, a former player for the St. Louis Browns, won all four games and collected $600 in prize money.

The horse races and the bicycle races ran smoothly until closing day of the exposition when Skip Tattersall, riding a horse named Semito, collided with P. E. Lewis, "the crack bicycle rider of Colorado," who was still on the racetrack. The *Citizen* reported that the jockey "turned a complete double somersault" over the fence but escaped with minor injuries.

The Peace Jubilee began with a street parade led by the First Regimental Band and included colorful floats, carriages, and young women riding bicycles. Speakers who praised the service of the Rough Riders in the war included New Mexico governor Miguel A. Otero and lawyers Ralph E. Twitchell of Las Vegas and Neill B. Field of Albuquerque.

Special guests at the ceremonies included two Rough Rider officers, Captain Max Luna of Los Lunas and Captain W. H. H. Llewellyn of Las Cruces. The Gaiety Comedy Four, a male quartet, sang a special tribute to Rough Rider William O. "Buckey" O'Neill of Arizona who lost his life in Cuba during the war.

The 1899 fair was moved away from the Old Town fairgrounds to take the form of a street fair and carnival in Albuquerque's business district. Downtown merchants decorated their stores with banners and bunting and displayed their wares in sidewalk booths. A "Midway Plaisance" for the carnival attractions was established on west Gold Avenue, along with a grandstand. Agricultural products and minerals from over the territory were exhibited in vacant rooms of a building at Railroad Avenue and Fourth Street.

One of the popular attractions on the midway was the famous "hoochie-kooche" dancer, Del Rose, whom the local newspapers said was "known in the swell set of New York as Little Egypt," and who had made a big hit at the Chicago World's Fair. Other midway attractions included vaudeville and minstrel shows, jubilee singers, trapeze artists, and the W. W. Gentry Dog and Pony Show.

Professor Zeno, who entertained crowds by parachuting from a gas-filled balloon, had a little trouble on the September 19 opening day when he got tangled in the balloon ropes and the parachute he was wearing opened as he was leaving the ground. He made a successful "illuminated" ascension that night, the newspapers said.

Tragedy struck on the second day of the fair when Charles Collins, who dived into a large container of water from a sixty-five-foot pole, struck the water in an awkward position and broke his back. He died two days later.

Cavalry maneuvers were performed by Troop H of the U.S. Ninth Cavalry, which rode in from Fort Wingate and camped on a vacant lot on west Gold Avenue. The troop also participated in street parades that included floats and bicyclists.

A Maypole dance proved to be a big hit at the exposition. As the *Albuquerque Citizen* reported: "The dainty appearance made by each of the little misses and the manly bearing of the boys as they went through the figures of the Maypole dance appealed to the eye and the innate love of the beautiful in everyone present." A recreation of the Battle of Manila, staged by a combination of mechanical and electrical effects, was presented each evening in front of the grandstand.

The 1899 fair proved to be a popular and financial success, and within a short time a Denver newspaper referred to the New Mexico Territorial Fair as "the great industrial exposition and festival of the Southwest."

# Chapter Nine

# END OF THE TERRITORIAL PERIOD, 1900-1912

## First Automobiles and Airplane Flights

**An Eventful Decade, 1900–1910**

New Albuquerque's population had reached 6,326 by the year 1900, and Old Town, which was counted separately, had a population of 1,191. The first decade of the twentieth century was to see some major changes in the appearance of the city and the lives of its citizens.

Automobiles were making their first appearances on Albuquerque streets, much to the consternation of city officials and lawmen who found that the horseless carriages were frightening the horses on horse-drawn carriages. Speed limits eventually were imposed, eight miles an hour for autos and ten miles an hour for horse-drawn vehicles.

J. L. Dodson, proprietor of a bicycle shop, was the proud owner of Albuquerque's first automobile, a Locomobile steamer that he picked up in Denver in 1897 in exchange for a debt that was owed to him. He drove it the more than four hundred miles to Albuquerque in about five days, pausing along the way to drive it up Colorado's Pikes Peak. Reaching snow during the mountain climb, Dodson wrapped the tires and rims with heavy ropes for traction. Finding that the brakes would not hold during the descent, he cut down a small pine tree and tied it to the back of the car for drag.

As Dodson continued south, his Locomobile became the first car to cross over Raton Pass on the Colorado–New Mexico border. Because the only available gasoline was shipped by rail, he had short layovers at several towns waiting for a train to arrive with the necessary fuel.

Dodson opened a garage in Albuquerque and sold the city's first automobiles, a few single- and two-cylinder Reos. The Wood Motor Company began selling Chryslers in 1907, and H. L. Galles began selling Cadillacs in 1908. The few automobiles on Albuquerque streets in 1900, in addition to the Locomobile, included a Yale, owned by T. C. Kern, and a secondhand Winton, shipped in by banker M. W. Flournoy. By 1910 there were more than thirty automobiles in the city.

The city took over firefighting duties in 1900, substituting a horse-drawn vehicle for the hand-drawn hose carts that had been used by the volunteer fire companies. The firefighting wagon was drawn by two horses named Frisky and Slim. The city fire department was located at 302 North Second Street, next to the city hall and police station that occupied a residence owned by Perfecto Armijo at the corner of north Second and Tijeras Avenue.

A large fire alarm bell, hanging in a tall, steel derrick in a vacant lot on the northeast corner of Railroad Avenue and First Street, also served as a curfew bell, sounding at eight o'clock each evening as a signal for young people under sixteen to be off the streets unless accompanied by an adult.

Albuquerque had sixteen churches of various denominations and one synagogue by the turn of the century. The Protestant churches included those of the Episcopalian, Presbyterian, Methodist, Lutheran, Baptist, and Congregational faiths.

About fifty Jewish families organized a congregation in 1897 and began construction of a synagogue, Temple Albert, at the northeast corner of south Seventh Street and west Gold Avenue. Named in honor of the late Albuquerque merchant Albert Grunsfeld, who died in 1893, the two-story synagogue with a large dome was dedicated on September 14, 1900, in ceremonies conducted by Rabbi Pizer Jacobs. President of the first congregation was Henry Jaffa, who had served as Albuquerque's first major in 1885.

Albuquerque's small black population organized the African Methodist-Episcopal Church in 1882 with services held at various locations.

Temple Albert, Albuquerque's first synagogue, was erected in 1899 on the northeast corner of west Gold Avenue and south Seventh Street and served the Jewish congregation at that location for sixty years. It was named for Albert Grunsfeld, a pioneer Jewish merchant. Courtesy UNM Center for Southwest Research, the Albuquerque Museum Photoarchive, PA1978.50.741.

It was a gala occasion in Albuquerque on May 11, 1902, when the Alvarado Hotel, said to be the finest railroad hotel in the country, had its grand opening with a dazzling electric light display. Built by the Santa Fe Railway, and operated by the Fred Harvey Company, the Alvarado was a part of a new complex that included an Indian building, a restaurant, railroad depot, and offices, connected by a brick promenade that stretched for two blocks alongside the railroad tracks.

Designed for the railroad by Chicago architect Charles F. Whittlesey, the three-story hotel was built in a California Spanish Mission style with arched arcades, balconies, and projecting parapets and towers. The outside walls were of cement covered with rough stucco. Interior features included carved beams, wood paneling, and huge fireplaces.

Decorating the hotel, which originally consisted of eighty-nine rooms, was Mary J. Colter, an interior decorator who was considered an authority on the culture of the American Southwest. Spanish and Indian motifs prevailed under her direction. Uniformed Harvey Girls served excellent cuisine to railroad passengers and locals alike. The adjoining Indian building housed a museum and curio shop filled with American Indian arts and crafts.

The Alvarado, designed to attract visitors of the wealthier class to Albuquerque, soon became the center of the city's social life and the scene of high society's annual Montezuma Ball. Whittlesey, the hotel's architect, built for himself a private home of logs and stone on a hilltop east of the railroad in 1903 and lived there with his wife and children until 1908. After a succession of ownerships, the home eventually housed the Albuquerque Press Club.

Public transportation in Albuquerque was modernized in 1904 when electric streetcars replaced the horse- and mule-drawn trolley cars that had been operating along Railroad Avenue since 1880. The new streetcar line was owned and operated by the Albuquerque Traction Company, organized in 1903 by William Greer and Henry Jastro, part owners of the Kern County Land Company of Bakersfield, California, which held extensive ranch interests in New Mexico and elsewhere.

Each of the ten green streetcars was served by a motorman and a conductor, and the service was expanded to include a line north on Twelfth Street to the American Lumber Company, and south on Second and Third streets to serve the Santa Fe Railway shops and Barelas. Later, another streetcar line began operating cars east to the University of New Mexico, and south on Edith Street to the city limits. Both lines later were acquired by the City Electric Company, which operated the streetcars until they were replaced by city buses in 1928.

Albuquerque, because of its high and dry climate, became a haven in the early 1900s for those suffering from tuberculosis and other respiratory problems. Several sanatoriums were erected in the sandhills east of the railroad for the increasing numbers of tuberculosis patients, along with small "lungers cabins" with sleeping porches.

The Catholic Sisters of Charity built the St. Joseph Sanatorium in 1902, and the Southwestern Presbyterian Sanatorium was founded in 1908, the forerunners of hospitals that remain in existence today.

Many TB patients who arrived in Albuquerque for the cure found recovery and lived long and productive lives, such as Clinton P.

Anderson, who eventually became a U.S. senator from New Mexico and secretary of agriculture under President Harry Truman.

A glowing description of Albuquerque as it appeared in 1906 was published in the January 1907 issue of *Out West* magazine. The article, entitled "A Bostonian Finds a New Home," consisted of a letter that the writer, identified only as Jim, sent to his wife in Boston, telling her that he had decided to settle in Albuquerque and urging her to come and bring the children.

In the letter, dated November 2, 1906, the Bostonian wrote that he arrived in Albuquerque on the Santa Fe Railway's "Flyer," and he began by describing the depot area: "A very large hotel called the Alvarado adjoins the depot here. These are of the old Moorish architecture, and with their quaint arches, towers and facades, for absolutely the most attractive group of buildings I have seen since I left Boston."

Albuquerque had nearly sixteen churches, he wrote, some of them costing upwards of $20,000, while one even had a $5,000 pipe organ. The public school system was well adapted to its purpose, he continued, with a Central School (at Lead Avenue and Third Street) and four ward school buildings. "The University of New Mexico is located here," he wrote, "and not only has a preparatory department and normal course, but offers a full college education, either classical or scientific. The number of pupils is only about 150, yet the college spirit is admirable. The Albuquerque public library [at Edith and Central] has 3,000 volumes."

The business district of the city was quite metropolitan in appearance, he continued, with wholesale and retail houses carrying extensive and varied stocks. He said he was especially impressed with the cleanliness of Albuquerque streets, the great number of brick and cement sidewalks, the beautifully kept lawns, and the abundance of flowers.

About one thousand men were employed at the Santa Fe Railway shops, and the American Lumber Company, employing about twelve hundred men, operated a large sawmill and a sash and door company. Major Albuquerque employers not mentioned by the Bostonian included the Albuquerque Foundry and Machine Works, the Albuquerque Scouring Mills and the allied Rio Grande Woolen Mills, and the Southwestern Brewery and Ice Company, brewers of Glorieta and other beers.

Traffic on Railroad (now Central) Avenue in downtown Albuquerque at the beginning of the twentieth century consisted mostly of horse-drawn carriages and horse-drawn streetcars. Courtesy the Albuquerque Museum Photoarchive, PA1973.12.4. General collection. Donated by Diane Gerow.

The name of Railroad Avenue had been changed to Central Avenue by 1908. Some promoters thought Railroad Avenue was too tacky a name for the city's main east–west thoroughfare. It took some Albuquerque residents a while to get used to the name change.

Albuquerque became the host city in 1908 for the sixteenth National Irrigation Congress, which drew several thousand delegates and visitors to the city from western states and territories and several foreign countries. The five-day congress was held from September 29 to October 3 to coincide with the opening days of the 1908 New Mexico Territorial Fair, which furnished entertainment for the visitors.

Sessions of the national conclave were held in the new Convention Hall on the northwest corner of Silver Avenue and Fifth Street, built especially for the occasion. The hall later was used as the National Guard Armory. Topics discussed at the general sessions included all aspects of irrigation, land reclamation, and water rights.

The principal speakers included California publisher William Randolph Hearst.

Serving again as Bernalillo County sheriff at the time was sixty-three-year-old Perfecto Armijo, brought out of retirement by New Mexico governor Miguel A. Otero in 1905 to replace Sheriff Thomas S. Hubbell, whom he removed from office for bestowing favors on his political friends. Hubbell had served as sheriff since 1895, and Armijo previously had served as sheriff from 1879 to 1884. Armijo was succeeded in office in 1909 by Jesús M. Romero.

New Albuquerque's population had grown to 11,020 in 1910, not counting about 3,000 tuberculosis patients in the city's eastern outskirts.

### Hanged in a Saloon

José P. Ruiz, convicted of murder in the fatal shooting of a young boy during a drunken spree, was hanged in Old Town on June 1, 1900. Oddly enough, the legal hanging took place in the vacant back room of a saloon.

The fatal shooting had taken place two years before, on May 27, 1898, after Ruiz and a companion had spent the day drinking at local saloons. Highly intoxicated, the two men mounted their horses and began racing up and down Albuquerque streets.

As they passed the home of Felipe O'Bannon on Barelas Road, Ruiz fired his revolver into the front yard of the residence where four young boys were playing, killing seven-year-old Patricio O'Bannon and slightly wounding another. Newspapers at the time identified the wounded boy as seven-year-old Desiderio Aragon, but it actually was six-year-old Arturo García, who sixty years later was still displaying the bullet scar across the back of his neck.

In a 1959 interview, the sixty-seven-year-old García recalled the events of that tragic afternoon. He said he returned to his home at 1418 South Fourth Street that afternoon after hunting for frogs along the river with some other boys. His mother, Mrs. J. A. García y Sánchez, wanted to punish him, but his grandmother, Mrs. Francisco Apodaca, intervened and took him to the O'Bannon home. García's mother and Mrs. O'Bannon were sisters.

"My grandmother went into the O'Bannon home to drink some coffee, and I remained out in the front yard," García recalled. "The other boys in the yard were Patricio O'Bannon, his brother, Andres, and Alex Green, our first cousin. Desiderio Aragon lived across the street, and might have been in the yard, too, but I don't remember him being there."

The boys were arguing over some frogs in the yard when Ruiz and his companion rode by late that afternoon. García said he never saw the two men, and did not hear the gunfire. "I must have been hit by the first bullet," he said. "I didn't see the two men at all, or hear any shots. I remember that I suddenly flopped over like a rabbit, then sat up on the ground. I could smell hair burning. I grabbed the back of my neck and found my hands covered with blood. I ran into the house, scared to death. I didn't have the slightest idea what had happened."

The women in the house ran into the yard, he said, and because of the confusion, it was several moments before it was discovered that Patricio had been shot through the back and was dying. "Ruiz had no excuse at all for shooting at us kids," García said. "We weren't in the street. In fact, there was a fence between us and the street."

García said he was called to testify at the trial of Ruiz, who was convicted of murder and sentenced to be hanged, but he did not attend the execution. Years later, as an adult, García owned and operated the A&B Liquor Store and Bar at the corner of Fourth and Bridge streets, just a few yards from where he was wounded as a child.

For obscure reasons, the hanging of Ruiz took place in a vacant back room of Pat Gleason's Gold Star Saloon, which stood on the south side of Railroad Avenue midway between the stone courthouse and the stone jail in Old Town. About fifty persons witnessed the hanging, all having received invitations from Sheriff Tom Hubbell.

Calm to the end, Ruiz pronounced these last words:

> Gentlemen, beware of drink, it has brought me to this
> scaffold. Fathers of families, train your children to respect
> everyone, and for the love of God keep them away from
> liquor for this is the cause of ruin. Now friends, in these
> my last moments, I ask you for the love of God to pray for
> my soul.

### Presidential Visits

President Theodore Roosevelt received a rousing welcome in Albuquerque on the afternoon of May 5, 1903, when he visited the city for several hours during a western rail tour. He was the first sitting U.S. president to pay a formal visit to Albuquerque, although President Rutherford B. Hayes had passed through town on a special train during the night of October 27, 1880.

A view of the Santa Fe Railway depot in Albuquerque in about 1930, with a train and the Alvarado Hotel visible in the distance. Courtesy the Albuquerque Museum Photoarchive, PA1982.180.211. Ward Hicks collection. Donated by John Airy.

Welcoming President Roosevelt to the city was a crowd of several thousand persons who were gathered at the Santa Fe Railway depot when the westbound train pulled to a stop at 2:50 P.M. Brass bands struck up martial music as Roosevelt stepped from his car to be greeted by local dignitaries including Bernard S. Rodey, New Mexico delegate to Congress.

Roosevelt was led through the crowds to a speaker's platform that had been erected outside the north door of the Alvarado Hotel. Standing guard in front of the stand were Rough Rider veterans who had served under Roosevelt during the Spanish-American War.

As a visual reminder to the chief executive that New Mexico was still a territory pressing for statehood, a special tableaux was staged on a platform next to the speaker's stand. Forty-five girls, representing the forty-five states, stood on the platform, while Miss Helen Butman, representing the territory of New Mexico, stood on the platform steps, pleading for admission.

In a brief talk, Roosevelt predicted that water utilization and irrigation would play a major role in the future of the region, saying:

The national government will aid you, you yourselves will
have done and will do so much, and I have no question that
in the lifetime of those I am now addressing we shall see
practically all the water that now goes to waste at times
stored and utilized and see this whole region blooming as
only the most favored regions of the earth can bloom.

Following his talk, the president was escorted to a line of waiting car-
riages for a tour of the city, led by brass bands and Troop F of the
Fourteenth Cavalry from Fort Wingate. The day had been declared a hol-
iday in Albuquerque, and flags and bunting decorated stores and homes.
"I am surprised to see such a neat and well appearing little city,"
Roosevelt said.

A large arch had been erected over Railroad Avenue at Second Street,
and as the procession passed under it, Miss Mildred Fox and Miss Elsie
Myers, who were stationed atop the arch, dropped flowers down on the
president's carriage. Roosevelt paused at Robinson Park to greet students
from the Albuquerque Indian School. There was a five-minute rest stop
at the home of Mr. and Mrs. Bernard Rodey at 802 West Kent Street,
where he was given a glass of punch and a cigar.

The procession stopped at the Commercial Club at Fourth Street
and Gold Avenue where Roosevelt was greeted by O. N. Marron, the club
president, who presented him with an honorary membership card in the
form of a Navajo saddle blanket. Woven by Elle, a noted weaver of
Ganado, Arizona, the blanket contained the words: "The President.
Honorary Membership Card. Commercial Club. Albuquerque, NM. May
5, 1903. "Why it's a Navajo, a real Navajo!" Roosevelt exclaimed as he
examined the gift.

As the procession moved along Gold Avenue, Roosevelt saw a huge
bearskin hanging from a second-floor window of a hotel. Rising from
his carriage seat, the veteran big game hunter bowed with hat in hand
and said, "I'm very glad to see you, my long sought friend."

Returning to the depot area, Roosevelt asked to be taken on a tour of
the Fred Harvey Indian Building. Here he was introduced to Elle, the
Navajo weaver. He also met and talked with Ray Morley of Datil, New
Mexico, then football coach at Columbia University, and Frederick Winn,
a cowboy artist of Magdalena, New Mexico.

Meeting veterans of his Rough Rider regiment, he called each by
name even though he had not seen them since the war. Roosevelt was

escorted back to his special train, and the crowds cheered as the train pulled out at 5:20 P.M. to resume the president's western tour.

President William Howard Taft received a rather cool reception when he arrived in Albuquerque on October 15, 1909. New Mexicans were losing patience with the federal government in their long and unsuccessful quests for statehood, particularly since Oklahoma had been admitted as a state in 1907.

Arriving by train late in the afternoon, President Taft was escorted to the Alvarado Hotel where he was scheduled to speak at a banquet that evening. Albuquerque police arrested one man who was headed for the hotel with a butcher knife, threatening to kill the president.

New Mexico territorial governor George Curry presided at the banquet and introduced a series of invited speakers, representing both the Republican and Democratic parties, who were asked to gently remind the president that New Mexico was ready for statehood. Not so gentle in his remarks was New Mexico rancher Albert Bacon Fall, who accused the president and the Republican Party of foot-dragging in New Mexico's campaign for statehood.

Taft, visibly shaken, jumped to his feet and defended his efforts on behalf of the territory and said that he was a staunch supporter of statehood for New Mexico. The *Albuquerque Tribune-Citizen* summed up the president's speech the next day with these words: "If the people of New Mexico are good, and if they do as President Taft tells them to do, and if they continue to hope, they will have the consolation that President Taft is using his influence to get statehood for them."

Taft, a man of large physical proportions, was best remembered in Albuquerque, however, for getting stuck in a narrow Alvarado Hotel bathtub.

True to his word, President Taft signed a proclamation on January 5, 1912, admitting New Mexico as the forty-seventh state of the union. Arizona was soon to follow.

### Last Territorial Fairs

Balloon ascensions gradually gave way to automobile races and airplane flights as featured attractions at the New Mexico Territorial Fair during the last decade before statehood. A daily balloon ascension with parachute jump was scheduled to be a featured attraction at the 1900 exposition that opened on September 18. Daily efforts, however, failed to get the balloon properly inflated.

Also failing to perform was the Chihuahua Military Band, said to be the finest band in Mexico. Fair officials waited in vain for days for the band to arrive, and thought it had arrived when a Mexican band arrived at the railroad depot. It proved to be what was considered a poor substitute, a band of boys from the School of Arts in Chihuahua, its repertoire consisting solely of a few operatic selections.

The 1900 fair consisted mostly of a street carnival in Albuquerque's downtown business district. The carnival included the usual vaudeville shows and acrobatic acts, along with a street parade and a fireworks display. Children of some of Albuquerque's most prominent citizens paired off to compete in cakewalk dancing, with the first prize going to Helen Hillyer and Willie Wroth. The other young couples were Pearce Rodey and Eleanor Whiting, Lillian Hesselden and Wallace Hesselden Jr., Tony Luna and Grace Borradaile, Paul Yewell and Hilda Grunsfeld, Marie Vorhees and Joe Walton, Reina Grunsfeld and Lizzie Taylor, and Madeline and Catherine Grimmer.

Just before the opening of the 1901 fair on October 15, the *Albuquerque Daily Citizen* published this brief item: "The approach of the Territorial Fair has brought together in the city quite a number of undesirable people, but City Marshal [Tom] McMillin has their records and has instructed his force to keep a watch on them."

Before the fair was over, the *Citizen* published another article reading:

> Pickpockets are in the city by the wholesale, while
> healthy looking beggars are here by the hundreds. Every
> visitor bilked by these miserable cattle is authorized to
> use their canes, clubs or butt ends of their pistols on
> their heads. Marshal McMillin is a very busy man these
> days, and cannot give personal attention to every com-
> plaint made.

Another thing that bothered the city marshal at the 1901 exposition was that it was scheduled so closely to the big street carnival at which celebrants were invited to wear masks, and he didn't like the prospect of a lot of people wandering around the streets at night wearing masks. He finally let the masquerade proceed on condition that the mask-wearers remained inside a roped-off area of the carnival.

A large San Juan County agricultural exhibit was brought to the fairgrounds from Farmington, New Mexico, in sixteen heavily laden wagons drawn by fifty horses. The caravan was joined at Pueblo Bonito in Chaco Canyon by sixteen more wagons of the Hyde Exploring Expedition, led by Richard Wetherill, and more than fifty Navajo Indians. The Navajos performed dances each evening around campfires in the downtown business district.

Serving as judges at rodeo events on the fairground were U.S. marshal Creighton Foraker and Colonel Alex Briersacker, whom the *Citizen* referred to as "two famous cow-ropers of the western plains." The main event was a wild steer roping contest, won by S. M. Craig of Magdalena with a time of one minute, forty-five seconds. Clay McGonegal of Roswell, later to become champion steer roper of the world, placed second with a time of two minutes, ten seconds. He did better the following year, roping and tying his animal in forty-five seconds.

An unscheduled stampede of wild rodeo horses proved to be a highlight of the 1902 fair that opened on October 14. Somebody accidentally opened the gate of a corral where they were being held, and they all stampeded into the outdoor arena where a cavalry troop from Fort Wingate was maneuvering and several other events were in progress. As the *Albuquerque Daily Citizen* reported:

> Wild broncs, shouting and yelling cowboys dashing all over the field, the line of the United States Cavalry, and a mass of fleeing humanity could be seen through the clouds of dust. To increase the perplexity of the frenzied animals, the shouts of several thousand human beings rent the dusty air.
>
> Numerous attempts were made to drive the broncos into the corral, but they would break through the line every time they came near the entrance. The confusion was so great that the attempt to corral the broncos was given up, and the crowd dispersed better satisfied with the performance than if the regular program had been carried out.

Carnival attractions on the downtown midway, meanwhile, included a Ferris wheel, merry-go-round, motion pictures, and the exotic dancer "Little Egypt," whom the *Citizen* said "furnished amusement for the unmarried men."

The first annual Montezuma Ball at the new Alvarado Hall on the evening of October 16 was preceded by a downtown parade featuring a representation of Montezuma, attired in gorgeous garments and a gilded crown, perched high on a replica of a bald eagle. Some recognized him as Sheriff Tom Hubbell. Miss Mabel Hunt, daughter of Mrs. Rose Hunt of Albuquerque, portrayed Queen Tecalco in the parade, riding in a pink and white float surrounded by her court of beautiful young women.

Pearl Ward of Denver, billed as "the champion lady rider of the world," was scheduled to compete in the bronc riding competition at the 1902 fair. She drew the number two horse, a long, lean bay with white feet that required five cowboys with ropes to bring it onto the field, kicking and bucking all the way. The *Albuquerque Citizen* reported that Miss Ward, after witnessing the performance of the outlaw bronc, "acted like a timid schoolgirl and refused to get within 10 feet of it after it had been roped."

That night, while attending an Elks masquerade ball, the champion lady rider was chided by some of the local boys who accused her of "turning yellow" at the rodeo. She became white with rage, the *Citizen* reported, and "the language she used made the black masks turn red."

+≈ ≈+

New Mexico's first automobile race, a timed event, was a feature of the 1903 fair that opened on October 12. Competing in the race were four Albuquerque residents, M. W. Flournoy with a twenty-horsepower machine, T. J. Curran with a ten-horsepower vehicle, R. L. Dodson driving his six-horsepower car, and Dr. John Tascher, whose eight-horsepower machine was driven by H. B. Hotelling. "Each machine ran against time," the *Citizen* reported, "Flournoy going the mile in 2:32, with Curran second and Dodson third. The Tascher machine failed to make the mile."

Horse races also were featured at the 1903 exposition, with the most interest shown in a matched pacing race between Marguerite, owned by Joe Barnett of Albuquerque, and White Beauty, owned by Samuel Gatlin of El Paso. "Marguerite kept up her good record and with apparent ease won the two heats, which were half-miles, in 1:15 and 1:18," the

*Citizen* reported. "White Beauty is from El Paso, and while speedy enough for the Pass City, demonstrated the fact that she is not speedy enough for Albuquerque."

Another feature of the fair was a football game between the University of New Mexico and the Albuquerque Indian School, with UNM winning 11–0.

William Randolph Hearst was a distinguished visitor to the fair, and Navajos from the Farmington area staged what the newspapers called a "Goblin in the Brush" dance in his honor one evening on Railroad Avenue between Second and Third streets in the light of six bonfires. Another fair visitor was Mayor Hayt of Santa Fe, who according to a newspaper account "was bitten a day or two ago by a rattlesnake, which he subsequently discovered to be a tarantula, and finally that it was only a red ant. But the bite was very painful."

The Albuquerque Traction Company acquired the territorial fairgrounds in 1904 when it inaugurated electric streetcar service in Albuquerque, and the grounds became known as Traction Park. The company improved some of the existing buildings, and erected a car barn that remained intact long after the fairs and the streetcars had ceased to exist.

Entertaining visitors at the 1906 fair was a trio consisting of a balloonist known as Professor King, his wife, and their pet monkey. Each afternoon, Professor King and the monkey would ascend in one balloon, while Mrs. King went up in the second one. When the two balloons reached an altitude of about one thousand feet, all three would parachute to the ground at the same time, the monkey involuntarily. The first to reach the ground each day was declared the winner. The *Citizen* said that it was the monkey's debut in the act, it descended head down during the drop, and it "didn't seem to enjoy it."

Another entertainer at the 1906 exposition was "Reckless Russell," a one-legged daredevil who performed each day at the corner of First Street and Railroad Avenue. From the top of a one-hundred-foot platform, he rode a bicycle down a steep slide to about twenty-five feet from the ground, then dove headlong into a six-foot tank of shallow water.

Four young Navajo men, brought to the fair by Paul Arrington of Farmington, raced their ponies around the racetrack each day. The opening day race was disrupted in the home stretch, however, because the Indians were camera shy. As the *Citizen* reported:

A lady with a Kodak caused the trouble. Just as she snapped
the shutter, three of the Indians caught sight of her and
wheeled off the race course, madder than wet hens. The
other Navajo continued on and won the race.

Named secretary of the Fair Association in 1907 was Roy A. Stamm,
member of an Albuquerque wholesale fruit company, who was a balloon enthusiast. With a partner, Joseph Blondin, they experimented in
1907 with a hydrogen-filled balloon. Since the small capacity balloon
would lift neither basket nor ballast when his weight was added to it,
Blondin, standing on the concentrating ring and hanging on to the
shrouds, managed to soar eighteen miles up Albuquerque's North Valley.
He was shot at eight times by terrified residents who had never seen a
balloon before.

At the 1909 fair, Stamm and Blondin tethered a gas-filled balloon to
the ground with a five-hundred-foot rope and offered to lift fair visitors
for a brief bird's-eye view of the city at $1 a head. Stamm said most of the
passengers came down "slightly white around the gills," but none
protested the time spent aloft.

Shortly after the 1909 fair, Stamm and Blondin took their longest balloon flight yet, soaring eastward on October 19 over mountains and
plains to a landing near present-day Moriarty, about sixty miles east of
Albuquerque. They reached an altitude of nearly thirteen thousand feet
above sea level during the nearly two-and-one-half-hour flight. Stamm
imported an airplane for the 1910 fair, but it sat on the ground as a sta-
tionary curiosity because it didn't have the engine power to take off from
Old Town's five-thousand-foot altitude.

<hr />

New Mexico's first airplane flight occurred during the 1911 fair in Old
Town, the exposition no longer called a territorial fair, but the Thirtieth
Annual New Mexico Carnival and First State Fair. Calling it the "State
Fair" was promoted by the *Albuquerque Morning Journal*, although actu-
al statehood for New Mexico was several months in the future.

Piloting the airplane on this historic New Mexico flight was Charles F.
Walsh, who was associated with the Curtiss Aeroplane Company. A former Santa Fe Railway fireman and professional baseball player who
had taken up aviation as a hobby, Walsh arrived in Albuquerque directly from Davenport, Iowa, where he had just completed a number of

Balloonists Roy Stamm and Joseph Blondin lift off their hydrogen balloon from west Central Avenue and Sixth Street in 1909 for a flight that took them over the mountains to a point about sixty miles east of Albuquerque. Courtesy the Albuquerque Museum Photoarchive, PA1980.75.9. Stamm collection. Donated by Bill Stamm.

flying demonstrations. His Curtiss biplane was shipped to Albuquerque by rail and taken to the exposition grounds where it was assembled by two mechanics. It was then placed in a special canvas hangar until ready for use.

The airplane had a thirty-six-foot wingspan and an eight-foot hardwood propeller of the pusher type that was turned at one thousand revolutions per minute by an eight-cylinder gasoline engine. It had bicycle-type wheels, and was guided by a steering wheel similar to those used in automobiles.

"When Walsh ascends into the higher altitudes," the *Albuquerque Evening Herald* reported, "he will be the first aviator who has ever conquered New Mexico air." A crowd estimated at seven thousand persons was on hand at Traction Park at four o'clock on the afternoon of October 11, third day of the 1911 fair, when the first flight took place. Walsh walked to his airplane, which was standing on the baseball diamond, kissed his wife and two children, climbed into the airplane, started the engine, sped across the field, and took off.

Rising gracefully into the air, the craft followed the Rio Grande as far south as the Barelas Bridge, circled east over the Santa Fe Railway tracks, flew west to the exposition grounds, and passed in front of the grandstand where the newspapers said the crowd cheered him ecstatically. Walsh landed his plane on the baseball diamond to the continued cheers of the crowd. Newspapers reported that he had been in the air fifteen minutes, had reached a speed of sixty-two miles an hour, and had reached an altitude of one thousand feet.

During a second flight the same afternoon Walsh circled north, nearly to Alameda, and landed after a thirteen-minute flight. Walsh made two more flights the next afternoon, this time circling over Albuquerque's West Mesa. On the third afternoon he flew over the Albuquerque Indian School, where Reuben Perry, the superintendent, had assembled several hundred students on the grounds so they could see the airplane fly over them.

The airplane flights were so successful that the Fair Association decided to hold Walsh over for a fourth day. This time he demonstrated how airplanes could be used in warfare by dropping small sacks of flour at players on the baseball diamond.

On that same day, October 14, Walsh took to the air with two passengers, Joseph McCanna and Raymond B. Stamm, younger brother of Roy Stamm, for flights over Albuquerque. The newspapers proclaimed that

McCanna and Stamm were "the first native sons of New Mexico to make flights into the air, arising from New Mexico soil."

Walsh, the toast of the 1911 fair, was killed a year later while performing aerial maneuvers at the New Jersey State Fair.

Replacing Walsh at the 1912 New Mexico State Fair was Lincoln Beachey, who was considered one of the foremost aviators in the world at the time. He began entertaining crowds with flights in his Curtiss biplane. Things went well until a race was arranged between the airplane and a motorcycle, both having about the same speeds. As the race got underway, Beachey failed to get enough altitude to clear the barbed wire fence just outside the fairgrounds. He walked away from the crash unhurt, but the plane was a total loss. The motorcycle was declared the winner.

Brought to the fair as a quick replacement was Roy N. Francis, who piloted what was called "the largest aircraft flying today." The *Herald* reported that the airplane was twenty-eight feet long and wide in proportion, and could carry 250 pounds in addition to the weight of the pilot. Accompanying Francis on one of his flights was Roy Stamm, who used a high-speed camera to take the first aerial photographs of Albuquerque.

## Some Pioneer Legacies

Charles Bernard Ruppe, a young pharmacist from New York, arrived in Albuquerque early in 1880, before the arrival of rail passenger service to the town, and founded a drugstore that was to continue operating into the twenty-first century.

According to an early newspaper article, Ruppe was heading for Mexico when he became stranded in Albuquerque. He had traveled west from New York by rail as far as passenger train service extended, then bought a burro, loaded his belongings on it, and walked to Albuquerque. Money that was to be forwarded to him failed to arrive, and he found temporary employment until 1883 when he opened the B. Ruppe Drug Store on the Old Town Plaza. A few years later he moved the store to the northwest corner of Railroad Avenue and Second Street in New Albuquerque.

Described as a short, stocky man of boundless energy, Ruppe was engaged in a wide variety of activities during his long residence in Albuquerque. He served five years as chief of the volunteer fire department, was manager of a baseball team and leader of an orchestra, and served in the New Mexico Territorial Legislature in 1907.

Ruppe rose to the rank of major in the New Mexico Militia, forerunner of the National Guard, served with General John J. Pershing's Punitive Expedition into Mexico in 1916, and served overseas during World War I. His hobbies included studying New Mexico history and archaeology and prospecting for minerals. In spite of all his outside activities, Ruppe managed to operate a popular and profitable drugstore, which he moved to south Second Street in 1924. It became well known for its large stock of herbal remedies.

Ruppe married Carrie Branford of Albuquerque, and they were the parents of five children. When he died in 1937, Ruppe was the oldest practicing pharmacist in New Mexico and the eleventh oldest in the United States. The B. Ruppe Drug Store continued in operation under new ownership after his death, and in 1964 was moved to the 800 block of south Fourth Street where it was to continue in operation for years to come.

The brothers Oren W. and Henry Strong, originally from Clinton, Illinois, arrived in Albuquerque early in 1881 while heading south for El Paso, Texas, in a prairie schooner drawn by six oxen. They decided to remain in Albuquerque when one of the oxen got sick and died, and they soon started a family mortuary business that was to continue into the twenty-first century.

The two brothers had left Illinois several years before with $60,000 and traveled west to Leadville, Colorado, where they invested in the mining business. They operated a mine with success for some time until water broke into the shaft and flooded them out. They went broke trying to reopen the mine, and decided to look for business opportunities in El Paso.

The Strong brothers had $200 between them when they reached New Mexico and camped on some vacant lots a short distance northwest of the new railroad depot. They bought three lots where they were camped for $75 when told that the lots would later become the corner of north Second Street and west Copper Avenue.

They erected a small wooden shack on the property, and lacking paint, Oren wrapped a rag around a stick, dipped it in axle grease, and painted "Strong Brothers" in grease across the front of it. They began selling merchandise from the shack, then bought some old wagon trains, reconditioned them, fattened the horses, and sold them at a profit. They opened a furniture store in a brick building they built on the site.

Oren had had some experience working for a mortuary in Illinois, and the brothers purchased some coffins from C. D. "Doc" Favor, a local gambler and part-time undertaker, and opened a funeral parlor as a sideline to the furniture business.

They remained in business at 201–211 North Second Street for fifty-five years as Strong Brothers General House Furnishers, Undertakers and Embalmers. Harry O. and Frank Strong, sons of Oren Strong, took over the business when they grew to manhood. The furniture line was discontinued in 1929, but the mortuary business remains intact.

In a 1955 interview, Harry Strong said that he was four years old when he arrived in Albuquerque from Illinois in the spring of 1882 with his mother, brother, and two sisters. He said they made the trip in the caboose of a railroad construction train.

Strong said there were fourteen saloons along Railroad Avenue when he was a child in the 1880s and that some of them were the scenes of periodic violence. Gamblers and transients who died with their boots on were often buried in unmarked graves in the sandhills east of the railroad tracks, he said. A rooming house that his father opened on Copper Avenue between Second and Third streets also was the scene of occasional violence, he continued. "I remember when one night four gamblers were playing poker at a table in the front room," he said, "when one of them suddenly jumped up and shot two of the others dead."

There was another time, too, when three gamblers rented beds at the house and tried to get away without paying. He said his father locked up their suitcases in a back room, and the three came back one snowy night to retrieve them. "I was alone in the house," Strong recalled, "when one of the gamblers came in and kept talking to me and keeping me occupied while his two companions tried to break in through a rear window. My father came back and caught them in the act. They started shooting at him, and he shot and killed one of them. The others escaped."

An exciting moment in Harry Strong's boyhood came in 1886 when he was permitted to ride Geronimo's horse, which had been brought to Albuquerque by General Nelson A. Miles following the Apache leader's surrender in Arizona. The small pinto horse was kept at Billy Trimble's livery stables on north Second Street. "I went over to the stables one day and the men there let me get up on Geronimo's horse and ride it around," he recalled. "I guess that was the proudest moment in my young life."

When Harry Strong retired the funeral business was passed on to his son, Oren Strong, and his son-in-law Richard Thorne, who operated it in new quarters east of the railroad tracks as Strong-Thorne Mortuary.

Chester T. French, founder of the French Mortuary, first arrived in Albuquerque on June 11, 1904, with a brother, Jesse, who was suffering from tuberculosis. They spent their first summer living in a small tent at the corner of north Tenth Street and Mountain Road. "People were wondering whether I came here for my health, or to evade the law," Chester French recalled in a 1954 interview. "Those were about the only reasons anybody moved to Albuquerque in those days."

During his first afternoon in Albuquerque, he recalled, he walked to the Rio Grande "to watch the boats passing back and forth." "I walked a mile west of the river before I realized that I had already crossed it," he said. "I was used to those big rivers back in Tennessee, and thought the Rio Grande would rival them."

Born in 1882 near Knoxville, Tennessee, French attended a country school near his home and later worked his way through Maryville College in Tennessee. Before moving to Albuquerque, he worked briefly at a mortuary and taught one year in a country school near his home. While he and his brother were living in the tent in Albuquerque, he secured work at the Albuquerque Lumber Company for 15¢ an hour. When his brother died, he went to New York and attended the Renouard Training School for Embalmers.

French returned to Albuquerque in 1907 and purchased a mortuary business from B. K. Adams that was located at Fifth Street and Central (formerly Railroad) Avenue. In 1908 he married Elizabeth Thomas, a native of Gallipolis, Ohio, who was teaching English at Albuquerque High School. They became the parents of two daughters.

The French Mortuary was located from 1922 to 1935 in the Commercial Club building at Fourth and Gold before moving to a modern location east of the railroad. Robert M. Fitzgerald became a partner in the business in 1941 and it was known for years as French-Fitzgerald Mortuary.

A prominent horticulturalist, French started one of the first large flower gardens in Albuquerque on east Central across from Albuquerque High School. He propagated and placed on the market a large, white morning glory he called "Pearly Gates."

Joe Barnett, a New Yorker of Italian descent, settled in Albuquerque in 1896 and began investing heavily in real estate projects, particularly in the vicinity of Railroad Avenue and Second Street. Many of his investments were in the entertainment business, and at one time he owned the only theaters in Albuquerque.

Barnett's business interests in the early 1900s included two office buildings, a saloon, a billiards parlor, and two theaters. Although he was known for years as a leading entrepreneur, his reputation was that of a quiet, unassuming man whose hobbies included hunting and fishing, horse racing, and an occasional game of billiards.

His first major project was the three-story Barnett Building, completed in 1903 on the southwest corner of Railroad Avenue and Second Street, which was considered one of Albuquerque's most modern office and store buildings at the time. Early ground floor occupants included O'Reilly's Drug Store, the Postal Telegraph Company, and the Levy Brothers' stock brokerage company. Among those occupying professional offices on the upper floors were Dr. L. G. Rice and Dr. J. A. Reidy.

Barnett also owned a smaller and earlier office building at south Second Street and Silver Avenue that housed the Albuquerque Post Office. Barnett's St. Elmo Saloon, on Railroad Avenue between First and Second streets, featured a flashing electric sign that read "Keno Tonight." His Palace Billiards Parlor was located at 118–120 South Second Street.

Barnett's earliest theaters were the Crystal and the Lyric. The Crystal Theater, in the 200 block of south Second Street, was erected by Barnett in about 1900 and was considered Albuquerque's leading theater for years to come. The varied attractions included touring road shows and silent movies.

In a 1952 interview, Barnett said that road show attractions at the Crystal ranged from opera singer Madame Schumann-Heink to comedian W. C. Fields. He said the auditorium sat 960 people, and the balcony another 360. During a home talent show in the early 1920s, enthusiastic patrons in the balcony began stamping their feet, causing the plaster ceiling on the bottom of the balcony to give way and fall upon patrons seated in the auditorium below, injuring scores of them. The theater had long been vacant when it was demolished in 1952.

In about 1910, Barnett bought the White Elephant Saloon on the southeast corner of Central (formerly Railroad) Avenue, which for decades had been Albuquerque's premiere drinking and gambling establishment. In operation since the early 1880s, the White Elephant had passed through a number of owners, including Abe Coon, Santiago Baca, J. K. Basye, Joseph Goldstein, Jacob Weinman, W. E. Talbot, and George K. Neher.

The White Elephant, with its ornate furnishings, catered to gentlemen of the upper class, with respectable women admitted on special occasions. The solid mahogany bar was long enough for fifty men to put their feet on the bar rail at the same time. The glassware was imported from Belgium, the beer glasses cost $12 a dozen, and the cuspidors cost $15 each. Paintings of scantily clad women adorned the walls. The gambling rooms offered roulette, keno, faro, monte, dice, open and draw poker, and other games until the city outlawed gambling in 1907. Later, prohibition ended the saloon's long tenure.

Barnett demolished the White Elephant building and in 1923 began erecting the six-story Sunshine Building on the site. Occupying the ground floor was the Sunshine Theater, which for years was one of Albuquerque's leading motion picture theaters. Professional offices occupied the upper floors.

During the remainder of his long life, Barnett maintained offices at the Sunshine Theater and his residence just down the street at the Alvarado Hotel. He and his wife, the former Lucille Travis, had no children, and his estate was inherited by a nephew. The Sunshine Building and its theater were to become his Albuquerque legacy.

╌╌╌ ╌╌╌

Leaving their marks in Albuquerque for years to come were Italian immigrant families who arrived in the city during the latter part of the nineteenth and early part of the twentieth centuries. Although most of these immigrants knew little or no English when they arrived, they founded family businesses that became a major part of Albuquerque's economy.

Regarded as the father of Albuquerque's Italian community was Italian-born Oreste Bachechi, who arrived in Albuquerque in 1885 at the age of twenty-five and set up a tent saloon near the railroad tracks. From this humble beginning he managed to expand the business into a profitable wholesale liquor dealership.

Bachechi kept in touch with his homeland during his early years in Albuquerque and persuaded many of his compatriots to settle in Albuquerque. He often lent them money for their passage, and helped them find work and a place to live when they arrived.

He also was a charter member of the Colombo Society, which was organized in 1892 to provide assistance to Italian immigrants in need. The society built a three-story headquarters building and social club at 410 North Second Street, known both as Colombo Hall and Columbus Hall, which included a bar, banquet room, dance floor, and card room.

Bachechi entered into a business partnership with Girolamo Giomi to form the Bachechi and Giomi Wholesale Liquor Distributing Company at 109 South First Street. Later, when prohibition ended the liquor business, he formed an amusement company, his interests including the Pastime Theater at 213 West Central Avenue.

Bachechi's lasting legacy, however, was the KiMo Theatre, a lavish motion picture palace which he opened in 1927 on the northeast corner of Central Avenue and Fifth Street. Constructed in an elaborate Pueblo Indian style, it featured Southwestern Indian designs and motifs inside and out.

In a contest to select a name for the Indian-styled theater, the winning entry, "KiMo," was submitted by Pablo Abeita, an Isleta Pueblo leader, and the word or phrase said to mean "king of its kind" in his native Tiwa language. Among names rejected in the contest was "Papago," the name of an Arizona Indian tribe, with its suggested slogan, "Mama go where papa go, let's all go to the Papago."

The KiMo and the Sunshine were Albuquerque's leading first-run movie theaters for years to come.

Italian immigrant Ettore Franchini was nineteen years old and could not speak English when he arrived in Albuquerque on May 4, 1899. He had traveled from Italy to join an aunt, who worked for the wholesale firm of Bachechi and Giomi. Franchini worked as a driver and porter for the firm until 1901 when he found employment as an engine wiper at the Santa Fe Railway shops. When railroad men sent the young immigrant to the tool crib for supplies, they often had to draw him pictures of what they wanted.

Franchini returned to Italy in 1903 long enough to marry eighteen-year-old Primia Bartolini and take her to Albuquerque. He continued his employment at the railroad shops as a boiler washer and machinist until 1910 when he entered a partnership with Arthur O. Bachechi, son of Oreste, in a general merchandise business known as the Bachechi Mercantile Company at 300 North First Street.

When the partnership was dissolved in 1922, Ettore and a younger brother, Ovidio, formed the Franchini Brothers grocery business at the same location. Specializing in imported groceries, fancy liquors, olive oil, and rare spices, Franchini Brothers was listed as Albuquerque's oldest grocery in the 1950s.

Also prominent in the grocery business was Italian immigrant Allesandro Matteucci, who arrived in Albuquerque on November 11, 1899, after service in the Italian Army and three years as a railroad construction worker in Nevada. Matteucci, who was twenty-seven at the time, journeyed to Albuquerque to join an uncle, Frediano Allessandri, owner of the Porto Rico Saloon and Grocery Store in Old Town. "My uncle called his business the Rancho Seco, or sick ranch, because business was so bad," Matteucci recalled in a 1949 interview.

Matteucci said he worked at the Porto Rico for $20 a month until his uncle's death in 1903, at which time he took over management of the business. A year or two later he entered a partnership with Pio Lommori to open the Lommori and Matteucci Grocery and Meat Market on the southeast corner of north Seventh Street and Tijeras Avenue.

Lommori left the partnership in 1907, and Allesandro and a younger brother, Amadeo, continued to operate the business as the Champion Grocery and Meat Market. Allesandro and his wife, the former Maria Stefani, lived upstairs over the grocery.

Amadeo left the Champion Grocery in 1915 to enter a partnership with Michael Palladino to open another grocery, Matteucci and Palladino, at 601 Tijeras Avenue. Allesandro continued to operate the Champion until his retirement in 1938.

Pompilio Matteucci, a brother of Allesandro and Amadeo, was a twenty-three-year-old shoe cobbler when he arrived in Albuquerque in 1904 from Lucca, Italy. He worked at a sawmill for seven or eight months, saving enough money to open a small shoe repair shop at 105 North First Street.

Pompilio soon opened a retail shoe store next door that he called the Paris Shoe Store, explaining in a 1951 interview that he chose this name because he was impressed with the beauty of the French capital on his way to America. As his business prospered, he moved the retail business to new and larger quarters on Central Avenue. The Paris Shoe Store continued in operation as a Matteucci family business for nearly a century, passing from father to son, and becoming one of the largest retail shoe store chains in the Southwest.

The first of four Del Frate brothers to arrive in Albuquerque from Italy were Giuseppe and Luigi, followed later by Guido and Frank. They founded a number of successful business enterprises, including the Savoy Bar and Pool Hall at 813 First North Street, and the Palms Beer Garden and Grocery in Old Town, the latter entering the twenty-first century as the Palms Trading Company, dealers in Indian handicrafts.

Other successful Italian immigrants included Siro Chiordi, whose grocery and bakery interests included the Italian Macaroni Factory on south Second Street, and the brothers Cherubino and Antonio Domenici, operators of the Montezuma wholesale grocery business on north First Street.

D. K. B. Sellers, an Ohio native who settled in Albuquerque in 1902, is remembered as the man who changed the name of Railroad Avenue to Central Avenue. He didn't do it during his 1912–1913 term as mayor, however, but as a prominent real estate promoter a decade before.

Soon after his arrival in Albuquerque, Sellers launched a petition drive to change the name of Railroad Avenue, which he believed was no longer appropriate for a street that originally connected Old Town with the railroad, but now extended far beyond. The change to Central Avenue was approved by the city government in 1904.

Although he was known as Colonel Sellers during his long and flamboyant career, he acknowledged that the title was an honorary one that had been bestowed upon him by a California governor. Late in his life he said that his long career in the west had included work as a cowboy, sheepherder, prospector, miner, grocery and tobacco salesman, telephone manager, newspaper publisher, realtor, banker, fair director, and mayor.

Born in Dayton, Ohio, on August 9, 1861, Sellers headed west at an early age and lived in various Colorado communities, including Trinidad, Leadville, Denver, Durango, and Ouray, helping to plat the latter town. He also spent time in California and Alaska. Before settling in Albuquerque he lived in Farmington, New Mexico, where in 1901 he founded the *Farmington Hustler*, a weekly newspaper.

In a 1950 interview at his Albuquerque home on the eve of his eighty-ninth birthday, Sellers recalled a brief encounter he had in the early 1880s with William B. "Bat" Masterson, famous frontier lawman, at Trinidad, Colorado.

"I was racing down the main street on horseback with another cowboy when Masterson, the city marshal, rushed into the street and tried to stop us by waving his arms," Sellers said. "When I failed to heed his warning, I heard two shots behind me, and bullets passing within a foot of each of my ears." Sellers said he stopped, and Masterson strode up to him.

"Look, son," the lawman said, "when I say stop, I mean stop. You wouldn't have heard my third bullet go by."

Sellers also recalled how a sham battle he arranged for entertainment at the 1903 New Mexico Territorial Fair almost resulted in tragic consequences. The make-believe battle was to be between a U.S. Cavalry troop from Fort Wingate and a group of Navajos from the Farmington and Chaco Canyon areas of northwest New Mexico.

"My plan was for the cavalrymen to march in formation past the racetrack grandstands and be ambushed by the Navajos," Sellers said. "Blank cartridges were distributed to the cavalrymen for their carbines, but it was found that there were no blank cartridges to fit the various sized guns the Navajos brought with them. I solved this problem by taking the side arms from the soldiers, loading them with blanks, and distributing them to the Indians."

Minutes before the make-believe battle was to begin, he continued, he was told by Navajo interpreter José Platero that Pesh-la-ki and some of the other Navajos had substituted something else for the blank cartridges that had been given them. "I walked over to Pesh-la-ki, engaged him in casual conversation, then suddenly jerked his gun from its holster and broke it open," Sellers said. "The blanks had been replaced with live ammunition."

Sellers said he called Albuquerque city marshal Tom McMillin to the scene, and he rounded up Pesh-la-ki and about six other Navajos who had changed their blanks to live ammunition and hauled them off to jail. He said the Navajos admitted that they planned to use the sham battle as a means of killing soldiers in front of a crowd of cheering spectators who thought it was all in fun. "Army authorities in Washington heard of the affair in Albuquerque and issued an order that American troops would never again be permitted to engage in sham battles with Indians," Sellers said.

While his principal occupation in Albuquerque was that of a real estate developer, Sellers was active in many promotional activities, including the staging of "wild west" entertainment at the territorial fairs. During that time he became acquainted with Tom Mix, a young New Mexico cowboy who competed in rodeo events at the annual expositions.

During the 1910 fair, Sellers staged a show in which Mix and other New Mexico cowboys came riding to his rescue after Navajos had captured him and tied him to a tree. Sellers said that a visiting motion picture company filmed the scene, and that the producer was so impressed with Mix's acting and horsemanship that he took him to California and started him on his movie career.

Sellers was an early automobile enthusiast and the owner of Albuquerque's fourth automobile. In 1912 he promoted the first automobile race between Albuquerque and Santa Fe, which he said was won by a car that completed the sixty-four-mile race in nine and one-half hours.

Sellers served as state fair president in 1912–1913, simultaneously with his term as Albuquerque mayor. As mayor he took credit for building a new city hall on north Second Street, paving Central Avenue and installing ornamental lighting along it, and uniforming members of the police and fire departments.

Sellers was challenged for reelection in the 1914 mayoral race by D. H. Boatright, a reformer who had recently moved to Albuquerque from Roswell. Boatright campaigned to close down Albuquerque's downtown red light district, while Sellers, fearing that this would result in a proliferation of unlicensed prostitution, believed that the licensed brothels should be kept intact under city supervision. Boatright won the election by 143 votes, the city outlawed prostitution in 1914, the leading madams left town, and the prostitutes moved to Old Town to continue their profession.

Sellers served as a state senator and continued to be active in real estate development, particularly in the University of New Mexico area, boasting in the 1930s that he had platted and sold nine different subdivisions in Albuquerque, comprising about half of the city at that time.

The Albuquerque pioneer was honored on his eighty-eighth birthday in 1949 at a hotel luncheon attended by about two hundred invited citizens who had lived in Albuquerque at least forty years.

# Chapter Ten

# EARLY STATEHOOD YEARS, 1913-1919

## Elfego Baca, Hooky Tom, and European Royalty

### Triumph and Tragedy

A sudden blare of fire and other steam whistles during the early afternoon of January 6, 1912, served as an announcement to Albuquerque's twelve thousand citizens that New Mexico was a sovereign state of the union at last. Only a few minutes before, President William Howard Taft had signed a proclamation admitting New Mexico as the forty-seventh state of the nation.

The brief ceremonies in the nation's capital came as no surprise as all steps toward statehood had been completed, including the adoption of a constitution and the election of the first state officials. American flags had been flying all day in Albuquerque's downtown business section in anticipation of the event. Late in the day, a group of citizens burned a symbolic coffin labeled "Territory of New Mexico," a reminder that New Mexico's sixty-one years as a U.S. territory had come to an end.

Albuquerque's statehood celebration, however, was dampened by a tragedy that was unfolding on a downtown street. Word soon spread that Alex Knapp, a popular Albuquerque police officer, had been shot and mortally wounded during a struggle with a transient who was said to be "either drunk, doped, or both."

The *Albuquerque Evening Herald* reported that Knapp had been shot in the chest during the struggle by a man who gave his name as Fred J. Watson, of Minneapolis, Minnesota, who had been in Albuquerque two days. The newspaper said that Knapp was attempting to take Watson to jail at three thirty in the afternoon when they began struggling in front of Shinick's blacksmith shop on Copper Avenue between Second and Third streets.

Early in the struggle, Watson drew a .25 Colt automatic revolver from his coat pocket and shot the officer in the chest. The newspaper article continued:

> Immediately following the firing of the shot, Knapp and Watson engaged in a life and death struggle. With his left hand Knapp grabbed Watson's right hand, in which was tightly clasped the bulldog automatic. With his right hand Knapp grasped Watson's throat, attempting with all his strength to crush the life out of the man.
>
> Equally desperate, Watson endeavored with all his power to free his right hand from Knapp's iron clutch and send a second bullet into the policeman's body. It was several moments before bystanders realized the situation. Those who arrived first thought Knapp was endeavoring to beat into submission an unruly drunkard.
>
> Knapp and Watson struggled for more than ten minutes while bystanders took turns in an attempt to wrest the revolver from Watson's hand. Watson seemed to have the strength of five men. There was murder in his face. With all the strength of his mind and body he seemed to be holding out in the hope the policeman would lose his strength and permit him to kill him.
>
> Finally one of the bystanders suggested that some one cut away the pocket of Watson's overcoat, in which he had put his hand with the gun. The suggestion was acted upon and finally a strangle hold was secured on Watson's wrist. By this time Watson was unconscious. The gun was taken from his clenched hand.
>
> After Watson had been choked into submission and the gun taken from him, Policeman Knapp collapsed. He fell over on top of Watson's body in a faint, saying in a low voice:

"I'm done, boys, I'm done. He got me." To nearly all those who watched the struggle, this was the first intimation that Knapp had been shot.

Watson was carried to jail, where it was learned later that his true name was Theodore Goulet. Knapp was taken to St. Joseph Hospital, where doctors said he had been shot through the pericardium, which surrounds the heart, and that there was no hope for his recovery. He died early on the morning of January 15. Goulet was convicted of second degree murder and given a prison sentence of ten years to life.

On January 15, 1912, New Mexico's first elected officials were inaugurated in Santa Fe. Sworn in as the first state governor was William C. McDonald of Lincoln County, a Democrat, who had defeated Republican Holm Bursum of Socorro in the 1911 elections. The first New Mexico state legislature convened in Santa Fe on March 11, 1912. Within four days, four of the legislators were in jail on charges of accepting bribes.

### Elfego Baca

Elfego Baca, who for years was considered Albuquerque's most colorful and controversial lawyer, achieved the reputation early in his life as a man handy with a gun. Three times he was tried and acquitted of murder charges, although his long career in New Mexico also included service as a sheriff, deputy sheriff, and district attorney.

Born in Socorro in 1865, Baca accompanied his parents a year later on a move to Topeka, Kansas, where he spent his formative years in an English-speaking environment. When he returned to Socorro in about 1880, he had some difficulty communicating with his Spanish-speaking relatives there.

In 1881, with the help of a young friend, Baca rescued his father Francisco Baca from the Los Lunas jail, twenty miles south of Albuquerque, by cutting a hole in the roof of his cell. The elder Baca had been jailed for shooting two boisterous cowboys in his role as town marshal of Belen. He was never recaptured.

Baca's principal claim to fame came in the fall of 1884 when at the age of nineteen he single-handedly fought off dozens of Texas cowboys who were attempting to dislodge him from a small and flimsy house in which he had taken refuge. The gun battle, which lasted more than thirty hours, occurred in the small Socorro County village

Elfego Baca, gunfighter and lawyer, among other occupations, was one of Albuquerque's most color- ful characters. He died in Albuquerque in 1945 at the age of eighty. Courtesy the Albuquerque Museum Photoarchive, PA1978.153.869. Brooks col- lection. Donated by Channell Graham.

of Upper San Francisco Plaza, also known as Milligans Plaza, now the town of Reserve.

Baca was working as a store clerk in Socorro when he was told that cowboys working for Texas cattleman John B. Slaughter were intimidat- ing and terrorizing the Spanish-speaking residents of the isolated village about 160 miles west of Socorro. Believing that he should do something about it, he headed west for the village. Although he claimed later that he did so as a "self-appointed" deputy sheriff, there is evidence that he was commissioned a deputy by Socorro County sheriff Pete Simpson.

With the help of some of the villagers, Baca arrested one of the cow- boys, Charlie McCarty, on a charge of disturbing the peace. When some of McCarty's cowboy friends demanded his release, there was a brief exchange of gunfire during which William Young Parham, Slaughter's ranch foreman, died when his wounded horse fell on him.

An estimated eighty cowboys were gathered in the village on October 30, 1884, when McCarty was taken before a justice of the peace and fined $5 on a charge of drunk and disorderly conduct. Baca, feeling threatened by the cowboys, hurried from the scene and sought refuge in a nearby small residence that had the form of a jacal, a flimsy structure with thin walls consisting of upright poles or slabs plastered over inside and out with mud.

Angry cowboys began converging on the small dwelling, and one of them, William B. Hearne, began kicking on the door and exclaiming, "I'll get that little Mexican out of there." Baca fired two shots through the flimsy door, both of them striking and fatally wounding the cowboy.

During the next thirty-three hours, according to some and probably exaggerated accounts, as many as eighty cowboys fired as many as four thousand shots into the dwelling, causing much harm to the house, but none to Baca, who returned their fire through cracks in the wall from a prone position on the dirt floor that was about eighteen inches below ground level. Unhurt, he surrendered to a deputy sheriff and was taken to Socorro to face murder charges.

Baca's trial on an indictment charging him with the fatal shooting of the door-kicking Hearne was moved from Socorro to Albuquerque, and took place May 7–9, 1885, in the adobe Bernalillo County Courthouse in Old Town. The jury acquitted him after a short deliberation, and a Socorro jury later acquitted him in connection with the death of Parham.

While standing trial in Albuquerque, Baca met and proposed to Francisquita Pohmer, sixteen-year-old daughter of Joseph and Dolores Chávez Pohmer, who promised to marry him if he was acquitted of murder charges. Despite the objections of her father, a native of Germany who owned an Old Town meat market, the two were married on August 13, 1885, in the San Felipe de Neri Catholic Church on the plaza. Baca and his bride established a residence in Old Town, and while he served for a while as county jailer, he got into enough scrapes that an Albuquerque newspaper referred to him as "an Old Town ruffian."

In 1886, for instance, he was charged with displaying a deadly weapon in a threatening manner against the person of Mrs. Josefa Werner, and with assaulting police officer E. D. Henry in an attempt to release a friend, Jesús Romero, whom Henry had just arrested. Baca said later that Judge W. C. Heacock sentenced him to the jail of which he was the jailer, giving him the distinction of being both jailer and prisoner in the same lockup.

After several years' residence in Old Town, Baca and his wife moved to Socorro, where between 1893 and 1906 he served successively as county clerk, mayor, schools superintendent, and district attorney.

While serving as county clerk he studied law in a private law office, and he was admitted to the practice of law in 1894.

Baca returned to Albuquerque in 1907 and opened a law practice in the N. T. Armijo Building on the northwest corner of Central Avenue and Second Street. Nominated by the Republican Party for election to the U.S. House of Representatives, Baca lost in the 1911 balloting to Democrat Harvey B. Fergusson of Albuquerque.

Baca, a veteran witness to hangings, was selected in 1913 to supervise all arrangements for what proved to be the last hanging in Bernalillo County. Hanged in Old Town on May 16, 1913, was Demecio Delgadillo, a twenty-eight-year-old native of Chihuahua, Mexico, who had been convicted of murder.

Delgadillo arrived in Albuquerque in 1912, got a job at a local lumber mill, and began dating twenty-six-year-old Soledad Sarracino de Pino. On the morning of September 22 of that year, she was found shot to death at her home on Mountain Road near Fourteenth Street. Police were told that Delgadillo had been seen with her the night before.

Delgadillo was arrested at Los Lunas the following day. He had a .38 caliber revolver in his possession with one cartridge fired. The bullet that killed Sarracino de Pino was a .38. Delgadillo was tried and convicted of murder, and sentenced to be hanged.

Baca supervised the erection and testing of a gallows in the yard of the Bernalillo County jail on the southwest corner of Central Avenue and Rio Grande Boulevard. The early morning hanging took place before a small crowd of about fifty spectators. Delgadillo's last words, spoken in Spanish, were, "I am not guilty. I did not kill that woman."

Once Delgadillo was pronounced dead, Baca announced, "Gentlemen, this is one of the nicest hangings I have ever seen. Everything went off beautifully." Baca's role in the hanging was recorded by William A. Keleher, a reporter for the *Albuquerque Journal* at the time.

While practicing law in Albuquerque, Baca became involved with various leaders of the Mexican Revolution that flared south of the border in 1910. When General Victoriano Huerta seized power in 1913, he hired Baca as his American representative in an effort to gain recognition by the U.S. government.

Baca was hired in 1914 to represent General José Inez Salazar, a Huerta loyalist who crossed into Texas and was arrested there on a charge of violating U.S. neutrality laws. Salazar was taken to a detention camp at Fort Wingate, New Mexico, where he also was indicted on a perjury charge.

Salazar's trial on the perjury indictment was scheduled to be held in Albuquerque on November 30, 1914, and on November 16 he was taken to Albuquerque and placed in the Bernalillo County jail to await trial. His confinement proved to be a short one. At nine thirty on the evening of November 20, two masked men entered the jail, overpowered Deputy Sheriff Carlos Armijo, released Salazar from his cell, and sped off with him in an automobile. Armed posses failed to find any trace of the three.

On January 31, 1915, in what appeared to be an unrelated incident, Elfego Baca shot and killed Celestino Otero of Albuquerque during an altercation on an El Paso street. An El Paso jury found that Baca had shot in self-defense. Newspapers said Otero was a well-educated man in his forties who sold patent medicine under the name don Pedro Abeyta, and who had been charged in Albuquerque with practicing medicine without a license.

On April 10, 1915, a federal grand jury in Santa Fe returned an indictment charging Elfego Baca and five others with conspiring to remove a federal prisoner (Salazar) from the custody of the U.S. marshal. Indicted along with Baca were Carlos Armijo, the deputy sheriff at the jail when Salazar was released; Manuel U. Vigil, the Bernalillo County district attorney; Trinidad C. de Baca, the state game warden; Monica Aranda and Porfirio Saavedra. The indictment also identified the late Celestino Otero as a conspirator.

The indictment charged that Baca initiated the conspiracy, that Deputy Armijo had permitted Otero and Aranda to remove Salazar from the jail, that Salazar was driven off in a car by C. de Baca to Vigil's home at Alameda on the northern outskirts of Albuquerque, and that Salazar remained hidden there until November 28, 1914, when Saavedra guided him on horseback south to the Mexican border.

The conspiracy trial of Baca and his five codefendants opened before a federal jury in Santa Fe on December 15, 1915, with U.S. district judge John C. Pollock presiding. U.S. attorney Summers Burkhart prosecuted the case, and the defense attorneys were A. B. Renehan and O. A. Larrazolo.

The prosecution sought to prove that Baca engineered the jail delivery, and that he later lured Otero to El Paso and killed him when Otero demanded immediate payment of the $1,000 Baca allegedly had offered him for his part in the conspiracy. The government also claimed that

Elfego Baca (left), while representing Mexican general José Inez Salazar (center), was accused of plotting the general's 1914 escape from the Bernalillo County jail. At right is Baca's law secretary, J. B. McGinnis. Author's collection.

Salazar had been hidden in a secret tunnel under the patio of Vigil's home in Alameda.

Defense witnesses testified that they saw Baca and C. de Baca at the Graham Brothers Saloon in downtown Albuquerque when the jail delivery occurred, and Vigil testified that he was trying cases in Gallup, New Mexico, at the time. The defense introduced testimony that investigators could find no trace of a tunnel or other opening beneath the patio of Vigil's home.

Judge Pollock dismissed the conspiracy charges against Saavedra and Armijo for lack of evidence, and the jury acquitted the remaining defendants on December 18. The mystery of the jail delivery was never officially solved.

Baca moved back to Socorro, served as sheriff of Socorro County in 1919 and 1920, and returned to Albuquerque in 1922 to resume his law practice. From 1925 to 1944 he occupied offices and living quarters in a one-story building on the northeast corner of Sixth Street and Gold Avenue, where he also operated a small printing plant for periodicals of a political nature.

Baca printed business cards that identified him both as a lawyer and private detective. One side of the card read: "Elfego Baca, Attorney-at-Law, License to practice in all courts from Justice of the Peace in New Mexico to the United States Supreme Court. Fees moderate." The other side read: "Elfego Baca, Private Detective, Discreet Shadowing Done, Civil and Criminal Investigations, Divorce Investigations Our Specialty."

Baca was a perennial but unsuccessful candidate for a wide variety of political offices on both the Republican and Democratic tickets during the remainder of his long life. He died at his home at 1501 North Third Street on August 27, 1945, at the age of eighty, and was buried in Albuquerque's Sunset Memorial Park. He was survived by his wife, one son, and five daughters.

### John Milne and Hooky Tom

When John Milne became superintendent of the Albuquerque Public Schools in 1911 he didn't realize that he would hold that position for the next forty-five years. During that period, school enrollment grew from about fifteen hundred to nearly forty thousand students. When he retired in 1956, Milne set a national record for length of tenure of a superintendent in a major school system.

Born in Scotland in 1880, Milne arrived in the United States three years later with his parents and was reared on a farm near Eldorado, Illinois. He received his early education there, and later graduated from Milwaukee State Teachers College and taught school for one year in Wisconsin.

Milne moved to Albuquerque in 1906 and found employment with the American Lumber Company. He resumed his teaching career in 1907 at the Third Ward elementary school on south Fourth Street, and in 1908 was appointed principal of Albuquerque High School, a position he held until 1911 when he was named schools superintendent.

Public school education in Albuquerque began in 1891 when citizens approved a $60,000 bond issue that provided for the construction of a two-story elementary school in each of the four wards of the city. These schools were not completed until 1893, and classes were held in temporary locations pending their completion.

John Milne, born in Scotland in 1880, served as superintendent of Albuquerque Public Schools from 1911 to 1956. He posed for this portrait in about 1930. Courtesy the Albuquerque Museum Photoarchive, PA1978.153. Brooks collection. Donated by Channell Graham.

The establishment of a public school system brought an end to the Albuquerque Academy, a tuition-based school that had been operating in Albuquerque and Old Town since 1879. The academy, with grades one through twelve, was operated by Colorado College of Colorado Springs, Colorado, and had an enrollment of 386 students when it closed.

Charles E. Hodgin, last principal of Albuquerque Academy, was named the first superintendent of the Albuquerque Public Schools in 1891. He served until 1897, when he joined the University of New Mexico as head of its Teachers Training Division.

Albuquerque's first public high school classes were held on the third floor of Perkins Hall, a three-story school building that the Albuquerque Academy had erected in 1890 at the northwest corner of east Railroad Avenue and Edith Street. The high school was moved in 1893 to a frame building in the 200 block of south Edith, and remained there until 1900 when it moved to the new Central School building on the northeast corner of south Third Street and Lead Avenue.

Mayo E. Hickey, superintendent of schools from 1898 to 1902, reported to the Board of Education in 1900 that he had administered twelve whippings, most of them for violations of his strict rule against smoking on school properties. He admitted with some embarrassment, however, that two of his victims had been whipped by mistake.

When two young men were seen lighting up cigarettes at the edge of the high school grounds at Third and Lead, some teachers grabbed them and rushed them to Hickey's office where they were both paddled. Only then was it learned that the two were not students, or even Albuquerque residents, but passengers on an Santa Fe Railway train that had paused for a lunch break at the depot a few blocks away. Out for a short walk to stretch their legs, they picked the wrong place to light up.

The public schools had a highly efficient truant officer during the early years of Milne's superintendency. His name was Thomas F. Morrin, but Albuquerque school children knew and respected him as Hooky Tom.

A slender Irish bachelor from New York, Hooky Tom Morrin served as the public schools truant officer from 1914 until his death in 1934. School attendance was remarkably high during those years. Hooky Tom saw to that.

Dressed in a smart khaki uniform with a shiny deputy sheriff's badge on his chest, the little Irishman was a familiar sight in Albuquerque for years as he plodded down the streets on his little brown horse on the trail of those who would play hooky from school. He carried a large billy club and a small leather quirt, but these were just for show, as he had a heart of gold under his stern exterior and avoided any violence.

Hooky Tom, who lived in the Korber Hotel on north Second Street, reported to work each morning at Central School when the schools were in session and was given a list of all the students who were reported absent that day. Armed with the list, he would climb on his horse and begin the task of checking up on every one of them.

He always leaned over to one side of his horse, putting all his weight on one stirrup, and the horse, to balance him, leaned the other way. When he got off his horse, he would toss the reins on the ground, and the animal would wait patiently until he returned.

Perhaps his first stop would be at little Mary's house, where Mary was said to be sick with the measles. But would Hooky Tom take her mother's word for it? Not on your life. Up the stairs he would go to see for himself. A former health department officer, he knew a sick kid when he saw one.

Next stop, little Bobby's house. Perhaps Bobby just overslept, or was feigning a sickness and hoped to duck out for a little fishing. Feel the bottom of the bed covers to make sure Bobby doesn't have his shoes on.

If Bobby is not in bed, get down on your hands and knees and peer underneath. If you don't find him there, check the closets.

When Hooky Tom saw a youngster on the street during school hours, he would stop and ask him his name. Then he would check the name against his list of absentees. If he was listed as absent, Hooky Tom would pull him up behind him on the horse and start off to school with him.

Milne recalled one time when Hooky Tom visited a home where a father was refusing to send his kids to school because he didn't want them vaccinated. Milne said he received a phone call from a neighbor requesting that he "come quickly before somebody is killed." He said he rushed to the home to find Hooky Tom and the father circling in the yard and preparing for battle.

"Hooky Tom was making menacing gestures at the father with his quirt," Milne recalled, "and the father was threatening Hooky with a pitchfork." Milne said the battle was averted, and the father agreed to send his children to school.

Hooky Tom also had the job of taking the annual census of school-age children. He visited almost every home in town each year, and when a child reached school age, he knew it. In 1930, he turned his faithful old horse out to pasture, and began making his rounds in a Ford roadster. He died in 1934 at the age of sixty-seven, and was taken to his home in New York for burial.

Central School at Third and Lead served as the high school from 1900 to 1914 when the new Albuquerque High School was built at the corner of east Central and Broadway avenues. Milne occupied administrative offices at Central School during his long career as superintendent.

Remarkable for his foresightedness, Milne anticipated the city's future growth and bought up vacant parcels of land in uninhabited areas in and around the city, which eventually became sites of new schools. He retired on July 1, 1956, at the age of seventy-six, and died of a heart attack the following September 5 while vacationing with his wife in Santa Monica, California.

## Auto Race to Gallup 1916

A highlight of the Fourth of July celebration in Albuquerque in 1916 was the start of a 170-mile automobile race west to Gallup. The event, sponsored by the Albuquerque Automobile Racing Association, offered a $700 prize for the winner, $300 for second place, and $200 for third place.

Nine drivers entered automobiles of various makes in the race, and they assembled at eight o'clock in the morning at Central Avenue and

Third Street. The entrants were Lloyd M. Cunningham driving a Maxwell, Roy Henry with a Chalmers, Leo Leyden with a Paige, V. L. Embery with a Haynes, Cliff Ulyatt with a Hupmobile, E. G. Nagle with an Overland, L. B. Malette with a Buick, Fred Merez with an Overland, and Zim Gibbon with a Reo.

The road to Gallup consisted of little more than a horse and wagon trail that for the most part paralleled the Santa Fe Railway tracks westward from a point south of Albuquerque. It was to be years before Route 66 followed closely the same path from Albuquerque to Gallup.

The automobiles, starting at three-minute intervals, headed south on Fourth Street, crossed the Barelas Bridge to the west bank of the Rio Grande, and continued south through Atrisco to the railroad tracks. Four of the nine cars that started the race didn't make it to Gallup. Roy Henry and his Chalmers didn't even get much past Albuquerque.

"Henry didn't last long in the race," the *Albuquerque Evening Herald* reported. "In taking a curve at Ranchos de Atrisco his Chalmers turned over and went to smash. Henry and his mechanic escaped serious injury." Three other cars didn't make it beyond Grants, about sixty miles short of the finish line, Malette dropped out at Laguna Pueblo when his Buick had used up all its spare tires, the Overland driven by Merez hit a telephone pole near Grants, and Gibbon and his Reo dropped out of the race at Grants.

Declared winner of the race was the Maxwell, driven by Cunningham, which reached Gallup with a time of six hours, fifty-three minutes, and thirty-one seconds. Recalling the event fifty years later, Cunningham said he took a shortcut at one point along the railroad bed, picked up a railroad spike in a tire of the four-cylinder Maxwell, and drove the last nine miles of the race on the rim.

"They wanted to disqualify me at first for coming into Gallup on the rim," he said. "Then they ruled that it didn't matter if I came in on four flat tires, just as long as I got there." Cunningham said the stripped-down Maxwell he drove was the smallest car in the race. "The Hupmobile should have won," he said. "It was the best car in the lot." The Hupmobile, however, came in fourth, with a time of seven hours and twenty-seven minutes. Placing second was the Paige, driven by Leyden, and placing third was the Haynes, driven by Embery.

Later that year, the 1916 State Fair proved to be the last of a long series of territorial and state fairs that had been held in Old Town since 1881. The demise was said to be due to financial problems, lack of funding by the state legislature, and America's 1917 entry into World War I.

## During World War I

In the summer of 1917, shortly after the United States declared war on Germany, a military training camp was established on University of New Mexico land in Albuquerque's eastern outskirts. Called Camp Funston, the installation was soon training more than thirteen hundred men for possible overseas duty. Male enrollment at the university dropped drastically that year as students rushed to enlist in the armed forces.

Camp Funston included barracks, tents, supply houses, hospital facilities, and horse corrals. Trenches were dug for trench warfare training. Commissioned officers occupied some of the university buildings.

The camp was given over to the Student Army Training Corps for a brief period in 1918 with the departure of more than fifteen hundred members of the New Mexico National Guard, who were called out for active duty. The worldwide influenza epidemic closed the camp and university in October. Due to the wartime shortage of manpower, women took over the operation of Albuquerque's electric streetcars. They were popularly known as "motorettes."

News of the end of the war was published in three "extra" editions of the *Albuquerque Evening Herald* on November 11, 1918. As the newspaper reported:

> When the momentous news of the end of the greatest war of all times flashed over the wire to Albuquerque shortly before one o'clock this morning the city instantly cast aside all other thoughts and thousands turned out at the early hour and began to stage the most hilarious celebration in the history of the state, a shouting commemoration of the downfall of autocracy.

News of the signing of the armistice came as no great surprise to the approximately twenty thousand Albuquerque residents. Everybody knew that the kaiser had abdicated, that revolution was spreading through Germany, and that peace envoys were negotiating the terms. So after the fire alarm started sounding shortly after one o'clock in the morning, everybody knew right away what it meant.

Residents sprang from their beds, dressed hurriedly, and ran out into the streets. The biggest of all Albuquerque celebrations was underway. It was to continue in high gear for twenty-four hours.

Many of the early risers converged on the downtown business section, where they soon had a bonfire roaring in the middle of the intersection of First Street and Central Avenue. The crowds invaded a blacksmith shop and hauled two heavy anvils to the intersection. They put gunpowder on top of one anvil, turned the other anvil upside down on top of it, and then ignited the gunpowder. The explosions tossed the top anvil several feet into the air, and it crashed down with a roar that shook nearby buildings.

The Albuquerque City Commission, which a year before had replaced the aldermen-mayor form of government, met in the morning long enough to declare the day to be a legal holiday. The city printed and circulated pamphlets urging all businesses to close for the day.

The commissioners also asked that all citizens assemble at First and Central at two thirty that afternoon for a "monster" parade to Robinson Park "where a celebration of Peace on Earth will take place." In the excitement of the day, the city officials apparently forgot about an order that had been in effect since October 5 banning public meetings and gatherings due to the influenza epidemic.

By mid-morning the streets were filled with horn-honking, flag-decked automobiles that paraded endlessly through the city. Riding in many of the autos were schoolchildren wearing red, white, and blue paper caps and waving American flags. Adding to the clamor was a fire truck that raced back and forth through the streets with bells clanging. Nestor Montoya, the county clerk, did his part by firing a cannon twenty-five times on the courthouse lawn.

Men employed at the Santa Fe Railway shops paraded through the streets beating on their dinner pails and upon washtubs that housewives along south Second Street threw into their path. Other young men beat on washtubs until the bottoms fell out.

Speakers at the Robinson Park celebration that afternoon included William A. Keleher, the city attorney; Mr. Montoya, the county clerk; Rabbi Moise Bergman; S. J. Briant, state director of the United War Work campaign; Miss R. L. Fish, overseas secretary of the YMCA; and Guido Papini, manager of the Pastime Theater.

The noisy celebration continued until late that night. Everybody in town felt a surge of patriotism, the newspaper reported, except maybe the thief who took advantage of the confusion to jimmy the doors of several dentists' offices and escape with several hundred dollars worth of dental gold.

Albuquerque's mayor-aldermen form of government had been in operation since 1891 when it was replaced in 1917 by a system providing for the election of three city commissioners and the appointment of a city manager. Amendments in 1919 increased the number of city commissioners to five.

The first three city commissioners in 1917 were Charles F. Wade, Walter M. Connell, and J. M. Raynolds. They elected Wade chairman, and appointed Paul G. Redington as the first city manager. Connell and Raynolds were reelected in 1919, and were joined on the commission by J. T. McLaughlin, Thomas Hughes, and E. B. Swope.

Albuquerque greeted European royalty on October 19, 1919, during a brief visit by King Albert and Queen Elizabeth of Belgium. They were on a coast-to-coast rail tour to give thanks to the American people for their help during the war.

A crowd of several thousand persons had gathered at the Santa Fe Railway depot when the eastbound train carrying the royal couple arrived in Albuquerque after a brief stop at Gallup. Welcoming the king and queen was New Mexico governor Octaviano A. Larrazolo.

The principal welcoming ceremonies, however, were held at Isleta Pueblo, and the king and queen were driven south to the pueblo in a motorcade. A special train transported hundreds of Albuquerque citizens to the pueblo, while others traveled south in cars and horse-drawn vehicles over a fourteen-mile road that recently had been graveled by convict labor.

Crowds filled the spacious plaza of the ancient pueblo and overflowed onto rooftops as Isleta and Laguna Indians performed ceremonial dances for the royal pair. Queen Elizabeth photographed some of the dances.

It was reported at the time that King Albert was interested in buying some American railroad equipment, that during his rail journey he sometimes pushed the engineer aside to pilot the train himself, and that in California, to better see the scenery, he even rode atop the baggage car.

# Chapter Eleven

# ALBUQUERQUE, 1920–1950

## The Depression and Wartime Years

**Clyde Tingley**

Few if any individuals exerted such a strong and lasting influence on Albuquerque as Clyde Tingley, a master politician of limited formal education whose political career in New Mexico spanned nearly four decades. His public service life, from 1916 to 1955, included years as chairman of the Albuquerque City Commission, two terms as governor of New Mexico, and chairman of the New Mexico State Fair Commission.

As chairman of the Albuquerque City Commission he referred to himself as "Mayor Tingley," as did many others, although Albuquerque had no official mayor under the city commission form of government. His wife called him "Buster," but nobody else did.

There was never any hint of dishonesty, misconduct, or scandal during Tingley's long and hard-fisted political career, although he was often the subject of criticism for his gruff and ungrammatical language. When a newspaper objected to his continual use of the word *ain't,* Tingley brought thunderous applause at a political rally when he exclaimed in his gravelly voice, "I ain't agonna stop using the word ain't!" This remark got him mentioned in *Time* magazine.

In addition to the many building projects and civic improvements Tingley promoted for Albuquerque, some of them bearing his name, he also came to be remembered for his mispronunciation of and unfamiliarity with many common words, resulting in anecdotes known as

"Tingleyisms." Some are true, some maybe not, but all reflected the backwoods character of the former Ohio farm boy.

While serving as governor, for instance, when a visitor entered his office and asked where his receptionist was, Tingley reportedly answered, "Oh, she's going to get married tomorrow, and she's out getting her torso ready." He meant *trousseau*, of course.

Clyde K. Tingley was born in a rural log cabin in Madison County, Ohio, on January 5, 1881, the son of George and Belle (Hanson) Tingley. He attended public schools at nearby London, the county seat, and at the age of nineteen got a job as a railroad construction worker and locomotive fireman.

As a machinist and toolmaker he worked for the National Cash Register Company in Dayton, Ohio, and at a number of automotive firms in Ohio and Michigan. He was employed as assistant superintendent of the Graham Motor Company in Bowling Green, Ohio, when he met and courted Carrie Wooster, an attractive redhead and member of a wealthy and prominent family there.

When Carrie was diagnosed with tuberculosis, her mother decided to take her to Phoenix, Arizona, for her health. When their train reached Albuquerque in 1910, mother and daughter got off the train, due to the illness of one or the other, and they decided to stay in Albuquerque upon learning that it was a center for tubercular patients.

Clyde followed them to Albuquerque, found employment at the Santa Fe Railway shops, and he and Carrie were married in 1911 (possibly 1912) when her health improved. The couple took up residence in a small health-seekers cottage, and in 1921 moved into a home at 602 South Walter that Carrie furnished with antiques brought from Ohio. In 1929 they moved into a modest home at 1523 East Silver that was to be their residence for the remainder of their lives.

Tingley began his political career in 1916 when he was elected to the city government as a Second Ward alderman, serving one term under Mayor Henry Westerfield. He was among the last of the city aldermen, for a city commission form of government was instituted in 1917. As an alderman, Tingley pushed successfully for city ownership of the privately owned water works at Broadway and Tijeras avenues. Citizens approved a $400,000 bond issue for purchase of the plant, the transfer of ownership occurring late in 1917.

Tingley was working as district maintenance engineer for the New Mexico Highway Department in the early 1920s when he resumed his

Clyde and Carrie Tingley established their first Albuquerque residence in a small health-seekers cottage in the sandhills east of the railroad tracks. They posed at home with their dog for this photo in about 1915. Courtesy the Albuquerque Museum Photoarchive, PA1976.142.4. Higgins-Tingley collection. Donated by Clarence Tingley.

political career and was elected to the Albuquerque City Commission. He served as a commissioner from 1922 to 1935, the last ten years as commission chairman.

Beautifying Albuquerque was one of Tingley's prime objectives during his years in city government. He worked to develop a city parks system, and he bought two thousand young Siberian elm trees that he offered free to property owners who agreed to plant them on their properties. He drove to all parts of the city, noting where street repairs and other improvements were needed.

One of Tingley's major accomplishments was the creation of an artificial lake, where a city dump had existed, near the east bank of the Rio Grande west of Old Town. Called Tingley Beach, and flanked by Tingley

Drive, it served as Albuquerque's first municipal bathing beach. Nearby was another Tingley promotion, Tingley Field, a baseball park that for years served as home for the Albuquerque Dukes, the city's minor league baseball team.

The story is told (with variations) that Tingley listened quietly as other city commissioners discussed the possibility of buying a fleet of gondolas for Tingley Beach. Finally, after asking how much each gondola would cost, and how many were needed, Tingley reportedly said, "Why don't we just buy two of them, and let nature take its course?" Years later, with the advent of public swimming pools, Tingley Beach was stocked with fish and became a popular fishing spot.

Tingley was elected governor of New Mexico late in 1934 on the Democratic ticket and was reelected to a second term in 1936, his two terms as governor extending from 1935 to 1938. During that period, he was credited with securing approximately $100 million in federal funds for public works projects in New Mexico.

Much of Tingley's success in obtaining the federal relief projects for New Mexico during the nation's Depression years came from the close friendship he formed with President Franklin D. Roosevelt, a fellow Democrat. Although worlds apart in education and the social graces, Roosevelt enjoyed Tingley's frequent trips to Washington, and was said to have roared with laughter when Tingley referred to Secretary of the Interior Harold Ickes as "that damned Itches."

Albuquerque's benefits from the Tingley-Roosevelt collaboration included Zimmerman Library and other University of New Mexico buildings, the Albuquerque Little Theatre building, grassy Roosevelt Park, buildings for the renewed New Mexico State Fair, a zoo, an airport terminal, and a Central Avenue underpass at the Santa Fe Railway tracks.

Roosevelt, a polio victim, lent his full support for construction of a million-dollar hospital for young polio victims at Hot Springs, New Mexico, now the town of Truth or Consequences. Completed in 1937, the Carrie Tingley Hospital for crippled children honored Mrs. Tingley for her selfless philanthropy and her compassion for sick and underprivileged children. The Tingleys had no children of their own.

While serving as governor, Tingley often was besieged by job-seekers who would sit for hours in the waiting room outside his Santa Fe office hoping for a chance to visit with him. He alleviated this situation by ordering a maintenance crew to saw two inches off the front legs of the chairs, causing them to slant forward. After slipping and sliding off the chairs, most of the visitors made hasty departures.

When Mrs. Tingley was entertaining some friends at a tea party at the governor's mansion, it was said, Tingley informed her guests that the cream they were pouring into their tea came from a crematory, rather than a creamery.

One of Tingley's first tasks as governor was to appoint a successor to U.S. senator Bronson Cutting, a Santa Fe Republican, who had been killed in an airliner crash in Missouri. He chose a fellow Democrat, U.S. representative Dennis Chávez of Albuquerque, who was to serve honorably as an influential senator from New Mexico until his death in 1962.

During his second term as governor, it was said, Tingley invited Senator Chávez to his office and asked for his support in amending the New Mexico Constitution to permit him to seek a third term as governor. "I don't know, governor," Chávez responded. "Before I could do something like that, I would have to consult with my God and my wife." Tingley, angered by the response, reportedly pounded on his desk and exclaimed, "By God, if I had consulted with my God and my wife, I never would have appointed you to the Senate!"

Unsuccessful in his quest for a third term, Tingley did not leave the governorship gracefully. As his successor, John E. Miles, was being inaugurated, Tingley reportedly locked all the doors and windows of the governor's mansion, put the keys in his pocket, and left for Albuquerque.

It did not take Tingley long to resume his career in city government once he had returned to Albuquerque. Elected to the Albuquerque City Commission in 1939 in the usual nonpartisan balloting, he served as a commissioner until 1955, most of the time as commission chairman.

His career as governor in Santa Fe did not refine his use of the English language. Reading from a speech that had been prepared for him, he told a political rally, "When I became your governor, I found that the Republicans had left New Mexico in a state of chaos," pronouncing *chaos* as "chowse."

Flamboyant in his public life, in contrast to his quiet and unpretentious private life, Tingley enjoyed meeting movie stars and other celebrities in Albuquerque and posing for photographs with them. His photo album included pictures of him with movie stars Mary Pickford, Douglas Fairbanks Jr., Ronald Reagan, and Fred McMurray; aviators Charles Lindbergh and Amelia Earhart; and physicist Albert Einstein.

Carrie Tingley, although noteworthy for her large hats and purple clothing, preferred to stay out of the limelight, and pursued her philanthropic work quietly. She loved motion pictures, and attended all the opening matinee performances of first-run movies at the Sunshine Theater.

When not in his City Hall office, Clyde Tingley often could be seen relaxing in an easy chair in the lobby of the nearby Hilton Hotel, where he was willing to discuss politics and city government with those who approached him.

One afternoon, while lounging in the Hilton lobby, he noticed that a group of bond buyers from out of town who were to submit bids at the City Commission meeting the next day were getting quite chummy, talking, laughing, drinking, and playing poker together. Collusion, Tingley thought to himself.

When the bond bids were opened at the City Commission meeting the next day, Tingley noticed immediately that they were all within a mill or so of one another. "Now you get out of here—all of you—and go back home!" Tingley shouted at the bond buyers. "When you get ready to present bids that have not been worked over, come back and we'll consider them then. That's all." The bond buyers left the meeting in a hurry.

Long regarded as a man who got things done, Tingley began losing his power and influence during his last years as a city commissioner. Much of this was due to Albuquerque's unprecedented growth, the population swelling from about thirty-five thousand in 1940 to nearly one hundred thousand in 1950.

The many newcomers who settled in Albuquerque during the wartime and postwar years felt no loyalty to Tingley, and regarded his style of politics as old-fashioned. They formed a nonpartisan Albuquerque Citizens Committee, and began making inroads in city government.

Tingley resented the newcomers who were taking their place in city government, opposed measures they introduced, and gained the reputation of a disgruntled old man. His long and prominent role in city government came to an end in 1955 when he decided not to seek reelection to the City Commission. Tingley retained his seat as chairman of the New Mexico State Fair Commission, a position he had held since 1948. Commissioners were not elected but served by gubernatorial appointment.

The annual expositions, first held in Old Town from 1881 to 1917, were resumed in 1938 on a 215-acre plot of land on Albuquerque's eastern

Clyde Tingley, shown here at this City Hall desk in about 1940, was often referred to as "mayor," although his official title was chairman of the Albuquerque City Commission. Courtesy the Albuquerque Museum Photoarchive, PA1976.142.44. Higgins-Tingley collection. Donated by Clarence Tingley.

outskirts, miles from the site of the original fairgrounds. Serving as state fair manager from 1938 to 1958 was Leon H. Harms, a former Kansas state legislator and founder of the Marion County Fair in Kansas.

The State Fair Commission announced plans in the spring of 1955 to erect a twelve-thousand-seat indoor rodeo arena on the fairgrounds at a cost of $800,000. The state fair rodeo shows at the time were being held outdoors in front of the racetrack grandstand. Tingley, as commission chairman, predicted that the proposed arena would bring in $30,000 a year for year-round events including stock, sports, and automobile shows.

The State Fair Coliseum, as it was initially known, was formally dedicated on September 28, 1957, opening day of the nine-day 1957 New Mexico State Fair. Entertaining crowds at rodeo shows during the exposition were Roy Rogers, "King of the Cowboys," and his wife Dale Evans.

The State Fair Commission, on November 26, 1958, voted unanimously to name the arena Tingley Coliseum in honor of the man who had contributed greatly to the welfare of New Mexico. "Through his efforts," the commission said, "the State Fair obtained practically all the money needed for State Fair buildings." Illness prevented Tingley from attending the meeting during which the coliseum was named in his honor. In another action, the commissioner dismissed Leon Harms as state fair manager and replaced him with Quenten "Tex" Barron.

Tingley, who had been an Albuquerque resident for nearly fifty years, died in an Albuquerque hospital on December 24, 1960, and his wife Carrie followed him in death about a year later. The "Tingley Era" of Albuquerque's history had come to an end.

A story is told that an Albuquerque visitor, after noting such landmarks as Tingley Beach, Tingley Drive, Tingley Field, and Tingley Coliseum, told Tingley that he was surprised the people of Albuquerque had not canonized him. "By God they tried to," Tingley responded, "but I beat them two to one."

### The Saga of Carl Magee

The following item appeared in an 1887 issue of Arizona's *Tombstone Epitaph*:

> An Albuquerque, New Mexico, editor, who expected a gang of lynchers to come for him about the middle of the night, took himself to the cellar, leaving a pet grizzly bear in his place instead.
>
> The lynchers did not bring any light, but made a plucky attempt to get out the bear and lynch it, but gave it up after three of them had lost an eye apiece, two of them had suffered the loss of thumbs chewed off, and the other six were more or less deprived of skin.
>
> The editor now has a great reputation as a fighter, and the bear did not mind the work one bit.

A doubtful story, but Albuquerque had some colorful and tough newspaper editors who managed to publish the truth as they saw it without the help of pet grizzly bears.

Tom Hughes, editor of the *Albuquerque Daily Citizen*, served sixty days in the Bernalillo County jail in Old Town in 1895 on a contempt of court charge for refusing to divulge the authorship of a front-page article attacking Judge Thomas Smith, chief justice of the New Mexico Supreme Court.

Hughes wrote daily columns from his jail cell, and upon his release, sympathetic Albuquerque citizens escorted him from the jail to a horse-drawn hack in a torchlight procession moving to the music of a brass band.

It was learned later that the article that had sent Hughes to jail was written by Thomas B. Catron, prominent Santa Fe attorney and Republican leader.

Hughes, a Kansas native, had owned the *Albuquerque Journal* in the early 1880s. He sold his interest in the newspaper in 1887, and with W. T. McCreight, began publishing the *Daily Citizen*.

It was not the intention of Carlton Cole "Carl" Magee to enter the newspaper business when he arrived in Albuquerque in 1919. The forty-six-year-old Iowa native, who for seventeen years had enjoyed a successful law practice in Oklahoma City, made the move to a higher and drier climate for the health of his wife Grace, who had a lung ailment.

Once settled in Albuquerque, Magee decided to remain, and believing that the city of fifteen thousand had little need for another lawyer, he used the opportunity to pursue a dream. As he recalled later: "For many years I had the idea in my head that some day after I had made my pile, I would try to run a newspaper that would tell the whole truth about everything as near as I could get the truth. Then I would see what would happen." It did not take him long to see what would happen.

Magee set his sights on the *Albuquerque Morning Journal*, the state's largest newspaper with a circulation of about seven thousand, which had gone through a succession of ownerships since its founding in 1880. He learned that the morning paper had been purchased in 1918 by Senator Albert Bacon Fall and a group of his wealthy Republican friends and supporters for the sole purpose of promoting Fall's reelection to the Senate. Once Fall was reelected, the owners had no further use for the paper.

Magee visited Fall at the senator's ranch at Three Rivers, in Otero County, and negotiated the purchase of the *Journal*. Fall, who had a $25,000 interest in the paper, told Magee he was willing to sell because he was broke, owed back taxes on the ranch, and needed the money for ranch improvements.

Carl Magee, controversial newspaper editor and publisher, founded the *Albuquerque Tribune* after owning the *Albuquerque Journal*. Upon retirement, he invented the parking meter. Courtesy Albuquerque Tribune.

Fall, a Kentucky native, had lived in New Mexico since 1883, and had been a prominent Democrat during New Mexico's territorial period before switching to the Republican party and becoming the leader of the Republican machine that exercised great influence in the state. Magee, a liberal Republican, sat in stunned amazement as Fall lectured him on the inner workings of machine politics in New Mexico.

In 1920 Magee bought the *Journal* at 310 West Gold for $115,000, spent another $20,000 on a new press, and in assuming control of the paper inherited an energetic young reporter, Clinton P. Anderson, who years later was to become a U.S. senator from New Mexico, and secretary of agriculture under President Harry Truman. Immediately, the two began investigating political corruption in New Mexico.

Magee said that he quickly learned that powerful political and business interests dominated New Mexico for selfish purposes and at the expense of impoverished citizens. "I found out, in a little while, that state officials went unchallenged," he recalled later. "They did as they pleased without criticism. Prisoners were cheated and starved of food. State institutions were run negligently. Public money was deposited in the banks, and state officials took the interest and put it in their own pockets."

Magee began his journalistic career by attacking the State Land Office, writing that money intended for the public schools was being diverted instead to Fall's political machine. This brought an angry Fall storming into the newspaper office, shouting, "Lay off the land office, or I'll put you on the rack and break you."

Magee also learned that five previous editors had been given the choice of going to jail, or shutting up and leaving the state, and that all had chosen the latter alternative. But Magee, a tall, rangy man with blue eyes and a square jaw, would not be intimidated, and kept exposing corruption in spite of death threats and physical assaults.

Early in 1921, Fall resigned from the Senate to accept appointment as secretary of the interior under Republican president Warren G. Harding. Magee, who switched his party affiliation to become a Democrat, soon learned that Fall was spending large sums of money to expand and build improvements on his Three Rivers ranch. Where, Magee wondered, did Fall, who said he was broke, get all the money?

Magee's initial investigation into the matter led eventually to what has become known as the notorious Teapot Dome scandal, in which Fall was accused of accepting hefty bribes from oil magnates Harry F. Sinclair and Edward L. Doheny in exchange for private leases on protected U.S. Naval Petroleum Reserves at Teapot Dome in Wyoming and Elk Hills in California.

Although he insisted until his dying day that the nearly half million dollars he received from the two oil producers consisted of loans, rather than bribes, Fall, who resigned his cabinet post in 1923, was convicted in 1929 of accepting a $100,000 bribe from Doheny. He was sentenced to one year in prison, and fined $100,000. In ill health, Fall served nine months of his sentence in the New Mexico penitentiary at Santa Fe, and was never able to pay the fine. He died in El Paso in 1944. Doheny, oddly enough, was found innocent of charges that he bribed Fall.

Magee's ownership of the *Albuquerque Morning Journal*, meanwhile, came to an end in April 1922 when financial institutions, pressured by Fall's political machine, put the squeeze on him by calling his notes and refusing to renew his loans. To avoid bankruptcy, he sold the *Journal* for $200,000 to the First National Bank of Albuquerque, but two months later was back in business by founding a weekly newspaper.

Establishing offices on the second floor of the Chester T. French Building, formerly the Commercial Club, on the southwest corner of Fourth Street and Gold Avenue, Magee began publication of *Magee's Independent* on June 22, 1922. Borrowing a phrase from Dante, the early Italian poet, Magee adopted the slogan, "Give Light, and the People Will Find Their Own Way," printed beneath the sketch of a rising sun.

*Magee's Independent* started life as a weekly paper, and continued so until February 6, 1923, when it was issued briefly as a semiweekly. On March 23, 1923, the name was changed to the *New Mexico State Tribune*, and a few weeks later, it became a daily newspaper.

Magee's attacks on political corruption helped result in Democratic victories in state elections. This drew the ire of powerful, old-guard Republican leaders in San Miguel County, including District Judge David J. Leahy and Secondino Romero of Las Vegas, New Mexico. They began making efforts to silence him.

In June 1923 Magee was ordered to stand trial in Judge Leahy's court in Las Vegas on trumped up charges that he had printed a libelous statement about a New Mexico Supreme Court justice. Even though the justice testified for the defense that he did not believe that he had been libeled, and made no complaint, Judge Leahy instructed the jury to return a guilty verdict, and then sentenced Magee to serve from twelve to eighteen months in the New Mexico penitentiary.

Immediately, New Mexico governor James F. Hinkle, a Democrat, pardoned Magee and set aside his conviction and sentence, calling the proceedings "a blot on the state and a disgrace to the good people thereof."

An angry Judge Leahy then found Magee in contempt of court for disregarding his orders not to write about the trial, and for calling the judge "corrupt" in public print. He ordered Magee to serve a one-year prison sentence and pay a $4,050 fine, but once again Governor Hinkle pardoned him immediately and set aside the sentence and fine.

Magee continued to express his strong opinions in his front-page newspaper columns titled "Turning on the Light," shedding light on many questionable activities that some wanted to keep in the dark. Impressed by Magee's determination and spirit, the Scripps-Howard newspaper chain bought the *New Mexico State Tribune* on September 24, 1923, retained Magee as editor, and adopted his "Give Light" slogan for all Scripps-Howard newspapers, later printing it under a sketch of a lighthouse. In 1925 the newspaper was moved a short distance west to a new plant on the southeast corner of Gold Avenue and Fifth Street.

While visiting Las Vegas on August 21, 1925, Magee was being interviewed by a reporter for the *Las Vegas Optic* in the lobby of the Meadows Hotel when Judge Leahy entered the lobby. Leahy, a Rough Rider veteran of the Spanish-American War, assaulted Magee without warning, knocking him down and kicking him, breaking several of his ribs.

Magee, prone on the floor, drew a .25 caliber revolver from his pocket, which he carried for self-defense, and fired two shots at his assailant, one of them striking Leahy in the arm. Unfortunately, one of the shots struck and killed an innocent bystander, John B. Lassater, a State Highway Department official, who was walking through the lobby. Magee was acquitted of a manslaughter charge, but he was haunted for the rest of his life by the knowledge that he had killed an innocent man.

Magee remained editor of the *New Mexico State Tribune* until the close of 1927, when Scripps-Howard transferred him to the editorship of the *Oklahoma City News*. In 1935, while serving as editor of that newspaper, Magee was instrumental in inventing the parking meter, marketing the new device as president of the Magee-Hale Park-O-Meter Company. He died in Oklahoma City in 1946.

Early in 1933, while the nation was gripped by the Great Depression, the *New Mexico State Tribune*, owned by Scripps-Howard, and the *Albuquerque Journal*, which had been owned since 1926 by Thomas M. Pepperday, entered into a joint operating agreement in order to survive.

Under this agreement, finalized on February 20, 1933, both the daily newspapers, while retaining separate ownerships, shared facilities under a single roof in a building the *Tribune* had occupied since 1925 on the southeast corner of Gold Avenue and Fifth Street. The *Journal* moved there from its former location at 310 West Gold. At the same time, the Albuquerque Publishing Company was formed to operate the mechanical, business, advertising, and circulation departments for both papers.

The *Journal* had been publishing both morning and evening editions, and the *Albuquerque Evening Journal* was merged with the *New Mexico State Tribune* and published as an evening paper under a new name, the *Albuquerque Tribune*. This joint operating agreement, known as the Albuquerque Plan, later was followed by other competing newspapers all over the nation, and continues in Albuquerque into the twenty-first century.

### Astride Route 66

The 1926 creation of U.S. Highway 66 as part of a new federal interstate highway system brought the first dramatic increase in out-of-state automobile traffic in Albuquerque and related roadside tourist facilities. Passing through Albuquerque, first on a north–south and later an east–west alignment, Route 66 played a major part in Albuquerque's growth and economy.

Stretching approximately twenty-four hundred miles from Chicago to Los Angeles, the new highway followed existing and mostly unpaved roads on its course through St. Louis, Missouri; Oklahoma City, Oklahoma; Albuquerque; and Flagstaff, Arizona. The heavily traveled thoroughfare, which eventually became paved all the way, became known unofficially as "America's Main Street" and the "Mother Road."

A desired east–west alignment of the highway across New Mexico was impossible at first because of the lack of suitable roads west from Santa Rosa, New Mexico, to Albuquerque, a distance of more than one hundred miles. As a result, the highway initially detoured north and west to Santa Fe, then south to Albuquerque, entering the city on north Fourth Street. The highway continued south through Albuquerque and Barelas to Los Lunas, then turned northwest to resume an east–west course through Grants and Gallup.

It was not until 1937, with the grading of new roads east of Albuquerque, that Route 66 achieved an east–west alignment across the state, entering Albuquerque through Tijeras Canyon and traversing the city on Central Avenue, the city's main east–west thoroughfare. The new alignment bypassed Santa Fe and Los Lunas.

Tourist courts along north Fourth Street suffered a loss of business as the tourist emphasis shifted to busy Central Avenue, where there was a proliferation of motels, restaurants, souvenir shops, and Indian trading posts designed to attract the Route 66 travelers. Many business owners erected large and brilliant neon signs to attract tourists to their establishments.

Westbound traffic through Albuquerque in the 1930s included carloads of destitute farm families who were fleeing to California from the severe drought that had turned their farmlands in the nation's southern plains into a veritable dust bowl.

Motorists on Route 66, when it crossed through the city on Central Avenue, saw much of what the city had to offer. The route took them by the entrances to the New Mexico State Fairgrounds and the University of New Mexico, through the heart of the downtown business section, and within a block of the historic Old Town Plaza.

The Federal-Aid Highway Act of 1956, which provided for a new system of interstate highways, sounded the death knell for Route 66. That portion of the highway extending from Oklahoma City west to Barstow, California, was replaced by Interstate 40, and the section of the original highway between Santa Fe and Albuquerque was replaced by Interstate 25.

Bypassing Central Avenue, Interstate 40 followed a new path across Albuquerque at varying distances north of the avenue, where tourist-oriented businesses began to fade. Motorists could now speed nonstop across Albuquerque on the Coronado Freeway, as it was called, without seeing the city's varied attractions.

### Mystery of the Missing Tourists

Albuquerque became the focal point of massive searches in 1935 following the disappearance of two middle-aged couples from Illinois who vanished in New Mexico during a leisurely motor trip to California. The missing tourists were Mr. and Mrs. George M. Lorius of East St. Louis and Mr. and Mrs. Albert A. Heberer of Du Quoin. Lorius was a coal dealer, and Heberer owned a barber shop.

The two couples, traveling in a 1927 Nash sedan owned by Lorius, spent the night of May 21, 1935, at a small hotel in Vaughn, about ninety miles southeast of Albuquerque. They apparently arrived in Albuquerque the next day, for a postcard Mrs. Heberer wrote to friends was mailed from Albuquerque on May 22.

The mystery of their whereabouts began to unfold six days later when the Lorius car was found abandoned on a street in Dallas, Texas, far off the path the tourists intended to take. An investigation revealed that the car had been left there by a lone man in his twenties, with dark hair and tattoos on his left arm, who had been posing as George Lorius and using Lorius's Shrine credentials to cash a string of forged checks from El Paso east to Dallas.

Further investigations revealed that the same unidentified man, driving the Lorius car, had veered off the highway six miles south of Socorro, New Mexico, about eighty miles south of Albuquerque, on or about May 23, that the car had been towed back to a Socorro filling station for servicing, and that the car had veered off the highway again forty miles south of Socorro and pushed back onto the highway by a truck. It was also learned that the same young man, appearing very nervous, had checked into a small hotel in El Paso under the name James Sullivan.

Governor Clyde Tingley, stating that the missing tourists would be found regardless of the cost, took personal charge of a massive search effort. Responding to his call for assistance were New Mexico State Police officers from all over the state, a detachment of the New Mexico National Guard, and an airplane from El Paso. Searchers scoured the countryside for one hundred miles and more east, west, and south of Albuquerque without finding any trace of the missing tourists. A number of suspects were questioned and released.

The Lorius car was taken to Albuquerque, where a bloodstained piece of bedclothing was found in the trunk. By checking the mileage on the car from the time it left East St. Louis until it was found abandoned in Dallas, it was determined that there were 232 miles that could not be accounted for on the car's known route.

Albuquerque Police Chief Pat O'Grady, believing that the tourists may have been killed in Albuquerque, ordered his officers to conduct a thorough search of the city, including business and vacant buildings and even a few private homes. No clue was found.

A new and surprising development occurred in Albuquerque on June 29 with the discovery of some charred luggage on vacant East Mesa land north of where the New Mexico State Fairgrounds soon were to be located. The partially burned items included some suitcase frames, a thermos jug, a medicine bottle, and some papers that were identified as having belonged to the Lorius party.

Adding to the mystery, however, was evidence that the items had been left there after a June 19 heavy rainfall that would have disturbed or washed away the ashes, nearly a month after the tourists were last seen.

"Today we have found the baggage," Governor Tingley announced. "Tomorrow we will find the bodies." In spite of renewed and massive searches of the area, however, no trace of the missing tourists was found. Periodic efforts in following years to locate traces of the missing tourists were in vain, and in 1942 Mr. and Mrs. George Lorius and Mr. and Mrs. Albert Heberer were declared legally dead.

Claiming to know the fate of the missing tourists, and asking close friends not to reveal her story until after her death, was Mrs. Josie Morgan Butler, who died in the early 1970s when she was in her late eighties. Her account was not verified by any other source.

Mrs. Butler said she was operating a small hotel on west Gold Avenue in Albuquerque in 1935 when the Lorius party arrived there and met with her friend Milton E. "Doc" Noss, a controversial chiropodist and treasure hunter whom she said she had known in Oklahoma as Milton Starr. Noss told the visitors that he had located an old gold mine and smelter in a cave in the Caballo Mountains, about 150 miles south of Albuquerque, and that the cavern was filled with gold bars and old relics.

When Lorius expressed an interest in buying some gold, she said, Noss agreed to take the tourists to his treasure trove, located on the lower west slopes of the Caballo Mountains directly across the Rio Grande from Hot Springs, New Mexico, now the town of Truth or Consequences.

When the four tourists arrived in Hot Springs, she said, one of the two women, whom she identified only as "the red-headed one," became ill and remained in a tourist court while the others, led by Noss and two unidentified young companions, proceeded across the river to the gold mine.

Once inside the cavern, she continued, a heated argument broke out concerning the gold, and the three visitors were shot to death, by whom she did not say. Their bodies were dumped in a hole in the cavern floor, she said, and Noss and his two companions left after further concealing the secret entrance to the cavern.

The woman who had been left behind in the tourist court was then killed, she said, and the young man who drove the Lorius car to Dallas buried her remains off the highway midway between Las Cruces, New Mexico, and El Paso, Texas. Weeks later, she said, a man picked up some luggage that the tourists had left at the Albuquerque hotel and burned it in an effort to destroy any evidence that it might provide.

Mrs. Butler, who said that she visited the Caballo Mountains cave on at least two occasions, said the contents included two rows of stacked gold bars, a number of human skeletons, and some artifacts including old Spanish coins.

She said that Noss, reluctant to remain around the cave following the murders, removed some of the gold bars and concealed them in other locations, including a shaft in Victorio Peak in the San Andres Mountains within what later became White Sands Missile Range in southern New Mexico. A large scale effort in 1977 to locate gold in Victorio Peak was unsuccessful, as were sporadic efforts to locate a treasure trove in the Caballo Mountains.

Whether or not Mrs. Butler's account of the mystery is reliable, it is a fact that the elusive Noss at one time was sought by authorities for questioning on word that "he knew something" about the missing tourists. He was shot to death in 1949 during an argument with another man over some gold bars that he allegedly possessed.

### Entering the Air Age

Albuquerque's first airport, a privately owned venture, began taking shape in 1928, the year that city buses replaced electric streetcars on Albuquerque streets. Since 1923, occasional pilots had been using a simple landing strip at the east edge of the University of New Mexico campus.

It was Charles Lindbergh's solo flight across the Atlantic in 1927 that inspired Frank G. Speakman of Albuquerque, a Santa Fe Railway employee, to become interested in flying and Albuquerque's future in aviation. He decided to go into the airport business, and took in as his partner William L. Franklin, also a railway employee.

Early in 1928, the two partners leased 140 acres of flatland for the project on Albuquerque's East Mesa, about six miles east of the downtown business section, near the western foot of the Manzano Mountains. Finding that the used tractor and grader they had bought was inadequate for runway construction work, they persuaded Clyde Tingley, then chairman of the Albuquerque City Commission, to lend them city road equipment for night work.

After two runways were completed, Speakman graded an extension of Ridgecrest Drive, then a wagon road, to provide access to the Albuquerque Airport, as it became known. Later, he opened Wyoming Boulevard south from Central Avenue to a junction with Ridgecrest at the airport.

Visiting and expressing an interest in the new airport was James G. Oxnard, a New York air transportation promoter, who bought Franklin's interest in the venture, established Aircraft Holdings, Inc. to operate it, and helped to provide financing for its expansion. The landing field was expanded to 480 acres, and airport facilities soon included a hangar, administration building, and a restaurant. When telephone service was inaugurated, Albuquerque residents learned that it was considered long distance to call the airport.

Wyoming Airways established a flight training business at the airport early in 1929. Two of the pilots, Clark Carr and William Cutter,

Albuquerque's first airport was opened in 1928 as a private venture by two Santa Fe Railway employees on East Mesa land later occupied by Sandia Base. Courtesy the Albuquerque Museum Photoarchive, PA1968.1.3. Speakman collection. Donated by Clark Speakman.

later established the Cutter-Carr Flying Service and became leaders in Albuquerque's air industry for years to come.

College sports history was made at the airport on October 10, 1929, when the University of New Mexico Lobos football team climbed aboard a Ford trimotor plane for a flight to Pasadena, California, to play Occidental College in the Rose Bowl, becoming the first such team to travel by air to a game. The Lobos lost 26–0.

Two fledgling airlines, Western Air Express (WAE) and Transcontinental Air Transport (TAT) used the airport for intermediate stops until merging in 1930 as Transcontinental and Western Air (TWA) in order to obtain a government airmail contract between New York and Los Angeles. The merger resulted in a move to a newly established airport on Albuquerque's West Mesa, the new location deemed closer to Albuquerque's business district and away from any mountain obstructions.

The East Mesa airport, becoming known as Oxnard Field, remained active during the 1930s, with its flight training school, an air charter service, and as a refueling and maintenance stop for military planes. The airport also attracted fly-in visits by many famous pilots, including Lindbergh and Jimmy Doolittle.

Some vacant land at the southeast corner of Central Avenue and Wyoming Boulevard, near the entrance to the airport, became the scene in the early 1930s of the First American Pageant, an annual but short-lived event that Albuquerque boosters staged late each summer in an effort to compete with the popular Inter-Tribal Indian Ceremonial at Gallup.

The programs included reenactments of events in New Mexico history, Indian ceremonial dances, Spanish fiestas, and rodeo events, staged in front of a large, false-fronted replica of a multistoried Indian pueblo. The pageant, which also included parades, closed after three seasons due to the Great Depression of the 1930s.

Airline passenger service moved back to the East Mesa in 1939 with the completion of the large Albuquerque Municipal Airport, about three miles west of Oxnard Field, with both TWA and Continental Airlines moving across town from the West Mesa. Built with the help of federal aid funds, the new airport boasted modern and sophisticated equipment and long runways needed by heavy aircraft at the near mile-high altitude. Yale Boulevard was extended south to the airport terminal, a Pueblo Revival–style building that included an elegant restaurant and cocktail lounge.

The new airport soon attracted the attention of military officials, and in 1941 the Albuquerque Army Air Base was established on land acquired adjacent to the airport as a training facility for bomber pilots and their crews. It was from this start that Kirtland Air Force Base evolved.

## A Popular Irish Cop

Patrick F. O'Grady, who served as Albuquerque's police chief from 1926 until his death in 1945, was a genial but tough Irish immigrant who did much to preserve law and order during his thirty-seven years with the Albuquerque Police Department. A handsome six-footer, with a thick Irish brogue, O'Grady was known to be handy with his fists, and never found it necessary to draw a gun in dealing with troublesome lawbreakers. Those who knew him said he was one of those Irishmen who were just naturally born to be policemen.

St. Patrick's Day always had a double meaning for Pat O'Grady, for in addition to it being an Irish holiday, it was also his birthday, having been born on St. Patrick's Day in 1875 in Ireland's County Waterford. He had but little schooling in his native land, but learned the facts of life as a young man working as a freight handler on the tough Waterford docks.

In the 1890s he accompanied his parents to the United States, going
first to Chicago to join his brother John, a Chicago police sergeant. Here
he got a job as a special officer in the freight yards of the Chicago and
Northwestern Railroad.

O'Grady moved to Albuquerque in 1906 to seek relief from an
asthma condition and obtained employment as a guard at a lumber
company yard. He joined the Albuquerque Police Department on
April 3, 1908, and was assigned to night patrol duty in the downtown
business district.

Albuquerque had fewer than a dozen police officers at the time. The
force consisted of Tom McMillin, chief; W. C. Kennedy, night captain;
and Alex Knapp, Billy Marquette, Frank Rossi, Charlie Mainz, Tony
Guevarra, José Ignacio Salazar, and George Highbargain.

Serving as night headquarters for the police force was the White
Elephant Saloon, on the southeast corner of Central Avenue and Second
Street, as there were no officers on night duty at the police station. John
Brady, night bartender at the saloon, took calls for police assistance on
the telephone, and summoned officers from their beats by running out-
side and whacking a metal lamp post with a meat cleaver.

O'Grady was promoted to night captain in 1909 and served in that
capacity until 1926, when he was named police chief, succeeding J. R.
Galusha, who resigned after serving as chief since 1916. O'Grady often
boasted that he pounded the night beat for eighteen years without a day
off before becoming police chief.

During his long career in Albuquerque law enforcement, O'Grady
came to know most everybody in town, and was said to have had an
uncanny ability to remember names, faces, and case histories. It was an
easy matter for him to stop and question strangers he saw walking the
streets at night.

Sometimes, when he reported for work in the morning, his officers
would tell him the particulars of a safe-cracking job or other crime that
had occurred during the night. After listening carefully to the details, he
would reach for his hat and say, "There's only one man in town who
could have done that." He usually came back with the offender in tow.
Often, when juvenile offenders were brought to his office, he would give
them a stern lecture, send them home to their parents, and tear up the
complaints against them.

Riding horseback at the head of various downtown parades, Chief
O'Grady brought cheers from bystanders as he paused at intervals and

tipped his hat to them. On St. Patrick's Day observances, he always wore a green tie with his uniform. Albuquerque mourned the loss of a popular and beloved police officer when Pat O'Grady died on June 19, 1945, at the age of seventy.

## Albuquerque During the War

Albuquerque began experiencing unprecedented growth during World War II due in part to a strong military training presence and related national defense facilities. The city's 1940 population had skyrocketed to 97,012 by 1950.

A bombardier school at the Albuquerque Army Air Base adjacent to the Municipal Airport trained thousands of crew members for the heavy B-17 and B-24 bombers and eventually the B-29 Flying Fortress. Practice bombing ranges were established southwest and west of the city.

The expanding air base was officially designated Kirtland Field in 1942 in honor of the late Colonel Roy C. Kirtland, a pioneer army aviator who had served in France in World War I. In addition to the bombardier school, Kirtland Field also established training facilities for aircraft navigators and glider pilots.

The Army Air Corps acquired an additional eleven hundred acres in 1942 adjacent to the east edge of Kirtland Field for the establishment of a training center for aircraft mechanics and air depot personnel, the acreage including the privately owned Oxnard Field. The new facility was referred to unofficially as Sandia Base, although that name did not become official until 1945. Near the end of the war, the base served as an Army Air Forces Convalescent Center for wounded pilots and their crews.

Kirtland Field experienced increased security measures following the 1943 establishment of Los Alamos, the highly secret laboratory community in the mountains northwest of Santa Fe, where scientists of the Manhattan Project were developing the first atomic bomb. The nuclear weapons were designed to be airborne by heavy bombers, and Kirtland possessed the nearest runways capable of handling such heavy aircraft.

A special military police unit was assigned to Kirtland to guard loading facilities for nuclear weapon test shapes, and Los Alamos military personnel and civilian technicians supervised an assembly and storage area for nuclear weapon components and hardware at Oxnard Field.

In spite of all the secrecy surrounding the Manhattan Project, some information about the atomic bomb was forwarded to the Soviet Union through an espionage network that included some military and civilian communist sympathizers at Los Alamos. Among them was David Greenglass, a soldier from New York, who was working as a machinist on the Manhattan Project.

Soon after Greenglass was assigned to Los Alamos in 1944, his wife Ruth moved to Albuquerque and obtained employment with the Office of Price Administration in the Rosenwald Building on the southeast corner of Central Avenue and Fourth Street. She rented an apartment on the second floor of a private home at 209 North High Street, a short distance east of the downtown business district, where her husband often spent weekends with her.

David was a brother of Ethel Rosenberg who, with her husband Julius, was engaged in Soviet espionage work from their apartment in New York. They persuaded him to reveal some information about the top secret work at Los Alamos, furnished him with half of an irregularly cut Jell-O box top, and said that a courier who would contact him in Albuquerque would possess the matching half.

On June 3, 1945, a Sunday afternoon, a stranger identifying himself as "Dave from Pittsburgh" knocked on the door of the Greenglass apartment in Albuquerque, presented the matching half of the box top, and said, "Julius sent me." The visitor later was identified as Harry Gold, a Philadelphia biochemist who was working as a Soviet espionage agent.

Greenglass sat down at the kitchen table and sketched from memory an atomic bomb and wrote several pages on the bomb and how it was to be detonated. In exchange for the information, Gold gave Greenglass $500 in a sealed envelope, and his wife banked it all except for $37.50 that she used to buy a U.S. War Bond.

Gold had arrived in Albuquerque from Santa Fe, where he had received additional information about the atomic bomb project from Klaus Fuchs, a German-born scientist and naturalized British citizen who was working on the Manhattan Project at Los Alamos. Their meeting had taken place on a bridge over the small Santa Fe River.

The Soviet spy ring was exposed in 1950, after the war, and resulted in federal indictments against those involved. All admitted their part in the espionage ring except the Rosenbergs, who were convicted and sentenced to death in New York and died in the electric chair in 1953. Greenglass served ten years of a fifteen-year sentence; Gold served sixteen years of a thirty-year sentence; and Fuchs served nine years of a fourteen-year sentence in England.

D. K. B. Sellers, pioneer Albuquerque real estate developer, civic leader, and former mayor, is shown promoting plans for the Nob Hill shopping center he developed in the 1940s on east Central Avenue. Courtesy the Albuquerque Museum Photoarchive, PA1978.141.282. APL collection. Donated by the Albuquerque/Bernalillo County Public Library System.

Meanwhile, the success of the Manhattan Project was demonstrated at five thirty on the morning of July 16, 1945, when Los Alamos scientists detonated an atomic bomb on desert terrain about one hundred miles south of Albuquerque at a spot known thereafter as Trinity Site. Similar bombs dropped on the Japanese cities of Hiroshima and Nagasaki three weeks later brought about Japan's surrender and the end of World War II.

Returning home to Albuquerque and other New Mexico communities at war's end were New Mexico National Guardsmen of the 200th Coast Artillery who were serving in the Philippines when the Japanese attacked Pearl Harbor and who had survived heavy fighting, the infamous Bataan Death March, and three and one-half years in Japanese prison camps. Only about nine hundred of the original eighteen hundred members of the antiaircraft regiment survived the long ordeals.

Not coming home to Albuquerque was Ernie Pyle, the Pulitzer Prize–winning war correspondent, who was killed by a Japanese sniper's bullet on the Pacific island of Ie Shima on April 18, 1945. Pyle, an Indiana native, was a roving columnist for Scripps-Howard newspapers in 1940 when he and his wife Jerry settled in Albuquerque and built a white frame house at 900 South Girard Boulevard, north of the Municipal Airport. This was to be his home base during his travels around the country, but America's entry into the war sent him first to European war fronts, and later to the Pacific, where he met his death at the age of forty-four. His wife died in Albuquerque seven months later.

The Pyle home was deeded to the City of Albuquerque for memorial purposes, and was opened in 1948 as the Ernie Pyle Library, the first branch library in the Albuquerque public library system. Included in the library are some of Pyle's personal possessions.

Albuquerque's future as a nuclear weapons research and development center was assured when the Atomic Energy Commission (AEC) took over Sandia Base in 1947 and established the Armed Forces Special Weapons Project. The Western Electric Company, as a prime contractor to the AEC, established Sandia Corporation at the base in 1949 and assumed management of Sandia Laboratory.

Providing tactical assistance to the nuclear weapons program was the newly designated Kirtland Air Force Base, formerly Kirtland Field, no longer a U.S. Army air base following the creation of the U.S. Air Force in 1947 as a separate branch of the armed forces. The Air Force Special Weapons Center was established at Kirtland in 1949 for the military conditioning of men and aircraft to handle atomic weapons.

Supersecret Manzano Base was established at the south edge of Sandia Base as the storage depot for nuclear weapons, the weapons concealed in tunnels constructed in foothills of the Manzano Mountains.

Sandia Base was expanded to include new technical buildings and laboratories, housing projects, and a school as employment on the base neared the five thousand mark. About 20 percent of the employees were on the technical staff, and recruiting programs for technicians and scientists brought many new and well-educated citizens to Albuquerque. Albuquerque's eastern outskirts, north of Sandia and Kirtland bases, began absorbing most of the newcomers to the city.

Major housing subdivisions began taking shape near the foothills of the Sandia Mountains.

Albuquerque's first outlying shopping center, Nob Hill, was established in 1947 on east Central Avenue east of the University of New Mexico campus. Covering a square block, it consisted of a series of connected stores flanking three sides of a small parking lot.

Albuquerque's second public high school, Highland High, was opened nearby in 1949 to serve the growing school enrollment in that area of the city. Other major building projects that year on Albuquerque's east side included the Bataan Memorial Methodist Hospital, near the air base, and the nearby Lovelace Clinic, operated by the Lovelace Foundation for Medical Education and Research, headed by Dr. William R. Lovelace and his son, Dr. William R. Lovelace II. Later, America's future astronauts were sent to Lovelace Clinic for a series of exhaustive medical tests performed by aviation medical experts.

# Chapter Twelve

# ALBUQUERQUE, 1950-1970

## 250 Years Old and Still Growing

### Celebrations and Tragedies

Albuquerque's tremendous wartime and postwar growth, ranking it as the fastest growing metropolitan area in the United States during the decade of the 1940s, continued at an accelerated pace during the years to come. Although the population had reached 97,012 by 1950, the city managed to retain much of the small town atmosphere it had known in the past.

Most all of the city's major retail businesses, hotels, restaurants, motion picture theaters, banks, and government offices were concentrated in the downtown business district, most retail stores observing evening hours only one night a week on weekends. Nightclubs featuring live entertainment were rare, as were fast-food outlets.

Central Avenue, both east and west of the downtown business district, was lined with motels, small restaurants, and stores that catered principally to the Route 66 motorists. One-way streets and parking meters were yet to make an appearance.

Women of Isleta Pueblo displayed Indian souvenir crafts on blankets on the brick walk at the Santa Fe Railway depot, selling them to passengers on the Chief, Super Chief, El Capitan, and Grand Canyon Limited passenger trains that paused there each day. Pueblo men, vending inexpensive Indian jewelry, were a familiar sight on downtown streets and in restaurants and hotel lobbies. Visitors to the railway depot often caught

Representing the new and the old, the Santa Fe Railway's Super Chief (foreground), powered by a modern diesel locomotive, and the Chief, hauled by a steam locomotive, stand side by side at the Albuquerque depot in about 1945. Courtesy the Albuquerque Museum Photoarchive, PA1982.181.4. Ward Hicks collection. Donated by John Airy.

glimpses of movie stars and other celebrities who rode the Chief and Super Chief before the airline industry entered the jet age. Most were willing to sign autographs as they left the trains to stretch their legs and visit concession stands.

The city's swelling population prompted the Albuquerque Junior Chamber of Commerce to sponsor monthly Newcomer Get-Acquainted Parties that were well attended at an east side ballroom. The common greeting among Albuquerque's new citizens was not so much "How do you do?" but "Where are you from?"

The Albuquerque City Commission approved name changes for more than six hundred Albuquerque streets, or sections of streets, effective July 1, 1952. Some were major changes, such as changing the name of most of New York Avenue to Lomas Boulevard, but many were minor, such as changing roads to streets, streets to avenues, or avenues to boulevards.

Some street names were merely shortened, such as changing Menaul School Road to Menaul Boulevard, and McKinley Avenue to Kinley Avenue. On Albuquerque's far west side, double-digit numbers were given to streets that had borne the surnames of such famous aviation pioneers as Amelia Earhart, Jimmy Doolittle, Roscoe Turner, and the Wright brothers. Earhart Avenue, for instance, became Eighty-sixth Street.

To better identify street locations, the city was divided into quadrants, consisting of northeast, southeast, northwest, and southwest, with the railroad tracks as the dividing point between east and west, and Central Avenue the dividing point between north and south. As an example, north Fourth Street became Fourth Street NW. Albuquerque residents began referring to the elevated lands east of the railroad as the Northeast and Southeast heights, to the lowlands along the Rio Grande as the North and South valleys, and to the elevated lands west of the river as the West Mesa.

In 1953, according to an *Albuquerque Facts* brochure published by the First National Bank, the city covered fifty-two square miles with 800 miles of streets, 240 miles of which were paved. There were 110 hotels, thirty-seven trailer courts, and four major hotels, the Alvarado, Hilton, Franciscan, and El Fidel.

Albuquerque also had ten indoor motion picture houses and six drive-in theaters, twelve parks and playgrounds, the Albuquerque Little Theatre for theatrical productions, and approximately two hundred professional and amateur artists. The brochure listed four radio stations, KGGM, KOAT, KOB, and KVER, and one television station, KOB-TV

(Channel Four), which had been operating since 1948. Not mentioned but added that year were television stations KGGM-TV (Channel Thirteen) and KOAT-TV (Channel Seven) and radio station KDEF.

There were 108 federal agencies and offices in Albuquerque in 1953 employing ninety-two hundred workers, of which Sandia Corporation employed five thousand and was recruiting specialists and replacements at the rate of about two thousand a year. There were 350 manufacturing firms employing ninety-eight hundred workers, and 300 general and specialized contracting firms employing from five to seven thousand workers.

The University of New Mexico, headed by Tom L. Popejoy as president, had a 1953 enrollment of forty-two hundred students and a graduate school enrollment of seven hundred. The university, featuring Spanish-Pueblo architecture, consisted of fifty permanent buildings on a 440-acre campus and a public twenty-seven-hole golf course. The College of St. Joseph on the Rio Grande, which was in its third year of operation on Albuquerque's West Mesa, had six hundred students enrolled. It was operated by the Poor Sisters of St. Francis Seraph, a Catholic order.

The public city-county schools system, headed by John Milne as superintendent, included two high schools, four junior high schools, and forty-five elementary schools with a total enrollment of thirty thousand students. Parochial schools included St. Mary's, with 600 high school and 940 grade school students, and St. Vincent Academy, with 100 high school and 300 grade school students. No enrollment figures were given for Menaul School, a Presbyterian high school with boarding facilities, and Harwood Girls School, a Methodist institution. Enrolled at the U.S. Indian School in Albuquerque were 650 boys and girls from various Indian reservations.

Albuquerque maintained its role as a leading health center with four general and four specialized hospitals, as well as the Lovelace Clinic. The general hospitals were Bataan Memorial Methodist Hospital, St. Joseph Sanatorium and Hospital, Presbyterian Hospital Center, and the Women's and Children's Hospital. Serving specialized groups were the U.S. Veterans Hospital, the Santa Fe Railway Hospital, the U.S. Indian Hospital, and the Sandia Base Hospital. Still under construction was the County-Indian Hospital.

Albuquerque experienced a major airline disaster when a TWA airliner, carrying thirteen passengers and three crew members, vanished

Tingley Beach, an artificial lake near the east bank of the Rio Grande
west of Old Town, served as Albuquerque's first municipal swimming
facility. It was the city's only public swimming pool when this photo was
taken in about 1945. Courtesy the Albuquerque Museum Photoarchive,
PA1976.142.35. Higgins-Tingley collection. Donated by Clarence Tingley.

shortly after taking off from Municipal Airport on the morning of
February 19, 1955. The airliner was bound for Baltimore, Maryland, with
a stop at Santa Fe, and air and ground searches were inaugurated when
the plane failed to reach Santa Fe. It was not until the next day that scattered wreckage of the missing plane was spotted high on the west slopes
of the Sandia Mountains, northeast of the airport. There were no survivors, and no official explanation as to why the airliner strayed two miles
off course to slam into the mountainside.

Albuquerque celebrated the 250th anniversary of its founding in the
summer of 1956 with twelve days of pageantry, parades, concerts, contests, arts and crafts shows, and fireworks displays. Male citizens had
been asked to grow beards for the occasion, and many who did proudly
showed off their whiskers at beard-judging contests.

The celebration, which began on July 3 and continued through July 14, featured evening performances of Enchantorama, a sixteen-part historical pageant depicting events in the city's long history. Performed outdoors at Zimmerman Stadium on the University of New Mexico campus, the pageant's two-thousand-member cast included Indian, Spanish, and folk dancers. A huge street parade, featuring floats, antique vehicles, marching bands, and horseback riders, moved west on Central Avenue from the university to Fourteenth Street on the morning of July 4. The celebration extended to all parts of the city, with street carnivals and a series of band concerts.

Coming from Spain as a special guest of the city was Beltrán Osorio y Díez de Rivera, the eighteenth Duke of Alburquerque, who maintained the extra *r* in his title that the city had dropped long before. He was accompanied by his wife, the Duchess of Alburquerque. The duke participated in various celebration activities, and presented the city with a large seventeenth-century tapestry, or *repostero*, bearing the coat of arms of his family. It later was displayed on a lobby wall of the new Civic Auditorium.

The Santa Fe Railway sponsored a special celebration at the depot on July 8 during which Fred Gurley, railway president, presented the city with a large steam locomotive that he said had been built only twelve years before but was already obsolete. Accepting the gift on behalf of the city was Maurice Sanchez, City Commission chairman, who said it would be displayed in Coronado Park as the nucleus of a proposed city transportation museum.

Christening ceremonies were held at the depot for two of the railway's new El Capitan Hi-Level passenger trains featuring double-decker cars. One had arrived from Chicago, the other from Los Angeles. Selected to swing heavy champagne bottles against the fronts of the two trains were Mrs. Gurley and Mrs. Sanchez. Instead of champagne, however, one bottle contained water from the Great Lakes, the other water from the Pacific Ocean. Both bottles failed to break after frequent swings at the trains and shattered only when the ribbons broke and they fell to the railroad tracks.

Albuquerque's anniversary celebration was deemed a great success, and once it was over, barbers were kept busy shaving off beards.

Albuquerque's new Civic Auditorium, owned and operated by the City northeast of the downtown district, consisted of an indoor arena topped by a round dome, more suitable for horse and ice shows than for theatrical performances. It proved to be rather short-lived, and eventually was demolished.

Visiting celebrities who performed there often joked about the design of the auditorium. Comedian Bob Hope compared it to a flying saucer, and asked when it was leaving for the moon. Comedy-pianist Victor Borge began his program by asking the audience when the bullfight was going to start, and later, when an office telephone could be heard ringing, he paused in his recital to announce, "The bull can't come."

Opera singer Lily Pons expressed concerns about singing at the auditorium upon learning that it had no sound shell and that there were drapes on the portable stage, which she said deadened sound. "No drapes, or no singing," she warned. A plywood sound shell was borrowed from the Albuquerque Little Theatre and placed behind her, the drapes were removed, and her May 9, 1957, recital took place with no acoustical problems.

Singer Frank Sinatra gave his only Albuquerque performance at the Civic Auditorium on June 1, 1957, but not before his staff rearranged the audience to fill up main floor seats, explaining that "the temperamental crooner might not sing if the crowd appeared to be scattered and main floor seats were empty." Ticket holders in the upper sections were moved to higher priced seats near the stage at no extra charge, and the show went on.

Movie producer Mike Todd spent the afternoon in Albuquerque on Wednesday, March 19, 1958, promoting his new film, *Around the World in 80 Days*, and attending a cocktail party at the Hilton Hotel. It proved to be his last public appearance.

Early the following Saturday morning, Todd and three others were killed in the crash of his private plane, a twin-engine Lockheed 10, in a mountain meadow about twenty miles southwest of Grants, New Mexico. The plane was en route from Burbank, California, to New York, and the pilot had reported moderate ice shortly before the predawn crash.

Todd's remains were taken to an Albuquerque mortuary and prepared for shipment to California. Survivors included his wife, actress Elizabeth Taylor, who had planned to accompany him on the flight but stayed home because of a cold. Also declining an invitation to join the flight was actor Kirk Douglas.

### Freeways and Malls Bring Changes

Census figures for 1960 listed Albuquerque's population at 201,189, and the population of Bernalillo County, which included some of the city's suburbs, at 262,199. Most of the city's population growth occurred in the Northeast Heights, where major housing subdivisions were being developed.

An exodus of retail stores from the downtown district began in the 1960s with the opening of two large shopping malls about five miles to the east. Winrock Center, so-called because it was developed by Winthrop Rockefeller, later a governor of Arkansas, was opened in 1961, and Coronado Center, a few blocks to the north, was opened in 1963. Smaller shopping centers, or strip malls, also were taking shape in eastern parts of the city, as well as hotels, restaurants, and motion picture theaters.

The completion of the interstate highway system through Albuquerque in the 1960s had an adverse effect on many tourist-oriented businesses by taking much of the tourist traffic off city streets. East–west Interstate 40, the Coronado Freeway, replaced Route 66 on Central Avenue, and north–south Interstate 25, the Pan-American Freeway, replaced U.S. 85 on Fourth Street. The cloverleaf junction of the two freeways northeast of the downtown section became known locally as the "Big I," the big interchange.

Department stores departing from downtown included Sears, Roebuck and Company, Montgomery Ward, and Dillard's. Downtown movie theaters were closed down or were used for periodic stage and musical productions, the city taking over the operation of the KiMo Theatre for theatrical productions. Downtown Albuquerque maintained its position as the city's principal government office and financial center with a long succession of new and ever larger city, county, and federal office and courthouse buildings where retail stores had once existed.

New building projects on the University of New Mexico main campus made it necessary to relocate the major athletic facilities there to university land south of the campus. Replacing Zimmerman Stadium in 1960 was a new football stadium, and a new basketball arena known as the Pit, because of its subterranean structure, was erected nearby in 1966.

Heavy traffic at Municipal Airport called for the 1963 construction of a new and much larger terminal building to replace the small, Southwestern-styled terminal building that had served air travelers since 1939. The expanding airport became known as the Albuquerque International Sunport.

Albuquerque winter sports came of age in the early 1960s when two Albuquerque residents, Robert Nordhaus and Ben Abruzzo, established the Sandia Peak Ski Area high on the east slopes of the Sandia Mountains where a ski run known as La Madera previously had existed. They expanded the area with new trails and a seventy-five-hundred-foot-long double chairlift.

Access to the ski area was only by a winding road on the east slope of the mountain until 1966 when the Sandia Peak Tramway, the longest in North America, began operating on the west side of the mountain. From the base terminal near the city's eastern boundary, two sixty-passenger coaches hauled visitors 3,878 vertical feet to the top of the mountain, where the elevation was 10,378 feet. The tram began operating year-round, hauling visitors on sight-seeing trips to the crest of the mountain, which offered panoramic views of Albuquerque and the Rio Grande Valley.

## Loss of Historic Landmarks

Albuquerque's postwar building boom coincided with the leveling of many of the city's historic landmark buildings. Most were the victims of demolition work rather than natural disasters.

One of Albuquerque's oldest known landmarks, a rambling adobe structure a short distance south of the Old Town Plaza, was demolished by the city in the early 1960s after it was damaged by fire. The building was of unknown origin, but was said to have housed a mercantile store operated by the Armijo family prior to the American occupation of 1846.

Thomas Post operated Post's Exchange Hotel in the building during the 1870s, and a nightclub known as the Sunnyside occupied it in the 1890s. The building also housed a number of other enterprises, the last tenant being a privately owned museum. The site became an Old Town parking lot.

Demolished nearby in 1959 was the large cast stone building with tower that had served as the Bernalillo County Courthouse from 1886 to 1924. The building, facing Central Avenue southeast of the plaza, later housed the San Felipe School, a Catholic elementary school, but was vacant when it was demolished. The site became a playground for the school that operated in new quarters to the north.

Huning Castle, the elaborate residence built by pioneer merchant Franz Huning in 1883, had long been vacant when it was demolished in 1955, the last occupant being a private school. Demolition of the large house on Central Avenue at Fifteenth Street began to the accompaniment of Albuquerque troubadour Eddie Gallegos, who stood in the yard with his guitar singing "Home on the Range." The site remained a vacant lot for years to come.

Many downtown landmarks fell victim to the wrecking ball, chief among them being the California mission–styled Alvarado Hotel near the railroad depot, demolished by the Santa Fe Railway in 1970 despite the protests of many Albuquerque citizens. The hotel had been in continuous operation since 1902. The site became a parking lot.

Demolished in 1971 was the six-story Franciscan Hotel, on the northwest corner of Central Avenue and Sixth Street. The Spanish-Pueblo–styled building had been built in 1925 by public subscription and had been operating ever since.

Downtown Albuquerque's oldest hotel, the two-story Sturges Hotel on the southwest corner of Central Avenue and First Street, was demolished in 1956 while serving as a rooming house. It had started life with the coming of the railroad in 1880 as Hope's European Hotel.

The Commercial Club building, a large, brownstone structure on the southwest corner of Gold Avenue and Fourth Street, was demolished in 1953 to make way for the Simms Building, a high-rise office building. The vanished structure had housed a number of enterprises since its construction in 1892.

The Albuquerque Elks Lodge, on the southwest corner of Gold Avenue and Fifth Street, was torn down in the 1960s to make way for construction of a thirteen-story federal courthouse building. It had started life in 1899 as the Elks Opera House.

Destroyed by fire in 1953 was the three-story Barnett Building on the southwest corner of Central Avenue and Second Street, a multi-purpose business building erected in 1902 by Joseph Barnett. Many other downtown business buildings were lost to posterity, as well as some of the older residences a short distance east and west of the business district.

## Revival of Old Town

Old Albuquerque, scene of the city's founding in 1706, remained a Bernalillo County entity outside the Albuquerque city limits until 1949 when it was annexed by the city that now surrounded it. Streets around the historic plaza were paved for the first time, and curbs and gutters were installed. The area was designated a historic zone, with strict limitations on new construction and sign sizes.

The revival of the Old Town Plaza district as a center of historic interest and a tourist attraction began in the 1940s following decades of decay and neglect. Once the center of Albuquerque's business and social life, the district began to deteriorate following the arrival of the railroad in 1880 and the establishment of a New Albuquerque near the depot.

By 1930, the only legitimate businesses on the plaza were a meat market operated by Florencio Zamora on the south side and a grocery operated by Charles Mann on the northwest side. A wire fence surrounded the plaza, and there was a small bandstand in the center. Except for the San Felipe de Neri Catholic Church on the north side of the plaza, most of the old buildings around the plaza were falling into a dilapidated condition.

A 1937 federal relief program to "beautify" the plaza resulted in the Works Progress Administration (WPA) construction of a three-and-one-half-foot stone wall around the plaza, consisting of large, reddish colored rocks held together by white cement. A small bandstand was erected in the center of the plaza of the same material.

Critics immediately complained that the rock construction gave the plaza the appearance of a fortress, that the bandstand looked like a three-layer cake and was not large enough to accommodate a band, and that the entire project was at odds with the New Mexico architectural style. Spearheading a drive to remove the so-called monstrosity was the newly organized Old Albuquerque Historical Society, headed by Richard Bennett as president. Other members included Irene Fisher, Mrs. Nelda Sewell, and Carmen Espinosa.

The Bernalillo County Commission declined to appropriate funds to demolish the project, but agreed that it could be removed on a volunteer basis. The Springer Transfer Company volunteered to remove the wall and bandstand, and the rocks were sold to contractor Edward Balcomb, who used them to construct a residence in Albuquerque's North Valley. "It took the WPA three months to build the rock wall and bandstand at a cost of about $50,000," Irene Fisher recalled later, "and we managed to have it torn down in three days at no cost."

The historical society financed construction of a new bandstand, or gazebo, in the center of the plaza, by selling "Old Town loafing permits." Albuquerque resident Albert G. Simms donated money to purchase cast iron benches in Chihuahua, Mexico, which were placed on the plaza, and pioneer families purchased lampposts for the plaza.

Nelda Sewell bought and restored Casa de Armijo, the historic Ambrosio Armijo hacienda on the east side of the plaza, and established a small art colony in a rear section of the building. Prominent local artists who took up residence there included Carl von Hassler, Ben Turner, and Clark True.

Old Town property owners and newcomers alike began restoring and renovating buildings around the plaza and converting them to tourist-oriented shops and restaurants. By 1949, Old Town was becoming a tourist attraction with three new restaurants and more than a dozen specialty shops.

The early restaurants were La Placita, operated by Wentworth Brown in the main part of Casa de Armijo; Molino Rojo, operated by Mrs. Alberto Domínguez on the south side of the plaza; and La Cocina, operated by Mr. and Mrs. Richard Bennett in the restored Manuel Springer residence on the southwest corner of the plaza.

A short while later, Brown opened a new restaurant, La Hacienda, in the restored Herman Blueher residence at the northeast corner of the plaza, and operation of La Placita was taken over by Elmer Elliott, who had been operating the Court Café on north Fourth Street in the downtown business district. Members of the Elliott family continued to operate La Placita for years to come.

Following the death of Richard Bennett, the space occupied by La Cocina was leased by Mannie Goodman, who operated his Covered Wagon trading post there for decades to come. The Indian trading post previously had been located in a structure shaped like a covered wagon near the mouth of Tijeras Canyon.

As Old Town gained momentum as a tourist attraction, business ventures, originally clustered about the plaza, expanded along streets leading away from the plaza. In addition to Indian trading posts and restaurants, the growing number of businesses included art galleries, gift and curio shops, antique shops, clothing stores, and ice cream and snack parlors. Most Old Town restaurants specialized in traditional New Mexican foods spiced with generous amounts of red or green chile. Menus in some restaurants warned customers that certain chile-hot dishes were "for fire-eaters only."

As had been the custom since the founding of Albuquerque, fiestas of the San Felipe de Neri Catholic Church continued on the plaza during the late spring of each year with parades, food booths, and Spanish and Mexican entertainment.

Christmas Eve luminaria displays on and about the plaza began attracting thousands of visitors who marveled at the thousands of glowing paper sacks, containing lighted candles, which outlined the streets, sidewalks, and nearby buildings. Smaller luminaria displays soon began appearing in other Albuquerque neighborhoods on Christmas Eve.

The Old Town Plaza was the setting in the summer of 1962 of the first annual New Mexico Arts and Crafts Fair, featuring 140 artists and craftspeople from around the state who displayed their wares in 120 booths set up on and around the plaza. The fair, which attracted an estimated seventy-five thousand visitors, became an annual event in Old Town before being moved to larger quarters at the New Mexico State Fairgrounds.

A relic from the past, a horse-drawn trolley car that had operated between Old Town and the railroad in the 1880s, reappeared on Old Town streets in the 1960s. Drawn by two horses, it transported visitors on sightseeing trips around the plaza. For many years, the old trolley car had been used as a chicken coop and corn storage bin behind a residence on Rio Grande Boulevard. Removed from that location in 1961, it was refurbished and repainted to its original condition and equipped with rubber tires.

Commercial ventures on the fringe of the Old Town Plaza district included the Old Town Shopping Center, a strip mall erected in 1961 on the northwest corner of Central Avenue and Rio Grande Boulevard on part of what had once been the New Mexico Territorial Fairgrounds. A large car barn on the site that had once housed Albuquerque's electric streetcars was demolished in the process.

Controversy erupted in 1966 when plans were revealed to demolish, or completely modernize, the historic San Felipe de Neri Church on the plaza. Opponents of the plan won the battle, and Albuquerque's oldest landmark was saved. The Old Town Plaza district became Albuquerque's most popular year-round tourist attraction and eventually consisted of more than one hundred businesses geared for the tourist trade.

### The Courtroom Wit of Judge Waldo Rogers

United States district judge Waldo H. Rogers, a native of New Mexico, managed to inject some western humor and informality into normally sedate courtroom proceedings during his nearly ten years as a federal judge in Albuquerque. His many barbs were directed at defendants, trial lawyers, and government prosecutors alike.

"I'm placing you on three years' probation," he told a young man who appeared before him for sentencing, "but if you are ever brought into this court again, I will send you so far away that it will take you a year to send your folks a telegram."

When a young man convicted of peddling narcotics appeared before him for sentencing, Judge Rogers asked him if he had anything to say for

Judge Waldo Rogers, whose federal courtroom candor and humor became legendary, is pictured here in an oil portrait by Albuquerque artist Wilson Hurley. Portrait courtesy of the artist.

himself, adding: "Before you start, I want you to know that I have read your long criminal record. I thought I would warn you before you start portraying yourself as the Chamber of Commerce Young Man of the Year."

Leafing through the criminal record of a man who appeared before him for arraignment, the judge looked at him and remarked, "If they brought a bloodhound into the courtroom it would walk right over and smell your feet."

Judge Rogers was appointed to the federal bench in Albuquerque in 1954 by President Dwight Eisenhower and served until his untimely death in 1964 at the age of fifty-five. His death was due to a recurrent lung ailment.

Born in 1908 in Las Vegas, New Mexico, Waldo Rogers was the son and grandson of distinguished New Mexico jurists. His father Albert T. Rogers was a prominent Las Vegas attorney, and his maternal grandfather Henry L. Waldo served as chief justice of the New Mexico Territorial Supreme Court in the 1870s. His great-grandfather, Lawrence L. Waldo, was an early Santa Fe Trail trader who was captured and executed by

New Mexico insurrectionists near Las Vegas in 1847 during the short-lived revolt against American rule.

Waldo Rogers was not yet three years old early in 1911 when he was kidnapped from his home by two masked men, who released him twenty-four hours later upon payment of a $12,000 ransom. The kidnappers were soon apprehended and the money recovered. One of them proved to be the boy's uncle, who said he wanted the money to impress a new girlfriend. Both men served prison terms. Due to his childhood experience, Judge Rogers declined to preside over any kidnapping cases during his service as both a state and a federal judge.

Rogers graduated from the University of Colorado Law School in 1931 and began practicing law in Albuquerque that year with former New Mexico governors Merritt C. Mechem and A. T. Hannett. He served as an assistant district attorney from 1932 to 1939.

A veteran of World War II, Rogers enlisted in the army as a private in 1942, saw active duty in the African and Italian campaigns, and was discharged with a rank of captain late in 1945. Returning to Albuquerque, he resumed his law practice and was named city attorney in 1947.

In 1951 Governor Edwin L. Mechem appointed him to the Second Judicial District Court in Albuquerque to succeed Henry G. Coors, who had been elected to the New Mexico Supreme Court, and for whom Coors Boulevard on Albuquerque's growing West Side was named.

When a second U.S. District Court judgeship for New Mexico was created by Congress in 1954, President Eisenhower appointed Rogers to the post to join Judge Carl A. Hatch on the bench. The contrasting styles of the outspoken Judge Rogers and the more somber Judge Hatch soon became evident.

As a federal judge, Rogers exhibited little patience with what he considered trivial charges brought against defendants by government attorneys. "What do you think I'm running here, a justice of the peace court?" he shouted during the arraignment of a man charged in connection with a $12 forged check. Turning to the defendant, he said, "I fine you a dollar and a half."

Judge Rogers also became angered when the U.S. Railroad Retirement Board brought before him a succession of Navajo and Zuni Indian men on charges of filing false claims for unemployment insurance. When a Zuni man was brought to court for filing a false claim for $30.24, the judge exploded. "So, a Railroad Retirement Board employee cuts another notch on his gun and another redskin bites the dust," he exclaimed as he assessed another $1.50 fine.

When a Zuni Pueblo religious leader pleaded guilty to a charge of leaving the scene of an accident at the pueblo, Judge Rogers placed him on one year probation on condition that he not get drunk. "That doesn't mean you can't take a few nips," he added. "Just don't get drunk."

The judge occasionally admonished trial lawyers he thought were becoming overdramatic in their remarks to the jury, telling them to "leave the arm waving to Perry Mason." During the course of a civil trial, he accused lawyers for both sides of "dragging their feet." "I told you yesterday that I wanted this trial to proceed with dispatch, and I'm telling you again today that I want this trial to proceed with dispatch," he told the attorneys. "If you don't, I'm going to light a firecracker under you." Moments later, he asked one of the attorneys to move to another location "because I can't see my wife in the back of the courtroom."

Judge Rogers thoroughly enjoyed a hearing in which a man who identified himself as Jesse James III, and who claimed he was the grandson of the outlaw Jesse James, testified in court as the plaintiff in a buried treasure suit. "Tell me more about Jesse James," the judge said, interrupting the man's testimony. "The only James I thought much about until now is Harry James's wife." (His reference was to actress Betty Grable, wife of bandleader Harry James.)

During a lull in one court session, on the top floor of the six-story Federal Building on the northeast corner of Fifth and Gold, Judge Rogers remarked from the bench that he thought some new, illuminated "Exit" signs that had been installed over the courtroom doors were a waste of money, adding that everybody knew that the doors were exits. "They are always doing something around here that I don't want done," he added. "I put my foot down on acoustical ceiling tile for my office. I can hear everything I want to hear in there."

Late in his career on the federal bench, Judge Rogers cautioned jurors that they should not get any wrong impressions from newspaper articles regarding his quips and comments. "I have appeared on the newspaper front page every day this week," he began. "It was accurate. I did say what the paper said I said."

He told the jurors that he began to worry that the articles would result in fears that he did not take his job seriously. "I do," he continued. "I am dedicated to my job. I think as much of this court, maybe more so, than I do of my church, and that is going a long way."

The judge said that if he made remarks during court that he thought were funny, or that the jury might or might not think were funny, he did it only to maintain their interest. "If you happen to see them in the newspaper, don't think I'm clowning, don't think I'm trying to make a three-ring circus out of this courtroom," he said. "When you pick up the evening paper, I want you all to realize that this court is as serious an institution as there is in America."

The judge said he once worked for a newspaper, and knew what newspaper reporters liked to hear. "I plead guilty to that," he added. He closed his remarks by saying that he was ever aware of the fact that the court is a place where justice is dealt out with an even hand. "I have dealt out two hundred to three hundred years of servitude during this term of court," he said. "If you think I like that, you are wrong."

Judge Rogers was held in such high esteem by the legal community that some prominent Albuquerque lawyers, including former district judge Bryan Johnson, began an unsuccessful movement to nominate him for a seat on the United States Supreme Court.

## Chapter Thirteen

# ALBUQUERQUE, 1970-2000

### The City's Population Nears the Half-Million Mark

Albuquerque's growing population reached 244,501 in 1970, according to the U.S. Census for that year. The count did not include inhabitants of suburbs adjacent to but outside Albuquerque city limits.

Periodic antiwar demonstrations that erupted in Albuquerque in the early 1970s occasionally turned violent and resulted in some property damage and a few minor injuries. Most of the demonstrations were centered on or near the University of New Mexico campus as young people protested America's involvement in Vietnam. Several persons, including a television cameraman, suffered slight bayonet wounds when New Mexico National Guardsmen were summoned to the campus to quell a disturbance. One of the campus demonstrations was led by actress and antiwar activist Jane Fonda.

War protesters who had gathered in Roosevelt Park swarmed out of the park and caused extensive damage to a nearby liquor store and an automobile dealership. A street brawl erupted in front of Albuquerque High School, at the corner of Central Avenue and Broadway Boulevard, when a group of high school students attacked war protesters who were marching west on Central from the university campus.

Kirtland Air Force Base, which also was the scene of periodic demonstrations near the entrances, absorbed Sandia and Manzano bases in 1971 to become a single Air Force facility. Nuclear warheads that had been

259

stored at Manzano Base later were moved to the Kirtland Underground Munitions Storage Complex.

The ten-story Hilton Hotel, which New Mexico native Conrad Hilton built in 1939 on north Second Street in downtown Albuquerque, changed ownership and name in 1971 with the construction of the Hilton Inn near the Big I. The original hotel, where Hilton and his bride Zsa Zsa Gabor were said to have honeymooned, became known as the Plaza, and was later renovated as La Posada de Albuquerque.

Albuquerque's reputation as the world balloon capital originated in 1972 when two local residents, Sid Cutter and Tom Rutherford, staged a balloon ascension event in the parking lot of Coronado Center as part of the fiftieth anniversary of KOB radio. Called the KOB Birthday Bash and Balloon Race, the event attracted thirteen hot-air balloons with their pilots and ground crews.

Balloon ascensions and races grew in size and popularity each year and culminated in the annual Albuquerque International Balloon Fiesta, attracting nearly one thousand hot-air balloons from all parts of the United States and more than a dozen foreign countries. An open space area in the north part of the city was set aside as Balloon Fiesta Park to handle the hundreds of balloons and thousands of spectators who began flocking to the ten-day event early each October. Said to be the most photographed event in the world, the fiestas included morning mass ascensions of multicolored balloons of all shapes and sizes, and evening balloon glows, when the tethered balloons are illuminated by their burners.

Three Albuquerque balloonists, Maxie Anderson, Ben Abruzzo, and Larry Newman, made history in 1978 when they completed the first successful trans-Atlantic balloon flight, landing their gas-filled balloon, the Double Eagle II, near Paris, France, on August 17.

Albuquerque's city government, which since 1917 had consisted of five elected city commissioners and an appointed city manager, reverted to the city council–mayor system in 1974, providing for nonpartisan elections of nine city council members and a mayor. Elected the first mayor under the revived system was Harry Kinney, an engineer, who was followed in office four years later by David Rusk, an economist and the son of Dean Rusk, who served as secretary of state in the 1960s during the Kennedy and Johnson administrations. Kinney defeated Rusk's reelection bid in 1981, served four more years, and later, in retirement, embarked on a new career as a taxi driver.

Efforts to revive the sagging downtown district in the 1970s included the establishment of the Civic Plaza on a square block of land, two blocks north of Central Avenue, which had been cleared of existing buildings. The open plaza, graced by a large water fountain, was flanked on the east by the new Albuquerque Convention Center, built in 1972, and on the west by new city and county government buildings. An underground parking area was established beneath the plaza.

The Albuquerque Public Library, which for years had been located at Central Avenue and Edith Street NE, was relocated in 1975 to new and larger quarters downtown at Copper Avenue and Fifth Street NW. The old library continued in use to house special collections.

During the summer, the city began sponsoring downtown Saturday night celebrations with a wide variety of entertainment features and food booths on Central Avenue between Second and Sixth streets. Years later, the Saturday night celebrations became known as Summerfest and were held on Civic Plaza, with each event honoring a different ethnic group of the city.

The All Indian Pueblo Council, representing New Mexico's nineteen Indian pueblos, established the Indian Pueblo Cultural Center in 1976 northeast of the downtown section on Indian trust land that previously had been occupied by the Albuquerque Indian School. The center, which soon became a prime tourist attraction, includes museum displays, gift shops, a restaurant, and meeting rooms. Indian ceremonial dances are performed periodically on the outdoor plaza.

The Albuquerque Museum, which had been housed temporarily in the former Municipal Airport Terminal, was relocated by the city in 1979 to much larger quarters at the northeast edge of the Old Town Plaza district, facing east over grassy Tiguex Park, which commemorated the Pueblo Indian province that once occupied the Albuquerque area.

Downtown Albuquerque lost another major business when the two daily newspapers, the *Albuquerque Journal* and the *Albuquerque Tribune*, moved in the summer of 1985 to a new plant established by the Albuquerque Publishing Company in the northern part of the city.

### Rio Rancho

Rio Rancho, which by the year 2000 had become the fourth largest city in New Mexico, began life in the early 1960s as Rio Rancho Estates, a small housing development near the northwest edge of Albuquerque, just north of the Bernalillo County line in Sandoval County. The site, high on the West Mesa overlooking the village of Corrales, had previous-ly been ranchland inhabited mostly by prairie dogs, coyotes, jackrabbits, and rattlesnakes.

Purchasing fifty-five thousand acres of land in 1960 was the American Real Estate and Petroleum Corporation (AMREP), a New York mail order business that also sold property in Florida and invested in oil exploration. AMREP opened a sales office on the site in 1961, after survey-ing and staking out roads and residential lots, and began promoting the proposed community to middle-income retirees in eastern and Midwestern states.

Early mail order solicitations failed to bring the desired results, however, and it was not until the corporation embarked on an aggres-sive sales campaign, which included meeting with and entertaining prospective buyers with luncheons, slide shows, and tours of the prop-erty, that Rio Rancho Estates began to take shape as a retirement com-munity. The principal selling points were inexpensive houses and building lots, mild winters, and scenic views. At one time, it was report-ed that there were as many as sixty retired New York police officers liv-ing in the new community.

Rio Rancho Estates included a small shopping center and a golf course by the early 1970s, and AMREP purchased an additional thirty-five thousand acres of land for future expansion. In 1980, when the popula-tion had reached about ten thousand, the community was incorporated as the City of Rio Rancho.

Rio Rancho's transition from a retirement to a high-tech communi-ty began in 1982 when Intel Corporation, the world's largest single pro-ducer of computer chips, established its largest manufacturing facility on 210 acres near the south edge of the new city. The huge Intel establish-ment was soon employing about five thousand persons in a cluster of buildings that included three fabrication plants.

Rio Rancho began experiencing a major population and building boom, the population soaring to 35,512 in 1990, and many of the new-comers consisting of young adults with children. Some found work at Intel and at other high-tech industries that had been established in the city, and some used Rio Rancho as a bedroom community, commuting to work in Albuquerque or Santa Fe.

Schools and city parks were established in the city, and Intel con-tributed $30 million toward construction of Rio Rancho High School, which was established in 1995.

The 2000 U.S. Census gave Rio Rancho a population of 51,576, making it the fourth largest city in New Mexico, ranking behind only Albuquerque, Santa Fe, and Las Cruces. By this time the city extended south to the Albuquerque city limits, and north along the west side of the Rio Grande to a point opposite the town of Bernalillo.

## West Side Development

Albuquerque's territorial expansion eventually was limited by the Sandia Mountains on the east, the Sandia Indian Reservation on the north, and the Isleta Indian Reservation on the south. Westward expansion soon followed, particularly on largely undeveloped lands along the west bank of the Rio Grande from Interstate 40 north to the southern boundaries of the city of Rio Rancho and the village of Corrales.

Much of the development occurred on the twenty-six-thousand-acre Black Ranch, also known as the Seven Bar Ranch, which Albert F. Black, a West Virginia entrepreneur, had purchased in 1929 for $50,000. The ranch, along the northern edge of Bernalillo County, measured about two and one-half miles north to south, and extended about ten miles west from the west bank of the Rio Grande.

Black, his wife June, and their five children struggled to make a living on the ranch, raising cattle, sheep, and a few crops. They built a ranch house, facing narrow and unpaved Coors Road, and established an airstrip nearby, which they called the Seven Bar Airport.

Financial success began in 1962 when the Horizon Land Corporation bought eighty-five hundred acres of the ranch for $1.7 million to develop the residential community of Paradise Hills. Later, as Albuquerque continued to expand west of the river, other portions of the ranch were sold or leased for commercial and residential development. Albuquerque's third major shopping center, Cottonwood Mall, was established in 1995 on what had been the Seven Bar Airport, and a restaurant, Chili's Grill and Bar, was built on the site of the Black ranch house.

By this time, the former ranch was bulging with major retailers including automobile dealerships, small shopping centers, a variety of restaurants, housing developments, and apartment complexes. What had been unpaved Coors Road became paved and widened Coors Boulevard NW, the busiest thoroughfare west of the river.

The tremendous growth of Albuquerque west of the river, and the growth of adjoining Rio Rancho, resulted in the building of two new bridges across the Rio Grande at Paseo del Norte and Montaño, and the replacement of the narrow Alameda Bridge.

Limiting commercial and residential development in some areas west of the river was the establishment in 1990 of Petroglyph National Monument, covering more than seven thousand acres of the West Mesa. The monument was created to protect more than twenty thousand centuries-old petroglyphs, or rock carvings, pecked or incised into dark volcanic rocks by early Pueblo Indians who inhabited the region.

The ancient petroglyphs are scattered along a seventeen-mile-long volcanic escarpment beneath long extinct volcanic cones that loom on Albuquerque's western horizon. The rock images include representations of humanlike figures, animals, birds, ceremonial masks, handprints, and geometric and abstract designs, all pecked into the rocks with stone tools.

Years before the monument was established, practical jokers would occasionally startle Albuquerque residents by building fires atop the extinct volcanic cones, causing columns of smoke to rise in the air, leading some to believe that the volcanoes had become active again.

### Downtown Revitalization, 1990s

Downtown Albuquerque, once the city's retail business center, was revitalized as a food and entertainment district through the combined efforts of city government and private enterprise. Ethnic restaurants, sidewalk cafés, nightclubs, specialty shops, and artists' studios began lining downtown streets that were spruced up with small trees, shrubs, and colorful wall murals.

The Hyatt Regency, a twenty-story luxury hotel, was established in 1990 on the south side of Civic Plaza on the fringe of what years before had been Albuquerque's red light district. The hotel's restaurant was given the name McGrath's Bar and Grill in recognition of the fact that it was located close to the site of a bordello that Lizzie McGrath, a prominent Albuquerque madam, had operated in the early days.

The Alvarado Transportation Center was erected by the city on the site of the Alvarado Hotel and designed to resemble the elaborate hotel that stood there from 1902 until 1970. Motion pictures returned to downtown Albuquerque with the building of a multiscreen Century Theatres complex on the southwest corner of Central Avenue and First Street, across the street from the transportation center and its bus station.

Residential apartments and lofts began taking shape in both old and new downtown buildings as part of the inner-city development. New apartments and lofts also were established near the downtown district.

The old Albuquerque High School building on the northeast corner of Central and Broadway, which had stood vacant since the early 1970s when a new school was built nearby, was refurbished to accommodate residential lofts and business pads. A two- and three-story apartment complex was erected on Central Avenue a short distance west of downtown on the site of Huning Castle, the elaborate residence of pioneer Albuquerque resident Franz Huning, which was demolished in 1955. The complex adopted the Huning Castle name.

Sections along the east bank of the Rio Grande west of Old Town were developed as the Albuquerque Biological Park. The park, established in 1995, included the existing Rio Grande Zoo and renovated Tingley Beach south of Central Avenue, and the creation north of Central Avenue of an aquarium, formal botanic gardens, and a period farm of the 1920s.

The Rio Grande Zoo, which has been ranked among the top zoos in the nation, had been developed over the years into a sixty-acre zoological park with more than thirteen hundred animals, including many in their natural habitats.

The Rio Grande Nature Center, a state park on the east bank of the Rio Grande north of the biological park, was established to provide visitors an opportunity to view waterfowl and stroll through the bosque, the thickly wooded area that lines both banks of the Rio Grande through the city.

### Entering the Twenty-first Century

Albuquerque's population reached 448,606 in 2000, according to the U.S. Census for that year, ranking it as the thirty-fifth-largest city in the United States. Albuquerque's metropolitan area, which included populated areas adjacent to or near the city limits, was listed as 712,738.

Los Ranchos de Albuquerque, a corporate village surrounded by Albuquerque, consists of a mostly rural area covering much of Albuquerque's North Valley along the east side of the Rio Grande. Regarded as one of New Mexico's most affluent communities, Los Ranchos, with a population of about five thousand in the year 2000, had become noted for large and expensive homes and horse farms.

The incorporated village of Corrales, north of Albuquerque on the west bank of the Rio Grande below the hilltop city of Rio Rancho, had a population of about seventy-five hundred, including many artists and writers who were attracted to the rural nature of the riverside village.

Although Albuquerque home building continued at a rapid pace, many of the city's business and professional people preferred to commute to work from homes they established along the eastern foot of the Sandia Mountains and in the South Valley as far south as Los Lunas. Albuquerque's economy continued to be based to a large extent on government and military payrolls, high-tech industries, and tourism.

Kirtland Air Force Base had become the nation's strategic weapons development center with about twenty thousand military and civilian workers, including those employed at Sandia National Laboratories on the base. Kirtland housed the nation's largest concentration of nuclear weapons, and although the Air Force was silent on the subject, the Washington-based Natural Resources Defense Council estimated that there were 2,450 nuclear warheads of various types stored at the Kirtland Underground Munitions Storage Complex.

Sandia National Laboratories, managed by the Lockheed Martin Corporation for the U.S. Department of Energy, had expanded beyond the development of nuclear weapons to include scientific and engineering research pertaining to the nation's defense, energy, and environmental needs.

Enrollment in the Albuquerque Public Schools district passed the eighty thousand mark. Student enrollment on the University of New Mexico main campus reached twenty-five thousand, while the Albuquerque Technical Vocational Institute (TVI), which was founded in 1965 as an accredited community college offering certificates in occupational fields, counted about twenty thousand students on four campuses.

Professional baseball in Albuquerque experienced a major change when the Albuquerque Dukes, for years a Triple-A farm club for the Los Angeles Dodgers, was replaced by the Albuquerque Isotopes, a Triple-A team in the Pacific Coast League.

The establishment of the outdoor Journal Pavilion, south of the Sunport, gave Albuquerqueans an opportunity to attend concerts by some of the nation's leading rock and country music stars. Similar entertainment became common at the new gambling casinos on Indian lands north, south, and west of the city.

The National Hispanic Cultural Center, celebrating more than four centuries of Spanish presence in New Mexico and the Southwest, was completed as Albuquerque prepared to observe in 2006 the three hundredth anniversary of the city's founding. The $40 million center, in the Barelas neighborhood a short distance south of downtown Albuquerque, consisted of a complex of buildings on a fifty-seven-acre campus that included three elaborate performing arts theaters, an art gallery, library, genealogy room, and a restaurant.

The expanded Albuquerque Museum, at the northeast edge of Old Town facing east over Tiguex Park, became part of a museum row with the establishment nearby of the New Mexico Museum of Natural History, the National Atomic Museum, and the Explora Science Center and Children's Museum, all facing south over the park.

Among new bronze statues scattered over Albuquerque were life-sized figures of a standing Clyde Tingley and a seated Carrie Tingley, created by Albuquerque artist Betty Sabo, near the entrance to the aquarium in the new Albuquerque Biological Park. So many visitors had grasped Clyde Tingley's outstretched bronze hand that the dark patina finish had worn off his index finger, perhaps a fitting tribute to the man who had accomplished so much for Albuquerque in the past.

### Some Albuquerque Celebrities

Albuquerque has served as home for a number of men and women, in addition to war correspondent Ernie Pyle, who gained national and even international fame in various professions. Only a few were born in Albuquerque, and some lived in the city for only short periods of time.

Pulitzer Prize–winning author Paul Horgan, who was born in 1903 in Buffalo, New York, moved to Albuquerque with his parents in 1915, attended the public schools, and launched his writing career in 1921 as a reporter for the *Albuquerque Morning Journal*. His Pulitzer prizes were for his books *Great River: The Rio Grande in North American History*, and *Lamy of Santa Fe: His Life and Times.*

Dr. Ralph J. Bunche, African American diplomat who won a Nobel Peace Prize, lived in Albuquerque in 1916–1917 as a youngster and attended the Fourth Ward (later Lew Wallace) elementary school. He won the peace prize in 1950 for his war mediation work as principal secretary of the United Nations Palestine Commission.

Vivian Vance, famed for her portrayal of Ethel Mertz on the long-running *I Love Lucy* television shows, began her acting career in the 1930s at the Albuquerque Little Theatre.

Broadway and film actress Kim Stanley was known by her true name of Patricia Reid when she lived in Albuquerque and attended the

University of New Mexico in the 1940s. Although nominated for two Academy Awards for her film work, she was best known for her starring roles in the Broadway stage productions of *Picnic* and *Bus Stop*.

George "Slim" Summerville, who was born in Albuquerque in 1892, ran away from home at the age of nineteen and became a famous comedy and character actor in both silent and sound movies.

Members of Albuquerque's Unser family won fame as race car drivers, winning nine Indianapolis 500 racing meets between 1968 and 1994. Bobby Unser won the Indy 500 in 1968, 1975, and 1981; his brother, Al Unser Sr., won in 1970, 1971, 1978, and 1987; and his son, Al Unser Jr., won in 1992 and 1994.

Award-winning author Tony Hillerman of Albuquerque won national and international acclaim for his series of mystery novels set on the Navajo Indian Reservation. His books appeared on national best seller lists, and several were dramatized as motion pictures for the Public Broadcasting System.

Jack Schaefer, who lived in Albuquerque in the 1970s, was best known for his western novels *Shane* and *Monte Walsh*, both filmed as Hollywood movies. Max Evans of Albuquerque also had two of his western novels, *The Rounders* and *The Hi Lo Country*, adapted to the silver screen.

Rudolfo A. Anaya of Albuquerque, award-winning author, playwright, and poet, is perhaps best known for his novel *Bless Me, Ultima*.

Cowboy artist Fred Harman, who lived in Albuquerque in the 1960s, was the creator of the cartoon strip *Red Ryder and Little Beaver*. Artist Wilson Hurley, nationally known for his large western landscapes, painted five large murals for the National Cowboy Hall of Fame and Western Heritage Center in Oklahoma City.

Albuquerque artist Pablita Velarde, a native of Santa Clara Pueblo, won national and international awards for her paintings depicting Pueblo Indian life and culture. The French government honored her with the coveted Palmes de Academiques.

Country music star Glen Campbell was yet unknown in the 1950s when he performed at Albuquerque nightspots with his uncle, Albuquerque radio personality Dick Bills, and the Sandia Mountain Boys.

John Lewis, the African American pianist who was reared in Albuquerque, became the founder and musical director of the Modern Jazz Quartet.

Bill Gates and a partner, Paul Allen, established headquarters in Albuquerque in 1975 and founded Microsoft, a computer software business. Reportedly turned down for a bank loan, they moved the business in 1979 to Seattle, Washington, where Microsoft became a giant in the computer industry, eventually ranking Gates as the wealthiest man in the United States.

# Index

Otero County, New Mexico: 223
Our Lady of the Angels School: 127
*Out West*: 173
Ovando, Capt. Francisco de: 12
Ovelin, S. M.: 127
Owen, Arnet O.: 115
Oxnard, James G.: 232
Oxnard Field: 233, 236

Padilla, Fray Juan: 4–5, 14
Páez Hurtado, Juan: 29
Page, Charles: 64
Parham, William Young: 202
Pajarito Land Grant: 87
Pajarito Pueblo: 37
Palace of the Governors: 42
Palladino, Michael: 194
Palms Beer Garden and Grocery: 195
Palms Trading Company: 195
Papago Indians: 94
Papini, Guido: 213
Paradise Hills: 263
Paris Shoe Store: 194
Parker, Peter "Shorty": 107
Pastime Theater: 213
Paul, Col. Gabriel: 75
Payupki Pueblo: 32
Pecos National Historical Park: 6
Pecos Pueblo: 5, 12–16
Pecos River: 15–16, 46, 113
Pena, José: 64
Peñuela, Marqués de: 32
Pepperday, Thomas M.: 227
Peralta, New Mexico: 76, 157–58
Peralta, Pedro de: 18
Parea, Escolástico: 112
Perea, Fray Esteban de: 19
Perea, José Leandro: 102, 123
Pérez, Albino: 44–45
Pérez de Villagrá, Capt. Gaspar: 17
Perkins Hall: 208
Perry, Rueben: 186
Pesh–la–ki: 196

Pétriz de Cruzate, Domingo
  Jironza: 24
Petroglyph National Monument: 264
Phelan, Thomas F.: 107, 143
Phillip II, King: 16
Phillips, Z. T.: 143
Pickford, Mary: 219
Picuris Pueblo: 23
Pierce, Franklin: 62
Pike, Zebulon: 37–39, 90
Pima Indians: 94
Pineda, Juan: 30
Pino, Facundo: 56
Platero, José: 196
Plaza de la Constitucíon: 42
Plaza de San Antonio: 43
Pohmer, Francisquita: 203
Pohmer, Joseph: 100, 147, 203
Pollock, John C.: 205–6
Pool, William: 64
Poor Sisters of St. Francis Seraph: 244
Popé: 20, 24
Pope, Brig. Gen. John: 90
Popejoy, Tom L.: 244
Porto Rico Saloon and Grocery
  Store: 194
Post, Thomas D.: 96, 123, 249
Postal Telegraph Company: 191
Post's Exchange Hotel: 249
Potter, Col. Charles: 111
Presbyterian Hospital Center: 244
Preston, Sadie: 114
Price, Daisy: 120
Prince, L. Bradford: 106
Puaray Pueblo: 15–24
Pueblo Bonito: 181
Pueblo Revolt, 1680: 20–22, 28–32, 36
Puerco River: 81
Puerto de Luna: 113
Puma, Joseph: 64
Putney, L.G.: 108
Pyle, Ernie: 239, 267
Pyle, Jerry: 239